Cengage Advantage
Books

A Creative Approach to
Music Fundamentals ELEVENTH EDITION

William Duckworth
Bucknell University

CENGAGE
Learning·

Australia • Brazil • Japan • Korea • Mexico • Singapore • Spain • United Kingdom • United States

A Creative Approach to Music Fundamentals, Eleventh Edition
William Duckworth

Product Director: Monica Eckman

Product Manager: Sharon Adams Poore

Product Assistant: Rachael Bailey

Media Developer: Chad Kirchner

Associate Media Developer: Elizabeth Newell

Marketing Manager: Jillian Borden

Senior Content Project Manager: Lianne Ames

Art Director: Faith Brosnan

Manufacturing Planner: Julio Esperas

Rights Acquisition Specialist: Jessica Elias

Production Service: MPS Limited

Text Designer: Jeanne Calabrese

Cover Designer: Wing-ip Ngan, Inkdesign, inc. ©

Cover Image: © iStockphoto.com/studiovision

Compositor: MPS Limited

For product information and technology assistance, contact us at
Cengage Learning Customer & Sales Support, 1-800-354-9706

For permission to use material from this text or product,
submit all requests online at **cengage.com/permissions**
Further permissions questions can be emailed to
permissionrequest@cengage.com

Library of Congress Control Number: 2013947726

ISBN-13: 978-1-285-44620-2

ISBN-10: 1-285-44620-8

Cengage Learning
200 First Stamford Place, 4th Floor
Stamford, CT 06902
USA

Cengage Learning is a leading provider of customized learning solutions with office locations around the globe, including Singapore, the United Kingdom, Australia, Mexico, Brazil, and Japan. Locate your local office at: **international.cengage.com/region**

Cengage Learning products are represented in Canada by Nelson Education, Ltd.

For your course and learning solutions, visit **www.cengage.com**

Purchase any of our products at your local college store or at our preferred online store **www.cengagebrain.com**

Instructors: Please visit **login.cengage.com** and log in to access instructor-specific resources.

Printed in the United States of America
6 7 8 9 10 11 12 23 22 21 20 19

For Will, Katherine, and Alison,
who grew with many of the songs in this book

Brief Contents

Contents

5 Pitch

6 Major Scales

7 Major Key Signatures

8 Intervals

9 Minor Key Signatures

10 Minor Scales

14 Chord Progressions

15 Writing a Song

Appendix A

Appendix B

Appendix C

Preface

As you start to study music in a more formal way, it might be helpful to know that you can take multiple pathways through the material you want to learn. No one "right" way to study music will ensure success. Instead, there are many parallel paths—some in this book, others online—all of which require about the same amount of commitment, dedication, and hard work. So, as you go forward, don't do so by rote. Endless practice with little to show for it over time is not a formula for success. If one method of study doesn't seem to work for you, try another. The goal is the same: to achieve your potential.

Practice

This is where this book and its online practice materials can help—by offering, as they do, alternate ways for you to practice and learn.

The textbook that you hold in your hands includes written work and listening examples to improve your musical skills, as well as periodic comprehensive review sections to help measure your progress. Its features are designed with you in mind:

Music in Action

In the Music in Action exercises, found in both the textbook and online at CourseMate, a variety of activities will encourage and enable you to become *musically* engaged, both on your own and as a class. They give you the opportunity to create music while learning the fundamentals of rhythm, melody, scales, intervals, and triads, in a creative framework.

Many Music in Action boxes are also devoted to ear training, sight singing, and songwriting—all skills that your instructor values highly. Their specific headings, "Ear Training," "Sight Singing," and "Song Building," each with a special icon, will help you and your instructor to locate them easily.

Music in Action 🎵 Song Building

Class Practice

You'll use these practice materials largely in class, while the end-of-chapter Practice materials, tabbed for easy reference, can be used *outside* of class and handed in to your instructor. You'll notice that the text includes many reminders to check the end-of-chapter Practice materials for further practice on a given topic.

> Practice naming pitches that use ledger lines in both treble and bass clef may be found in Practice 4-2 and 4-3.

Tips & Tools

Originally found in the comprehensive print book, these have been moved online in the advantage edition and provide reminders and help with particularly difficult concepts/point the way to extra assistance on the web.

Focus on Skills

These major review sections, also tabbed for easy reference, come after Chapters 2, 4, 5, 7, 8, 11, and 14. Each one is coordinated with interactive Focus on Fundamentals exercises online.

CourseMate

In addition, an interactive website—*CourseMate*—contains thousands of Focus on Fundamentals practice materials, as well as a complete eBook, podcasts from the author, videos, and sound files of musical examples in the text. *ƒ* icons in the text will remind you about online CourseMate materials that are available for your study and practice. Now, online at *Music Fundamentals in Action* and CourseMate, as well as in your text, you can practice the material you need to learn, at a pace that's right for you.

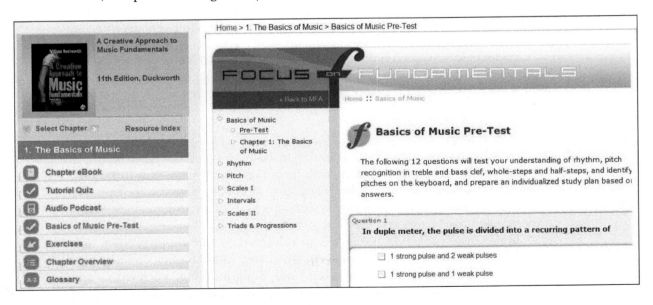

To get started with CourseMate, simply go to login.cengage.com's or cengagebrain.com's student registration area, and create a new account by entering the code on the CourseMate card (available separately).

In this eleventh edition, you have access to practice materials that will not only allow your teacher to focus class attention on the topics that are most important to the group, but also allow you to customize your own individual learning experience to better suit your schedule. What you need to learn—the fundamentals of music—may be fixed, but how you set about acquiring this knowledge is now, more than ever, in your hands. Though regular practice and study are absolutely necessary—no musician ever gets any better otherwise—the variety of musical experiences and practice materials in this package will make your work seem easier and less repetitive and, perhaps, go a little faster as well.

How to Practice

You will begin to learn music by learning how to practice. Nothing is more significant; it is the most important activity a musician undertakes. The good ones practice every day; you will need to as well, if you want to improve. So, regular practice is emphasized, and specific techniques for *how* to practice are discussed throughout the text. You will also find plenty of practice exercises designed to help you grow and improve musically, plus skill assessment materials to help you gauge your progress along the way.

Being Musical

It is equally important that you experience the more creative aspects of music—the listening, performing, and composing activities—as early in your studies as possible. This, after all, is the *fun* side of music, the part that makes all the studying and practicing worthwhile.

As you proceed through this material, all the way to writing a song in Chapter 15, remember that music isn't something you begin to make after you complete the class. It can, should, and must happen all along the way.

Focus

The focus of your work in music fundamentals will be to understand and learn to use the basic set of musical building blocks, or elements, that inform all music. This is important regardless of the type of musician you consider yourself to be, because no matter what the style, the fundamentals of music always stay the same. What changes are the many different ways that composers have emphasized and combined these elements. To put it more succinctly, musical styles change over time, but the fundamentals of music do not. So, no matter what kind of music you listen to, and want to write and play, the way to begin is to learn the fundamentals. You will always be able to apply them to any style of music you may come to love, including ones that haven't even been imagined yet.

To Instructors

For instructors who have used *A Creative Approach to Music Fundamentals* in a previous edition, there are several changes in this new eleventh edition, beyond its updated design:

- A new Annotated Instructor's Edition is available, with answers to all text exercises, as well as an introductory section of teaching tips and the answers to the additional practice sheets located (and downloadable from) on the Instructor's Companion Site for ease of reference.
- A new Cognero computerized Test Bank (created by Elizabeth Pauly at Minneapolis Community and Technical College) is now available through the Instructor's access at login.cengage.com
- A new Chapter 2 on keyboard fundamentals has been created from the previous edition's Chapter 1.
- The text itself has "cut to the chase," avoiding extra verbiage and focusing even more on practice.
- The connection between eBook, CourseMate, and text practice materials is strengthened via web cross-references integrated into the beginning of each chapter and each Focus on Skills.
- The text's Focus on Skills review exercises have now been aligned with the online Focus on Fundamentals exercises in CourseMate's Music Fundamentals in Action tutorials.
- All pages are now punched and perforated to facilitate class handouts and assignments.

The results of the changes to this new eleventh advantage edition are that, thanks to an integrated set of print and online courseware, music fundamentals classes can become more customized, more interactive, and more fun to teach (and learn from) than ever before. *A Creative Approach to Music Fundamentals*, Eleventh Advantage Edition, is a new approach to learning music. It is designed for today's students, tomorrow's musicians.

Acknowledgments

I would like to thank the following reviewers for their assistance in revising *A Creative Approach to Music Fundamentals*:

Robert Brownlow, University of Akron

Jefferson Campbell, University of Minnesota, Duluth

Chris Coulter, East Los Angeles College

Brenda Lang, Cincinnati Christian University

John Lindberg, Minnesota State University, Mankato

David Patterson, University of Massachusetts, Boston

Elizabeth Pauly, Minneapolis Community and Technical College

Matt Schaffner, Bellarmine University

As teachers responsible for making this material come alive in the classroom, their ideas and suggestions have been invaluable in helping me reshape and reorder the content of this edition into the strongest and most useful courseware yet.

Finally, a very special thanks to Wally Gunn, without whose excellent work there would not be an Annotated Instructor's Edition this time around.

Bill Duckworth

Introduction

Introduction

The purpose of this book and companion website is to help you to become a better musician. You are already *musical* to some degree. Most of us sang and danced as children, and many of us play musical instruments today, some by ear, others by reading notes. And although you may never have performed on stage or toured with a band, you certainly have amassed a good deal of knowledge about the music you know and love. So regardless of how far you have come in your pursuit of music, you should begin to consider yourself a musician and to think of this book and website as helping you to become a better one.

But what exactly do we need to learn that will make us more musical? Fortunately, there are certain aspects of music so fundamental that all musicians, regardless of the style of music they play, will profit from a deeper understanding of them. These are the four characteristics of musical sound and the six basic elements of music. So no matter what style of music you like—from metal, rap, electronic, and hip hop, to Broadway, gospel, Tin Pan Alley, and pop, all the way to classical music by Bach, Mozart, Beethoven, and Mahler—all musical sound has the same four characteristics and all styles of music use the same six basic elements. Learning about these building blocks of music (this musical DNA, if you will) will help all of us to become better musicians.

Looking at Music

Everybody likes to listen to music. It's a natural thing to do. Looking at music, however, is an acquired taste. Some of the world's best musicians learned by rote and play by ear. Here, our work will require us to understand music as written on the printed page, and we will learn to interpret the various notational signs and symbols and what they tell us about how the music should sound. What you will find is that different styles of music often look different on the page. Here, for example, is a piece of classical piano music by Beethoven. Notice how precisely the musical gestures appear to be controlled.

Example 1: Beethoven, "Moonlight" Sonata

Compare that with this lead sheet for a popular song in which improvisation and personal interpretation are not only allowed, but expected.

Example 2: Traditional, "Careless Love"

As we continue, we will learn about both types of notation as we learn to translate the *look* of music into *sound.*

The Characteristics of Musical Sound

There are four characteristics of all musical sound. These are:

- Pitch
- Duration
- Volume
- Timbre

Pitch results from the movement of air molecules and the vibratory patterns they create. The word *pitch*, however, is more of a musical term than a scientific one; the sound created by vibrating air molecules is called *frequency* by scientists and acousticians.

Duration concerns the length of a sound in time. Durations consist of three distinct parts: the initial attack, the period of time the sound is sustained, and the decay (dying away) of the sound. Musical instruments express these three aspects of duration in a variety of ways, and this variety is a major factor in the uniqueness of each sound.

Volume is a term used to identify the relative loudness of a sound. It is called *amplitude* by scientists, who measure it in decibels. Most musicians, however, use the term volume, and refer to musical loudness with less precise terms such as *forte* (loud) and *piano* (soft).

Timbre describes the *color* of sound. It is that characteristic of sound that allows us to identify a guitar, flute, or violin, even though they may all be playing the same pitch. It is important, incidentally, that musicians be able to identify instruments by their sound, and you should begin now to develop this ability. Next to practicing, listening is one of the most important things a musician can do.

The Elements of Music

The six basic elements of music are:

- Rhythm
- Melody
- Harmony
- Timbre
- Texture
- Form

Both rhythm and form deal with music in time. **Rhythm** extends from the steady pulse underlying the music to the unlimited array of rhythmic patterns riding above the pulse. Think of rhythm as the engine that moves the music forward and gives it the feeling of always going somewhere. **Form**, on the other hand, is about how an entire piece of music unfolds in time, that is, how the various parts or sections go together to create a musical shape that is both recognizable and pleasing to the ear.

Melody and harmony are also related; they deal with pitch and its musical manipulation. **Melody** is the sequential unfolding of pitch over time. It creates the shapes that we identify as songs. **Harmony**, on the other hand, involves simultaneous sounds (or chords) that create pleasing and interesting combinations (or chord progressions). Because our work deals with tonal music, we will spend much of our time exploring these two areas.

Timbre and texture are related to the sounds of instruments and voices. **Timbre**, as we have seen, refers both to the sounds of individual instruments and voices, such as the piano or guitar, as well as to various combinations of instruments, such as the rock band or string quartet. All of these individual instruments and ensembles have their own unique timbre. **Texture**, by contrast, refers to the number of voices or instruments a piece of music may contain. When discussing musical texture, we speak of a thick or thin texture, and whether it is monophonic (a single melody line), homophonic (a melody with accompaniment), or polyphonic (two or more equally important melodies, as in a fugue or a round).

Our work with these six elements will focus primarily on rhythm, melody, and harmony, but will touch on all of them to one degree or another. As we go forward, you will find that each style of music has developed its own way of defining, weighing, and combining these elements; if you can identify these differences, your understanding of music, as well as your ability to perform it, will increase dramatically.

How to Practice

Musicians must practice; it's a fact of life. They do it every day. Almost no one is sufficiently talented to be able to skip this step. For you, just beginning the formal study of music, your growth will depend upon how successful you are at learning to connect the *study* of fundamentals with *practicing* them. It is not enough to put knowledge about music into your head; you must put the sound and "feel" of it into your body, as well.

All musicians are a composite of musical skills and understandings. The process of creating your unique musical personality is one of learning to emphasize the skills you have, and to work around those you don't. In order to be successful, we need to develop all of our skills as much as we possibly can.

But how do we go about learning to practice musical fundamentals? What is involved? Is there a right way and a wrong way? Although there may not be a "wrong" way, there are certainly ways that work better, and produce success faster, than others. These center on setting realistic goals, frequency of practice, and a variety of materials.

Set Both Short- and Long-Term Goals

What do you want to learn today, tomorrow, next week? Who do you want to be musically by the end of this course? By the time you graduate? In ten years? Throughout your life? Goals will give you a standard against which to measure your progress. As you proceed from exercise to exercise and chapter to chapter, keep your goals in mind and try to see how each topic relates to helping you carry out your plan.

Practice Frequently

We learn by doing. Think about learning to ride a bicycle, speak a foreign language, or play a new online game—our skill at all three improves with focused, consistent practice. The same is true in learning the fundamentals of music. With music, just as with other skills, it is important to remember that improvement doesn't develop in a straight line. Instead, we get better in plateaus. Success comes with daily practice, but not at the same rate every day.

Practice a Variety of Materials

Not only is it less boring to practice a variety of exercises, it also helps you to learn faster, because you approach the same material from different points of view. As we continue, remember that all fine musicians, no matter what style of music they play, are a unique blend of musical talent and musical knowledge, and that they encourage and develop both skills through hard, consistent work. As your musical knowledge grows and accumulates, it will influence and better inform your natural talent. You can't be sure exactly how or when this will happen, but you'll know it when it begins. And when it starts, it never stops: becoming a good musician is a lifelong journey. There is always more to learn, no matter how accomplished you are.

The Basics of Music

Introduction

This chapter could have been titled *The Two Things You Really Need To Know,* because that is what it's about: an intro to the two most important building blocks of tonal music—rhythm and pitch. These two areas are the place where almost everyone begins, because no matter what kind of musician you plan to be, you're going to need to know how to manipulate pitches and maneuver through rhythms. This chapter introduces these two topics. And although they will be covered in greater detail in Chapters 3, 4, and 5, the purpose of introducing them here is to get you on the road to making music as quickly and easily as possible.

Rhythm

Let's begin with the element of **rhythm**. All music has a rhythmic component. Sometimes it is front and center, sometimes in the background, but whether fast and furious or slow and subtle, rhythm always represents a measuring and a parceling out of time. When we talk about rhythm, we are always talking about how music flows through time.

For some reason, most of us feel more secure with our rhythmic skills than with our ability to hear and sing pitches. Perhaps it is because our pitch skills seem more individual and, therefore, more personal. Also, because it is often thought of as easier, rhythm is sometimes given less attention and drill than pitch. Perhaps for this reason many people, even those with a significant amount of musical training, have misconceptions about rhythm's contribution to a piece of music. As you begin, keep in mind that rhythm plays a fundamental role in all of the world's music, and that a mastery of rhythm (no matter what the style) and of rhythmic notation (for most Western styles) is a necessary first step in becoming a good musician.

So what is musical rhythm? All of us can feel it; it's one of the musical elements we respond to first. Most of us can even single out the instruments most involved in creating rhythm. But when asked to define rhythm, we have trouble; we give only a partial definition. Although each individual definition contributes to our understanding of musical rhythm, none, by itself, explains the concept entirely. A true explanation of musical rhythm is intricate and complex, changes from culture to culture, and involves the interaction of a large number of rhythmic components, or elements.

We will begin by examining these rhythmic elements individually, both here and in the following chapters. What you will discover is that all of these components—pulse, meter, measure, note values, dotted notes, and ties—are relatively simple concepts when studied individually. It is the many ways in which they combine that create the mystery of musical rhythm.

As you continue with this chapter, as well as the two which follow, remember that all of the individual rhythmic elements combine within a piece of music to produce a rhythmic feeling unique to that piece. Remember also that most of us already have a high degree of sensitivity and an intuitive appreciation of those rhythmic qualities. There is the place to begin.

Music in Action ◀)) Ear Training

Listen to a piece of music that you have heard many times before. It may be a solo work or a piece for a small or large ensemble. It can be something from the past, such as a symphony or string quartet, or something more current, such as a pop song, dance mix, or rap. What is important—whatever style you choose—is that it be a piece of music that you "know." When listening this time, however, try to concentrate primarily on the rhythm. Are you able to direct your musical attention this selectively? If you have never tried this before, it may take several attempts before you are successful.

How different does the music sound when you listen to it this way?

- Do you hear things that you have never really paid attention to or thought much about before?
- Is there a steady pulse?
- Can you hear rhythmic patterns?
- Do the rhythmic patterns repeat?
- Are there a lot of different patterns, or just a few?

Try to put your thoughts and feelings about the *rhythmic* qualities of this music into two or three sentences.

Now, with help from your teacher or another student, choose a piece of music from another culture and listen to it, again paying particular attention to the rhythm.

- Are there obvious rhythmic similarities or differences between this and the more familiar music you heard first?
- Are the rhythmic elements of this second piece more or less prominent?
- Do the questions about pulse, patterns, and repetition that you considered for the first piece apply equally to this style of music?

Try to summarize your thoughts about the rhythmic qualities of this unfamiliar music in two or three sentences. Then, compare what you have written about these two dissimilar styles. ●

Pulse

Most of the music we hear around us every day has a steady **pulse**. The pulse, which is both constant and regular, can be felt when you tap your foot to music. This steady pulse in your foot can be represented visually by notes of any value. Here, it is represented by a line of whole notes.

o   o   o   o   o   o   o

Here by half notes, quarter notes, and eighth notes.

The point is that any note value can be used to visually represent the pulse. This even includes dotted notes, which we will study later.

♩. ♩. ♩. ♩. ♩. ♩. ♩. ♩. ♩.

But regardless of the note value chosen—the quarter note is probably used most—it is important to remember that a steady, proportional relationship is established by the pulse, against which the combination of sounds and silences that makes up the actual music moves.

Meter

As you listen to and feel the pulse in various pieces of music, you will notice that some pulses sound stronger than others. This combination of strong and weak pulses forms a recurring pattern known as the **meter**. When musicians talk about the meter of a piece, they are referring to a particular pattern of strong and weak pulses. The three most common patterns or meters are duple meter, triple meter, and quadruple meter. As the following illustration shows, in **duple meter**, the pulse is divided into a recurring pattern of one strong and one weak pulse, **triple meter** divides the pulse into a recurring pattern of one strong and two weak pulses, and **quadruple meter** divides the pulse into one strong and three weak pulses.

duple meter   ♩ ♩ ♩ ♩ ♩ ♩ ♩ ♩ ♩ ♩ ♩ ♩
                   >   >   >   >   >   >

triple meter   ♩ ♩ ♩ ♩ ♩ ♩ ♩ ♩ ♩ ♩ ♩ ♩
                   >   >   >   >

quadruple meter   ♩ ♩ ♩ ♩ ♩ ♩ ♩ ♩ ♩ ♩ ♩ ♩
                   >   >   >

The sign > is an **accent mark**. It indicates that the note under which (or over which) it appears is to be given more stress than the surrounding notes.

Feeling the Meter
Clap each of the metrical patterns just shown twice—first slowly, then faster—accenting the notes indicated. Notice that the speed you choose does not in any way alter the meter. What matters is that you keep the pulse steady and accent the proper notes. ●

Measures

As you performed the different meters, you may have lost your place momentarily. Even if you didn't, you can see that it would be difficult to play a long piece of music without losing one's place. For this reason, music is divided into **measures** with vertical lines called **bar lines**.

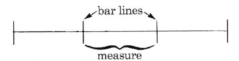

A bar line occurs immediately before an accented pulse. Thus, duple meter has two pulses per measure, triple meter has three pulses per measure, and quadruple meter has four pulses per measure. The following example shows the common meters again, this time with bar lines included. Notice how much easier it is to read and perform the meter when it is written this way.

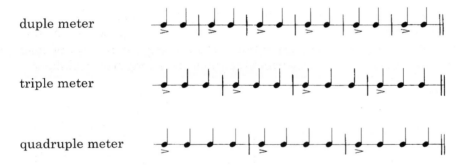

duple meter

triple meter

quadruple meter

Music in Action

Hearing Pulse and Meter
As members of the class listen, clap a steady pulse without any noticeable accents. Slowly change the pulse to duple, triple, or quadruple meter. You may want to have a contest to see how quickly members of the class can detect the shift to a measured pulse. ●

Note Values

Learning to read music involves mastering two different musical subsystems: pitch notation and rhythmic notation. Pitch is indicated by the placement of a note on a five-line staff (the higher the note on the staff, the higher the pitch). You will learn about that later in this chapter. Rhythm, on the other hand, is written with note-value symbols, which show duration. The following note values are the most commonly used:

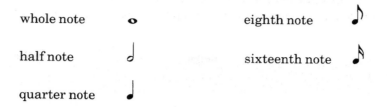

whole note   o   eighth note

half note   sixteenth note

quarter note

Notice that only the whole note exists as a notehead. Half notes and quarter notes consist of both a notehead and a stem,

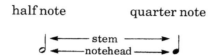

half note   quarter note

while eighth notes and sixteenth notes consist of a notehead, a stem, and either one or two flags.

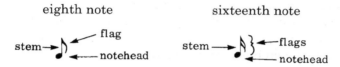

eighth note   sixteenth note

By combining these note values into various rhythmic combinations, the steady pulse of a piece of music is divided into an endless variety of patterns. The following example shows both the steady pulse and a rhythmic division of that pulse. Can you see how one line appears to support and strengthen the other?

quadruple meter

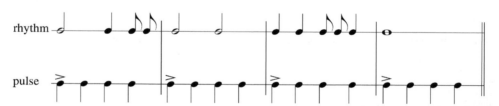

When several notes with flags occur together, the flags are usually replaced by beams that join the notes together at the tops of the stems. Generally, these note groupings are put into combinations of two, three, four, six, or eight. This is done to reflect the location of the pulse in relation to the rhythm. That is, a new beam is used at the beginning of each pulse. This makes it visually easier to tell where the beats are.

When beams are used, they indicate the rhythmic value of the notes in the same way as flags do for individual notes.

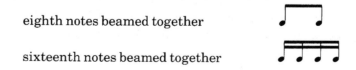

eighth notes beamed together

sixteenth notes beamed together

Sometimes sixteenth-note beams stop in the middle of the pattern and then begin again. This is usually done to make the rhythm clearer to the eye and does not affect the value of the notes in any way. The rule is that if a stem is touched by a beam, it becomes that value, even if the beam touches only one side of the stem. Thus, in the following example, the two sixteenth-note patterns would sound identical, even though they look slightly different, because each stem is touched by two beams.

Once you begin working with rhythms of different note values, you will notice that short, incomplete beams are often used.

In this example, the second and fourth notes are sixteenth notes, and the first and third are eighth notes (the function of the dot will be explained later in this chapter). Just remember that if a stem is touched by a beam, it becomes that value, and you should not have any trouble deciphering the rhythmic patterns that appear throughout the rest of this book.

Class Practice

Before proceeding further, you should practice drawing note values. This is not difficult but it does require some practice if you have not worked with them before. Keep the following points in mind:

1. Note heads are oval rather than round.
2. The flags on eighth and sixteenth notes always point to the right, no matter which side of the note the stem is on.
3. Notice also that when the stem points down, it is always located to the left of the notehead, and when it points up, it is always on the right.

Now try some on your own. Remember to draw examples of the stems both above and below the notes.

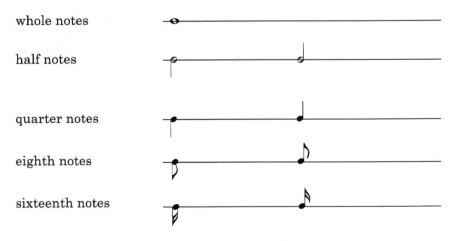

Regardless of the speed (tempo) at which a piece of music moves, the note value symbols are proportionately related to each other. Thus, if the quarter note receives one pulse, the half note will receive two pulses and the whole note four pulses. This proportionality can be illustrated in the following way:

𝅝 = ♩ ♩ ♩ ♩   One whole note is equal in duration to four quarter notes.

𝅗𝅥 = ♩ ♩   One half note is equal in duration to two quarter notes.

Notes of lesser value than the quarter note are proportioned in the same way:

♪ ♪ or ♫ = ♩   Two eighth notes equal one quarter note in duration.

♬♬ or ♬♬ = ♩   Four sixteenth notes equal one quarter note in duration.

The proportionality of note values may be easier to understand if we put them into a rhythm tree. Here, each horizontal line of notes lasts the same amount of time, that is, four pulses.

whole note

half notes

quarter notes

eighth notes

sixteenth notes

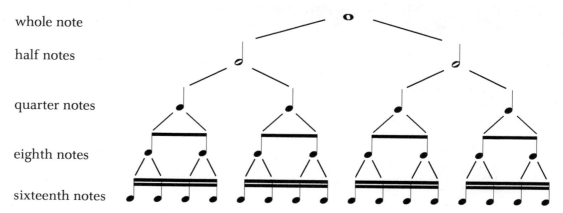

As mentioned earlier, different note values can represent the pulse. If, for example, the eighth note receives one pulse, the quarter note will get two pulses and the half note four pulses. Similarly, if the half note receives one pulse, the whole note will get two pulses and two quarter notes will be needed to complete one pulse.

Music in Action 🔊 Ear Training

Your instructor will select three examples from the following rhythmic patterns and play them on the piano. In the space provided, indicate whether the examples are in duple, triple, or quadruple meter. Remember to listen for the basic, underlying pulse.

1. _____

2. _____

3. _____

Duple Meters

Triple Meters

Quadruple Meters

Rests

Just as the symbols for note value represent duration of sound, **rest** signs are used to indicate durations of silence. Each note value has a corresponding rest sign.

whole rest (fourth line of staff) ▬

half rest (third line of staff) ▬

quarter rest 𝄽

eighth rest 𝄾

sixteenth rest 𝄿

We can create a rhythm tree for rests similar to the one we made for note values.

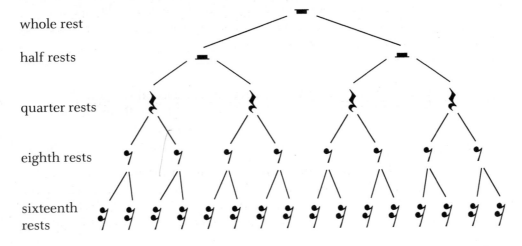

whole rest

half rests

quarter rests

eighth rests

sixteenth rests

Note that the whole rest is often used to indicate one complete measure of silence. It can serve this purpose for any meter, and when used in this way, it is centered within the measure.

Practice drawing the following rest signs:

whole
rests

half
rests

quarter
rests

eighth
rests

sixteenth
rests

Pitch

The Staff

In Western music, pitch is written on a **staff**. The music staff (pl., *staves*) consists of a group of five parallel lines. In music notation, the five lines, the four spaces between the lines, and the spaces above and below the staff are all used. The lines and spaces are numbered from bottom to top: the lines 1 through 5, the spaces 1 through 4.

Noteheads

The lines and spaces of the staff, from the bottom to the top, indicate successively higher pitches. In technical terms, **pitch** is the frequency at which a given sound vibrates. The faster the vibration, the higher the pitch is said to be. (A more detailed explanation of the physical characteristics of sound is given in Appendix I.)

Noteheads are the small oval shapes drawn on the staff to represent particular pitches. They may appear either on a line or in a space, as in the following staff. Notice that the second notehead represents a slightly higher pitch than the first one, because the third space is above the third line.

Previously, you were asked to practice drawing notes on a single line. Look back at that effort now. Are your noteheads clearly on the line? To indicate pitch, noteheads must be placed exactly on a line or in a space. Practice notehead placement once more, this time on the staff, by drawing the following noteheads. Remember to make the noteheads oval rather than round and to draw them small enough so that they sit clearly centered either in a space or on a line.

1.

2.

Music in Action 🔊 Ear Training

Your instructor will play, in random order, various two-note sequences from examples 1 through 6 below. Listen carefully to each of the sequences and indicate in the numbered spaces below the examples whether the second note is higher in pitch (*H*) or lower in pitch (*L*) than the first. Remember, these examples are being played in random order.

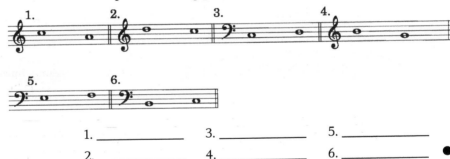

1. _____   3. _____   5. _____

2. _____   4. _____   6. _____

Music in Action 🔊 Ear Training

Your instructor will randomly select and play various three- and four-note sequences from those given below. Listen carefully to each of the sequences, and in the spaces below the examples, indicate whether the last note is higher in pitch (*H*) or lower in pitch (*L*) than the first.

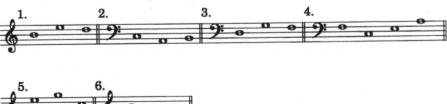

1. _____   4. _____

2. _____   5. _____

3. _____   6. _____

The first seven letters of the alphabet (A through G) are used to name pitches. The staff by itself does not represent any particular set (or range) of pitches; this is the function of **clef** signs. Each clef sign locates a particular pitch on the staff. Two clef signs are used the most: treble clef and bass clef.

The Treble Clef

The **treble clef**, or **G clef**, identifies the second line of the staff as the location for the note G that is five notes above middle C (the C approximately in the middle of the piano keyboard). Notice that the lower part of the treble clef sign encircles the second line:

Class Practice

Practice drawing the treble clef sign. First, draw a vertical line; then, draw the remainder of the clef, starting at the top of the vertical line. Remember to encircle the second line with the lower part of the clef.

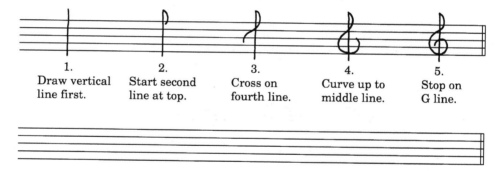

1.	2.	3.	4.	5.
Draw vertical line first.	Start second line at top.	Cross on fourth line.	Curve up to middle line.	Stop on G line.

Once a particular pitch is identified on the staff by a clef sign, the other pitches on that staff follow automatically in alphabetical sequence. Remember, only the first seven letters of the alphabet are used. After that, the sequence of letters repeats.

Class Practice

Because the musical alphabet consists of only the letters A through G, it is important to become fluent in using these seven letters in various combinations. As a class (and later on your own), practice the following sequences using the letters A through G. Notice that some of the sequences move up the alphabet whereas others move down.

(continued)

When you begin, try to keep a steady pulse as you say the sequences. As you improve, try to say each pattern in either duple, triple, or quadruple meter, clapping your hands on the downbeats, that is, the first beat of each measure, as you say each sequence.

1. B C D __ __ __ __ __ __ __ __ __
2. G F E __ __ __ __ __ __ __ __ __
3. D E F __ __ __ __ __ __ __ __ __

For additional practice naming pitches in the treble clef, see Practice materials 1-1 and 1-2 at the end of this chapter.

Music in Action  Sight Singing

Try to sing the following two songs using the syllable *la*. Then try singing them in rhythm, with letter names. For each song, see whether some pitches occur more frequently than others, and identify the pitch that seems to produce the most restful feeling or clearest sense of completion. If you play piano or guitar, once you are comfortable singing these melodies, try playing one or both of them on your instrument.

"Michael, Row the Boat Ashore"

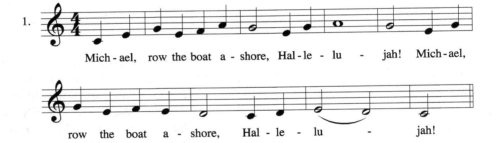

"Go Tell Aunt Rhody"

The Bass Clef

The **bass clef**, or **F clef**, identifies the fourth line of the staff as the location for the note F that is five notes below middle C on the piano.

F → 𝄢

Practice drawing the bass clef sign. First, draw a dot on the fourth line; then, draw the curved sign, beginning at the dot; and finally, place two dots to the right of the sign, one just above the fourth line and one just below.

As with the treble clef, the pitches of the bass clef are arranged in alphabetical sequence.

F   F   G   A   B   C   D   E   F   G   A   B

For practice identifying pitches in the bass clef, see Practice materials 1-3 and 1-4 at the end of this chapter.

Music in Action ● Sight Singing

Sing the following two songs, both written in the bass clef, first using the syllable *la*, then with the letter names in rhythm. For each song, identify the pitch that seems to produce the most restful feeling or clearest sense of completion. Then, if you play piano or guitar, try playing one or both of these songs on your instrument.

"This Old Man"

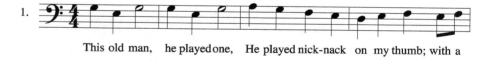

1.

This old man, he played one, He played nick-nack on my thumb; with a

nick-nack pad-dy-whack, Give a dog a bone, This old man came roll-ing home.

"Sweet Betsy From Pike"

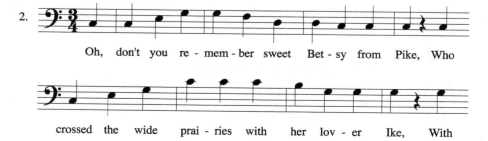

2.

Oh, don't you re - mem - ber sweet Bet - sy from Pike, Who

crossed the wide prai - ries with her lov - er Ike, With

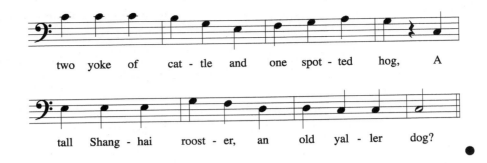

two yoke of   cat - tle and   one spot - ted   hog,   A

tall   Shang - hai   roost - er,   an   old   yal - ler   dog?

The Great Staff

The **great staff**, also known as the grand staff, consists of a treble clef staff and a bass clef staff joined together by a vertical line and a brace.

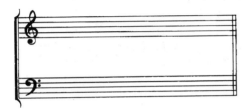

The great staff is used primarily for piano music. It is also sometimes used for choral music or any other type of music requiring a range of pitches too wide for a single staff.

In the following example, notice that one pitch, *middle C*—so called because of its location in the middle of the piano keyboard and on the great staff—does not touch either staff. Instead, it sits on a short line, called a *ledger line*, that is not part of either staff. Ledger lines are explained in more detail in Chapter 5.

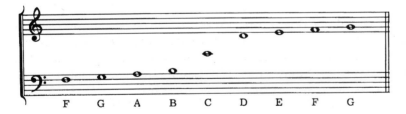

In actual music, however, middle C does not appear, as it does here, in the center of the great staff. Rather, it is located closer to one staff or the other.

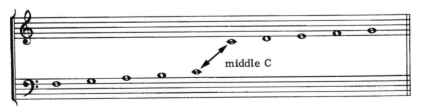

In piano music, the notes on the treble staff are usually played by the right hand, and the notes on the bass staff are played by the left hand. As shown in the following example, the location of middle C indicates which hand is to play it.

Bach: Courante from French Suite No. 2

right hand

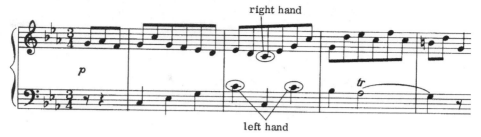

left hand

In choral music, the location of middle C indicates which voice should sing it.

Bach: Chorale from Cantata No. 180

Deck thy - self, my soul, — with — glad – ness,
Come in - to the day - light's splen – dor,

Tenor

For practice identifying notes on the great staff, see Practice materials 1-5.

A Final Note

Think of music written down on paper as a storage and retrieval system. In this system, musical information is stored by the composer in a code of shapes and symbols. A performer wishing to turn this written code back into sound must understand not only which musical elements are being dealt with but also how they are encoded.

The key to reading and writing Western music is to realize that the written music of our culture focuses on and encodes two major musical elements: pitch, which is the basis of melody and harmony; and duration, through which the rhythm flows. Although a lot of additional information is given in music notation, these two elements—rhythm and pitch—are the primary ones.

Music in Action

Applying Your Skills

The following rhythms and melodies are taken from Appendices A and B. Clap and count the rhythms, and try to sing the melodies using a neutral syllable such as *la*. (In Chapter 5, you will learn another way to sing melodies called movable *do*.) After you have tried to sing these melodies, play them on the keyboard to check for accuracy. These two appendices contain a lot of practice material. As you continue with this book, it would be extremely helpful to practice one or two rhythms and melodies at the beginning of each study session.

Rhythms

(continued)

Moderate   Asia

3.

Fast   Africa

4.

Melodies

1.

2.

3.

Practice

Practice materials are for use outside of class. Think of them the same way you do your instrument. To get better, you must practice every day. Similar Practice materials will appear at the end of each chapter.

Practice 1-1

Identify by letter name the following pitches in the treble clef. Remember that the treble clef is also known as the G clef because it identifies the second line of the staff as the note G.

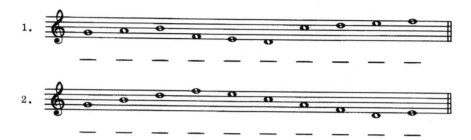

Practice 1-2

Identify by letter name the pitches of the following songs written in the treble clef. Keep in mind that the treble clef identifies the pitch G. When you have finished, try singing these songs using the letter names in place of the lyrics.

Practice 1-3

Identify by letter name the following pitches in the bass clef. Remember that the bass clef is also known as the F clef because it identifies the fourth line of the staff as the note F.

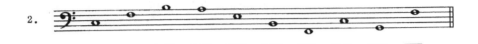

Practice 1-4

Identify by letter name the pitches of the following songs written in the bass clef. Keep in mind that the bass clef identifies the pitch F. When you have finished, try singing these songs using the letter names in place of the lyrics.

"Nine Hundred Miles"

"Skip to My Lou"

Practice 1-5

Identify by letter name the following pitches on the great staff. Remember that middle C will never be exactly in the middle of the great staff, but, rather, closer to one staff or the other. Remember also that the treble clef identifies the second line as the G above middle C, while the bass clef identifies the fourth line as the F below middle C.

1.
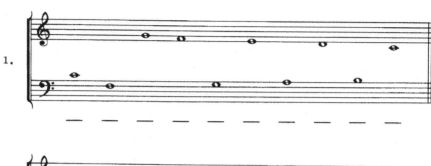

2.
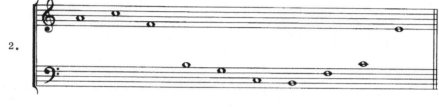

2

The Keyboard

𝄐 **Visit Music Fundamentals in Action, at CourseMate, to:**

• Take a Pretest on the basics
• Hear the author's Let's Talk About Music podcasts on the basics
• Find many more practice exercises to help you succeed in this course
• See Tips&Tools for each chapter

Introduction

Learning music theory is easier if you know your way around the keyboard. Either an acoustic piano or an electronic keyboard will work. With either of them, you will be able to both hear and see concepts of musical sound such as intervals, scales, and triads. Although it is possible to do this to some extent on other instruments, such as the fingerboard of the guitar, it is far easier to work with these concepts at the piano keyboard. This section will introduce the keyboard and help you begin to understand it. Future chapters will frequently refer to the keyboard when clarifying particular points. Some exercises will help you become familiar with the keyboard.

The standard piano keyboard has 88 keys: 52 white ones and 36 black ones. (Synthesizers and electronic keyboards are generally smaller, commonly five-and-one-half octaves, as opposed to slightly more than eight octaves for the piano.) The black keys on both pianos and synthesizers are arranged in alternating groups of twos and threes. Moving from right to left on all keyboards produces successively lower pitches, while moving from left to right creates successively higher ones.

The White Keys

As explained earlier, only the first seven letters of the alphabet are used to name pitches. These seven letters name the white keys of the piano, beginning at the left end of the keyboard with A and successively repeating the sequence A through G up to the other end of the keyboard.

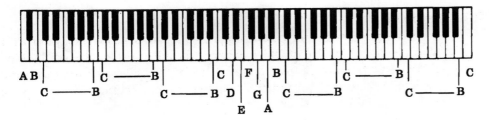

AB | C —— B | C | F | B | C —— B | C
C —— B | C —— B D | G | C —— B | C —— B
E | A

Learning the keyboard is easier when you locate and remember two landmarks. The first is the note C. In the following illustration, notice that the note C always occurs immediately to the left of a group of two black keys. The pitch called *middle* C is the one approximately in the middle of the keyboard.

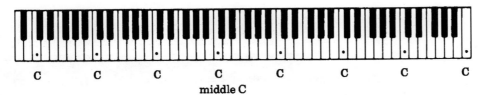

C   C   C   C   C   C   C   C
middle C

The second landmark to locate is F. This is the pitch that occurs immediately to the left of a group of three black keys.

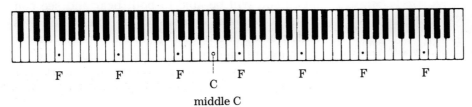

F   F   F   F   F   F   F
C
middle C

With these two landmarks, you should be able to learn the rest of the keyboard more easily. Remember, too, that only the letters A through G are used, and that the alphabetical sequence runs from left to right.

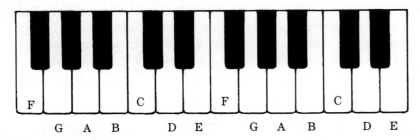

F   C   F   C
G   A   B   D   E   G   A   B   D   E

It is sometimes helpful to memorize other landmarks such as G or B. But be careful not to rely too heavily on landmarks at the expense of learning all the keys equally well. Landmarks are convenient at the beginning, but you only know the keyboard when you can name any key at random.

For additional practice naming the white keys, see Practice materials 2-1 and 2-2.

Music in Action

Keyboard

These pitch sequences are the opening notes of four songs you may know: "He's Got the Whole World," "On Top of Old Smokey," "She'll Be Coming Round the Mountain," and "Frere Jacques." Find and play these pitches at the piano, naming each song if you can. When you can play them, practice singing each song fragment with letter names.

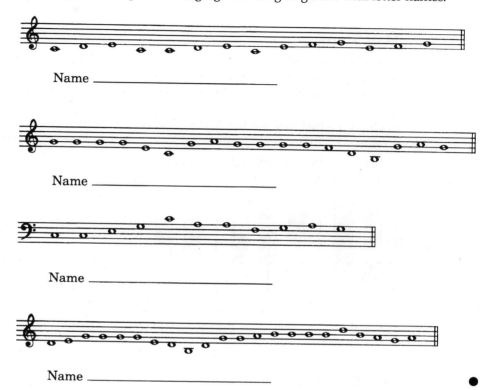

Name _____

Name _____

Name _____

Name _____

The Black Keys

The black keys of the piano are named in relation to the white keys that they stand between. Furthermore, each black key can be identified by two different names. For instance, the black key between F and G is called either *F sharp* (F♯) or *G flat* (G♭). F♯ identifies that black key as the pitch *above F*, while G♭ tells us it's the pitch *below G*.

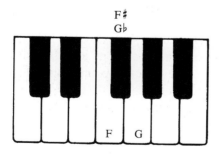

At first, it may seem needlessly confusing that one black key can have two different names, but once you understand the pattern, it will make sense. It is important to remember that each of the white keys has its own letter name (A through G), while each of the black keys is related to, and takes its name from, the white key on either side of it.

For practice naming the black keys, see Practice materials 2-3.

Musical Distances

The piano keyboard has the important characteristic of allowing us to visualize musical distances. The musical distance between two pitches, whether sounded or written on the staff, is called an **interval**.

Half Steps

The smallest interval on the piano is a **half step**. This is the distance from any key to the key immediately above or below it. The following example shows the three situations in which half steps can occur: (1) between a white key and a black key, (2) between a black key and a white key, and (3) between a white key and a white key. Notice that the third possibility, between a white key and a white key, appears in only two places in each octave—between E and F and between B and C. As you look at this example, remember that an interval is the distance *between* two notes.

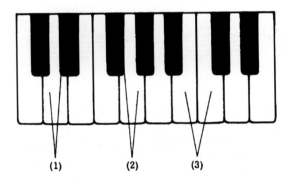

Whole Steps

A **whole step** consists of two half steps. On the keyboard, there will be one key between the two pitches that are a whole step apart. Whole steps can appear (1) between a white key and a white key, (2) between a black key and a black key, and (3) between a white key and a black key. In each instance, the whole step has one pitch in between.

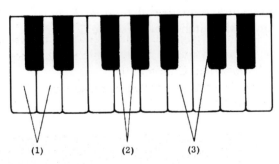

Whole steps *usually* involve pitches of adjacent letter names, as in the following cases:

For additional work with whole steps and half steps, see Practice materials 2-4.

Accidentals

In written music, the following signs, called **accidentals**, are used to alter the pitch of a note chromatically:

♯	**sharp**	raises the pitch to the next adjacent note (that is, a half step)
♭	**flat**	lowers pitch by a half step
✗	**double sharp**	raises pitch by two half steps (one whole step)
♭♭	**double flat**	lowers pitch by two half steps (one whole step)
♮	**natural**	cancels a sharp, double sharp, flat, or double flat

When pitches are written as words, the accidentals follow the note (as when spoken); for example C♯ is read C sharp. When pitches are notated on a staff, however, all accidentals are placed to the left of the pitches they affect and on the same line or space as the note.

Right   Wrong

Double sharps and double flats can be confusing. As you know, the sharp sign raises a pitch by a half step. In most instances, this means that a pitch will be raised from a white key to a black key—for example, F to F♯, C to C♯. Because a double sharp raises a pitch *two* half steps, or one whole step, quite often the resulting pitch is a white key. Thus, F to F✗ appears on the keyboard as F to G. In the same way, E to E♭♭ appears on the keyboard as E to D.

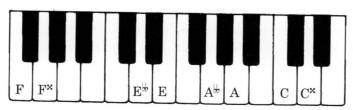

You may be wondering why we can't simply ignore double sharps and double flats. In fact, these signs seldom appear in music, but when they do, they have a specific function, which we will discuss in Chapter 10.

For additional practice locating notes on the keyboard, including those with double sharps and flats, see Practice materials 2-5.

A Final Note

As you probably are aware by now, the piano or electric keyboard is extremely useful in helping us visualize abstract musical concepts like intervals, scales, and chords. Knowing the keyboard is also important for a number of other reasons, such as understanding harmony, learning voicing for arranging, and composing. Many musicians study piano or synthesizer as a second instrument because of this versatility. These people feel that improving their abilities on the keyboard helps them to *understand* the music better.

Even if you do not play piano or synthesizer, you should spend some time each day becoming familiar with the keyboard. The Class Practice and Practice materials in this book are useful for this purpose, as are simple songbooks and beginning sight-singing books. Another good place to begin is Appendix D, Graded Melodies for Sight-Singing and Playing. Remember, becoming musical requires your active participation. Remember, too, that being able to *hear* what you play *before you play it* is one of the goals of becoming more musical. Your skill at sight-singing will improve if you practice it for a few minutes each time you sit down to practice your instrument. Try singing each exercise before you play it. Then play it. Then sing it again. This may seem difficult at first, but you will get better as you practice, and the skill you will learn will be invaluable.

Practice 2-1

Locate and write each given pitch on the keyboard. Remember that each pitch will occur in more than one place, because these keyboards span more than an octave. Begin by locating the F and C landmarks. When you have located all the pitches, practice finding and playing them on the piano.

1. F, C, G, D, B

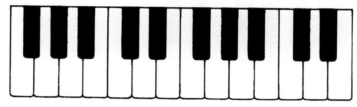

2. A, E, B, F, D

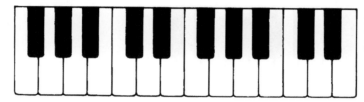

Practice 2-2

Identify these pitches by letter name. Then, write the name of each pitch once on the keyboard that follows in the location where it occurs. Finally, find and play each of the pitches on the piano. Remember that the treble clef identifies the pitch G, while the bass clef identifies the pitch F.

1. 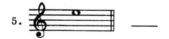   4.

2. _____   5.

3.  _____   6.

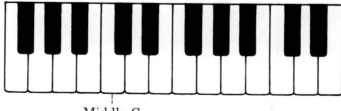

Middle C

Practice 2-3

Locate the following pitches on the black keys of the piano by drawing a line from each pitch name to the appropriate place on the keyboard. Remember that each pitch will occur in more than one place, because these keyboards span more than an octave. Begin by locating the F and C landmarks. When you have located all the pitches, practice finding and playing them on the piano.

1. C♯, G♭, B♭

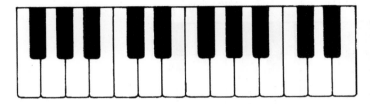

2. E♭, F♯, A♭

Practice 2-4

On the following keyboards, identify each indicated interval as either a whole step or a half step. Use the letters *W* or *H* to indicate the interval and write them in the spaces provided. Remember that the half step is the smallest distance on the keyboard, and that a whole step consists of two half steps.

1.

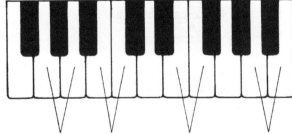

_____   _____   _____   _____

2.

_____   _____   _____   _____

Practice 2-5

Locate the indicated pitches on the following keyboards by drawing a line from the written pitch to the key it represents. Begin by naming the notes, making sure that you are thinking in the right clef. Pay particular attention to the double sharps and flats. Then, play each of the pitches on the piano.

1.

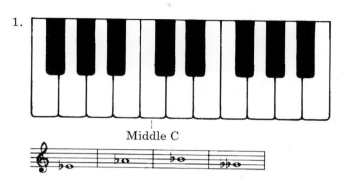

Middle C

2.

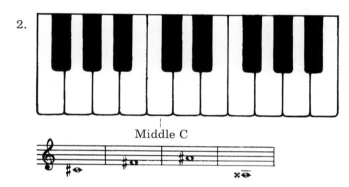

Middle C

3.

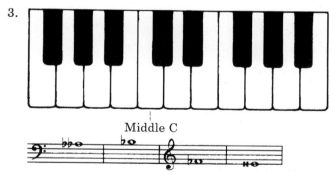

Middle C

Focus on Skills 1: **The Basics**

 Visit Music Fundamentals in Action, at CourseMate, for interactive Focus on Fundamentals exercises.

As you can see, musical knowledge is cumulative. The various facts fit together like a jigsaw puzzle, and you have to remember a great deal of the previous information to fully understand the new concepts. That makes it important to check periodically, to learn whether we have fully grasped the material we've covered so far. This is the first of seven such checkpoints; the others come after Chapters 4, 5, 7, 8, 11, and 14.

The questions in this section ask you to provide information you learned in the first two chapters. If you discover weaknesses in any of these basic areas, be sure to review the relevant sections of those chapters before beginning Chapter 3.

1. In the space provided, draw a treble clef sign and a bass clef sign, as well as a flat sign, sharp sign, natural sign, double sharp sign, and double flat sign for the given notes.

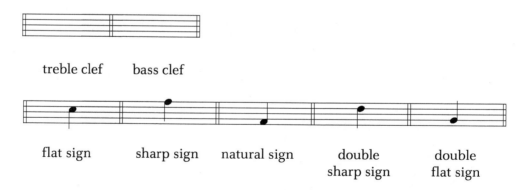

treble clef   bass clef

flat sign   sharp sign   natural sign   double sharp sign   double flat sign

2. Identify the six basic elements of music. They may be in any order.

    a. _____

    b. _____

    c. _____

    d. _____

    e. _____

    f. _____

3. Locate the following pitches on the keyboard. Each pitch can be found in more than one place on these keyboards. Make sure you locate them all.

a.
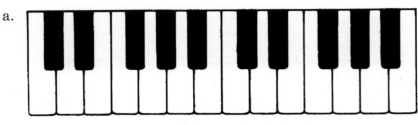

D, G, F, E, A

4. Locate the indicated pitches on the black keys of the keyboard by drawing a line from each pitch to the appropriate key. Remember that the same black key may have two different names.

a.
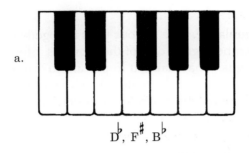

D♭, F♯, B♭

b.
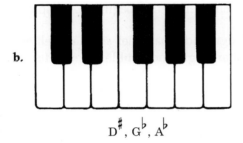

D♯, G♭, A♭

5. Locate the indicated double sharps and double flats on the keyboard by drawing a line from each pitch to the appropriate key.

a.
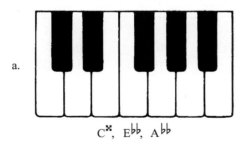

C𝄪, E♭♭, A♭♭

6. Identify the following pitches by letter name.

7. Write each indicated pitch in four different places on the grand staff. The easiest way to do this is to locate two in the treble clef and two in the bass clef.

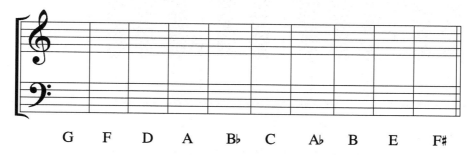

G   F   D   A   B♭   C   A♭   B   E   F♯

8. Complete the following:

   a. Duple meter contains _____ pulses per measure.

   b. Quadruple meter contains _____ pulses per measure.

   c. Triple meter contains _____ pulses per measure.

9. Complete the following:

   a. One whole note is equal in duration to _____ quarter notes.

   b. One quarter note is equal in duration to _____ eighth notes.

   c. One quarter rest is equal in duration to _____ sixteenth rests.

Rhythm I: Simple Meter

 Visit Music Fundamentals in Action, at CourseMate, to:

- Take a Pretest on rhythm
- Hear the author's Let's Talk About Music podcast on rhythm
- View a Hands On Music video on simple meter
- Find many more practice exercises to help you succeed in this course
- See Tips&Tools for each chapter

Introduction

In Chapter 1 we learned the basics of rhythm and meter, but that is only the beginning. Here, and in the following chapter, we will learn that there are two distinct types of meter—simple and compound.

Music based on steady recurring pulses can be divided into two types:

- simple meters that divide the basic pulse into two parts, and
- compound meters that divide the basic pulse into three parts.

In this chapter, we will learn about simple meter, including a method for counting it; in Chapter 4 we will study compound meter and how it is counted.

We will begin, however, by building on what we learned in Chapter 1. We will learn about dotted notes, which is a way of increasing the time value of any note, regardless of the meter, and time signatures, which tell us both the meter of the music plus the note value that gets the beat.

Dotted Notes

Musical rhythms can become extremely complex at times, making use of note values that go far beyond the whole, half, quarter, eighth, and sixteenth notes studied so far. One such new note value is the **dotted note**.

When you first begin to study dotted notes, they can seem very confusing. But if you will keep in mind that the dot always means the same thing, you will have less trouble. A dot to the right of a notehead gives that note a longer duration. Furthermore, the dot always increases the time value of that note by one-half. For example, a half note is equal in value to two quarter notes.

$$\half = \quarter + \quarter$$

When a dot is placed beside a note, this new note, called a dotted note, becomes equal to the original value plus one-half the original value. In the case of our half note, adding a dot creates a dotted half note with a time value equal to three quarter notes.

$$\text{♩.} = \text{♩} + \text{♩} + \text{♩}$$

Rests as well as notes can be increased in value by adding a dot, although dotted rests are used less often than dotted notes. As with notes, a dot placed to the right of a rest increases its value by one-half.

Time Signatures

The **time signature**, or **meter signature** as it is also called, is made up of two numbers, one above the other. It always appears at the beginning of a piece of music. The time signature gives us two different pieces of information: The top number tells us the meter of the piece; the bottom number identifies the note value that represents the pulse. For example, in the time signature ¾:

  3 indicates triple meter—that is, three pulses per measure.
  4 identifies the quarter note as the pulse beat.

Remember that although the quarter note represents the pulse for many pieces, other note values can also serve this purpose. Both the eighth note and the half note are frequently used.

  Here is an example of triple meter with the eighth note representing the pulse,

while this is a triple meter with the half note representing the pulse.

Notice, incidentally, that the meter signature is *never* written as a fraction: ¾.

Identify the meter and indicate the note value that represents the pulse for each of the meter signatures below.

EXAMPLE: **4** quadruple meter
     4 quarter-note pulse

1. $\frac{2}{8}$ _____

2. $\frac{3}{4}$ _____

3. $\frac{4}{2}$ _____

4. $\frac{3}{8}$ _____

5. $\frac{2}{4}$ _____

6. $\frac{4}{8}$ _____

7. $\frac{3}{2}$ _____

8. $\frac{2}{2}$ _____

Simple Meter

Thus far, our discussion of meter has dealt entirely with what is called simple meter. In **simple meter**, the basic pulse is normally divided into two equal parts. For instance, in $\frac{2}{4}$ meter, each quarter note (the note representing the pulse) is divisible into two eighth notes:

$\frac{2}{4}$ ♩ ♩ | ♩ ♩ | = ♫ ♫ | ♫ ♫ |

This division of the basic pulse into two equal parts is the mark of a simple meter. Metrical patterns such as $\frac{3}{8}$ and $\frac{3}{2}$ also subdivide in this way:

$\frac{3}{8}$ ♪ ♪ ♪ | ♪ ♪ ♪ | = ♫♫♫ | ♫♫♫ |

$\frac{3}{2}$ 𝅗𝅥 𝅗𝅥 𝅗𝅥 | 𝅗𝅥 𝅗𝅥 𝅗𝅥 | = ♩♩♩♩♩♩ | ♩♩♩♩♩♩ |

The common simple meters are:

simple duple	$\frac{2}{8}$	$\frac{2}{4}$	$\frac{2}{2}$
simple triple	$\frac{3}{8}$	$\frac{3}{4}$	$\frac{3}{2}$
simple quadruple	$\frac{4}{8}$	$\frac{4}{4}$	$\frac{4}{2}$

Note that in all cases the top numeral indicates the number of pulses in each measure, and the bottom numeral indicates the note value that represents the pulse.

For each of the following simple meters, write one measure of notes representing the pulse and one measure of notes representing the division of the pulse. Follow the example.

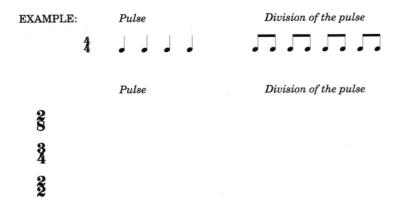

EXAMPLE: *Pulse*   *Division of the pulse*

          Pulse   *Division of the pulse*

A Counting Method for Simple Meters

In learning rhythms, it is helpful to know a method of counting that can be spoken aloud as you are clapping rhythms. The value of such a system is that it can be transferred to "mental" counting when you are playing or singing actual music. Although several systems are in use, the following one is recommended.

The Basic Pulse

In this system, the basic pulse is identified by the numbers "one, two, three, four," as needed. (This is true for both simple and compound meter, which we will learn later.) Practice counting the following examples in simple meter until you feel comfortable with the basic pulse. Remember to always keep the pulse steady.

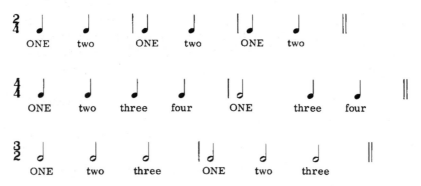

Divisions of the Pulse

When dividing simple meters, *and* is used to indicate the division of the pulse. Practice the following examples until they feel comfortable.

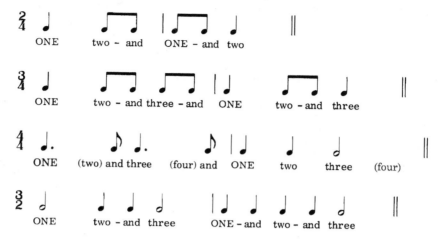

When a further subdivision is needed—that is, if you need to indicate one-quarter of the basic pulse—the syllables to use are *e* and *a* (or *da*). Here are some examples to practice.

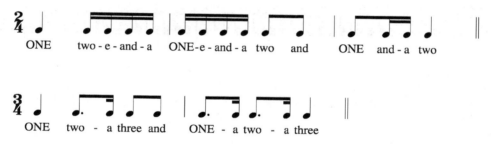

Class Practice

As a class, clap and count the following rhythmic examples taken from folk songs. You will probably know some of these pieces, and that will help you decide whether you are doing them right or not. Begin by saying two measures of the divided pulse (1-and 2-and) aloud before clapping. When you are comfortable with the counting system, also try playing the rhythms on an instrument or keyboard while counting mentally. Remember to always keep the basic pulse steady.

(continued)

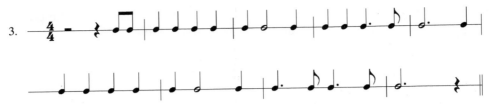

3.

For additional practice with counting syllables, see Practice materials 3-3 at the end of this chapter.

Music in Action

Performing Simple Meters

As a class, clap and count aloud the following two-part examples in simple meter. Half the class should clap the top part and half the bottom part. When you are comfortable with your part, try switching parts. Then, by yourself, try tapping the examples on a desk or tabletop, one part per hand.

1.

2.

3.

Conducting Simple Meters

So far, the rhythmic patterns you have been asked to clap can be performed by the class without a conductor. To perform more complicated patterns, or patterns consisting of three or four separate parts, however, you will probably need a conductor to keep everyone together. Indicating the beats and keeping the group together are important functions of the conductor.

The conductor indicates the beat with movements of the right arm. The following are the basic arm movements for duple, triple, and quadruple meters.

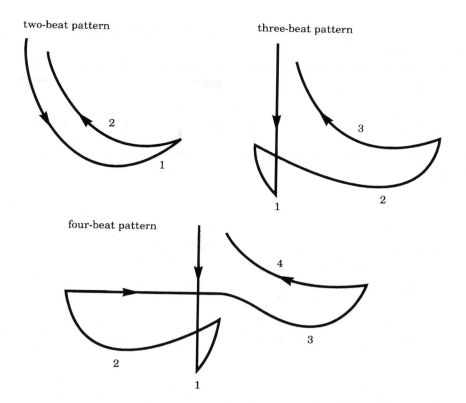

two-beat pattern

three-beat pattern

four-beat pattern

When practicing these patterns, remember the following points:

1. The beat pattern is always performed by the right arm only. This is true even if you are left-handed.

2. Always practice standing up. It is difficult to conduct correctly while sitting down, and almost no one does.

3. The first beat of each pattern is called the **downbeat**; the last beat is called the **upbeat**.

4. Keep the beat pattern high enough for everyone to see. The center of the pattern should be level with your chest, not your waist.

5. The arm motion should always be fluid and smooth. Never let the arm come to a complete stop.

6. When beginning a pattern, always prepare for the first beat of the exercise by giving the beat that comes directly before it. Assume, for instance, that you are going to conduct an exercise that uses a three-beat pattern starting on the downbeat. To begin, you would give the previous upbeat as a preparation. This is called the *preparatory beat.*

7. Not all pieces of music begin on the downbeat. Sometimes the piece begins with an incomplete measure of one or more pickup beats. Formally, this is called an **anacrusis**, a word from poetry that means the lead-in syllables. When conducting a piece that begins with an anacrusis, give the beat before it (whatever it is) as the silent preparatory beat.

Conducting

The following melodies are in simple meters. Practice conducting each of these melodies while you sing each of them on *la*. Keep practicing until you are comfortable singing and conducting simultaneously.

"Hush, Little Baby"

"Scarborough Fair" *

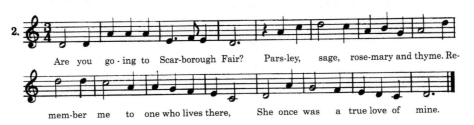

"Sourwood Mountain"

Music in Action 🔊 Ear Training

Your instructor will choose two rhythmic passages in simple meter from Appendix A and play them for you several times. You will be told the meter of each example. Listen carefully to each passage, and try to notate it in the space provided below. If the passages seem too long, your instructor can divide them into shorter segments. Use the counting method to help clarify the rhythmic patterns you hear.

1._____

_____

2._____

_____

Beams in Simple Meter

Although it is still common in vocal music (where it is important to align notes precisely with the lyrics) to see individual eighth notes or sixteenth notes with separate flags, in instrumental music these notes rarely appear individually. Instead, two or more eighth or sixteenth notes will be grouped together, according to beats, with a connecting beam. A vocal rhythmic pattern such as

will appear in instrumental music as

Notice that eighth notes are grouped by a single beam and sixteenth notes by a double beam.

When connecting notes with beams, it is important in all but the simplest patterns to begin each beat with a separate beam. A musician trains his or her eye to see such patterns of beats within a measure. A poorly written arrangement, such as the following, is momentarily confusing:

This pattern is confusing rhythmically because the beaming has hidden the second, third, and fourth beats of the measure. The following shows a much clearer way of writing the same pattern:

Here, each of the four beats begins with a new beam. Remember, the reason we beam notes together is to make the rhythmic patterns easier to recognize, not more difficult.

Extra care must be taken when beaming irregular divisions of the beat, particularly dotted rhythm patterns, because these can be especially tricky. First, try to determine where each basic beat begins. This is more or less a process of adding up the note values. Then, combine groups of notes so that each basic beat is beamed together. Make sure, however, that you do not combine two beats into one group. Each beat should be beamed separately.

The following examples may make the above explanation clear. In a simple meter, such as $\frac{2}{4}$, the basic beat is the quarter note. This quarter note can be divided into two eighth notes or four sixteenth notes.

But the quarter note can also be divided into any combination of eighth notes and sixteenth notes that total one beat. In simple meters, for instance, there are three ways that the combination of one eighth note and two sixteenth notes can be written.

Notice that in each case the combination of notes is equal to one beat in simple meter. Notice also that the beaming (one beam for eighth notes, two for sixteenth notes) clearly indicates the beginning of each beat.

The beaming of dotted notes in simple meter is simply an extension of this same principle. Because a dotted eighth note is the equivalent of three sixteenth notes, the dotted-eighth-and-sixteenth pattern is frequently found and can be written one of two ways:

Notice that, in both cases, a complete beat is combined under one beam.

Class Practice

As a class, clap and count each of the rhythms given below. Then, rewrite them by beaming the eighth notes and sixteenth notes together, taking care not to place beams across beats. Next, clap the patterns you have written. Does being able to see clearly the beginning of each beat make it easier to read the patterns?

For additional work with simple meters, see Practice materials 3-1, 3-2, 3-4, and 3-5.

Tempo

How fast the pulse of a piece of music moves is called the **tempo**. Whereas today we might use the terms *fast* and *slow* as indications of speed, many pieces of music use Italian terms to assign the tempo. The following is a list of the most important terms and their meanings:

Slow Tempos

largo	broad, very slow
lento	slow
adagio	slow

Moderate Tempos

andante	slow walking speed
moderato	moderate walking speed

Fast Tempos

allegro	fast
vivace	quick, lively
presto	very fast

In addition, the following two terms are important because they indicate gradual changes of tempo:

ritardando (*rit.*)	gradually becoming slower
accelerando (*accel.*)	gradually becoming faster

A Final Note

Rhythm is such an important and fundamental part of music that it must be mastered in order for you to become a successful musician. This mastery must include the ability to recognize note values, count meters and rhythms, and perform intricate patterns using a variety of durational symbols.

In this chapter, we have concentrated on simple meters, which divide the basic pulse into two equal parts. Before moving on to compound meter, make sure that you understand and are comfortable recognizing note values in simple meters, and that you can clap and count the various examples in this chapter.

Always keep in mind that what at first may seem difficult or confusing will, with consistent practice, become easier. The key, of course, is practice. Whether alone, with friends, or in class, the more you practice the better you will become. Above all else, keep the pulse steady. This may require that you practice at a slow tempo at first, but this is okay. Like everything else, speed and proficiency comes with practice.

Music in Action

Performing Simple Meters

As a class, clap or perform on instruments the following two- and three-part rhythmic examples, paying particular attention to the tempo of each example. Then, experiment with tapping out the examples on a desk or tabletop, one part per hand. If you are particularly adventurous, you might also like to try tapping out the three-part example: Tap out the top part with your right hand, the middle part with your left hand, and the bottom part with one foot. You may find the three-part example difficult at first, but remember that organists and trap-set drummers use this kind of rhythmic coordination every day.

Andante

Moderato

Allegro

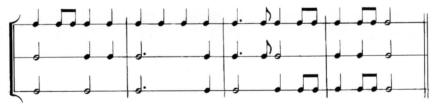

Music in Action

Composing

Below are two melodies in simple meter: one from a minuet by Bach and one from Russian folk music. You may have heard one or both of these pieces before. Clap the rhythm of each melody several times. Then, in the space provided, write a second rhythmic part that, when clapped with the rhythm of the melody, will complement it and create a two-part clapping piece. Your teacher may wish to work on this as a class or assign it as homework. If used as homework, perform these clapping pieces in class and discuss their strengths and weaknesses.

Bach: Minuet in G Minor

Russian Folk Song

Practice 3-1

Divide each of the following sequences of notes into measures by placing bar lines in the appropriate places. Begin by looking at the time signature to determine the number of beats per measure and the note value that gets the beat. Remember to put a double bar line at the end of each sequence. When you have correctly placed the bar lines in each of these examples, practice playing each one on an instrument or keyboard. If you sing, choose a comfortable pitch in the middle of your range. Remember to keep the pulse steady and to hold each note for its full value.

Practice 3-2

The following rhythmic passages are barred and notated correctly. Study them carefully and write the meter signature for each in the appropriate place. Begin by deciding the number of beats each measure contains. When you have correctly identified the meter signature of each example, practice playing the passages on an instrument or keyboard. If you sing, choose a comfortable pitch in the middle of your range.

Practice 3-3

The following examples in simple meter are taken from Appendix A. For each, write the counting syllables below each line. Begin by looking at the time signature and deciding the number of beats per measure. Then, practice clapping and saying the syllables aloud. Be sure to keep a steady pulse.

1.

2.

3.

4.

Practice 3-4

Rewrite each of the following rhythmic patterns in the indicated simple meter. Begin by determining the note value that gets the pulse. Then determine the number of pulses per measure.

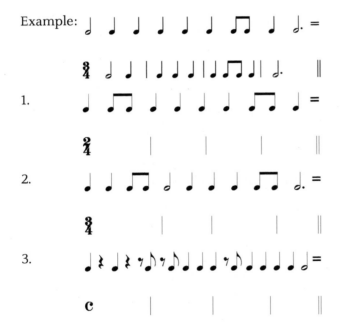

Practice 3-5

Rewrite the following rhythmic patterns by beaming the eighth notes and sixteenth notes together. Remember: Do not place beams across beats. Remember also that dotted eighth and sixteenth notes that occur within one beat in simple meter are joined in one of the ways shown in the example.

EXAMPLE: ♩. ♫ or ♩ ♫.

Rhythm II: Compound Meter

𝄐 **Visit Music Fundamentals in Action, at CourseMate, to:**

• Take a Pretest on rhythm
• Hear the author's Let's Talk About Music podcast on rhythm
• View a Hands On Music video on compound meter
• Find many more practice exercises to help you succeed in this course
• See Tips&Tools for each chapter

Introduction

In addition to the two-part division of the pulse in simple meter that we learned in Chapter 3, there is another common way to divide the pulse. A division into three equal parts is called **compound meter**, and we will learn about that here.

Compound Meter

Compound meter may be confusing at first because the 𝄕 meter signature seems to indicate that there are six pulses in a measure and that the eighth note gets the pulse. This is true, but 𝄕 meter is normally counted and played with the six eighth notes grouped into two sets of three. As a result, 𝄕 meter "feels" like duple meter, with the primary pulse represented by a dotted quarter note and each of the primary pulses divisible into three parts:

Pulse   *Division of the Pulse*

$$\frac{6}{8} \quad \jmath. \quad \jmath. \quad | \jmath. \quad \jmath. \quad | \quad = \quad \text{♫♫♫} \quad | \quad \text{♫♫♫} \quad |$$

The correct term for 𝄕 meter, therefore, is *compound duple*.

Practice clapping the following pattern in 𝄕 meter. It will help you begin to feel the divisions of compound duple meter. Be sure to emphasize the accented notes.

A problem that often arises is how to distinguish between $\frac{3}{4}$ meter and $\frac{6}{8}$ meter, because both contain six eighth notes. The difference is in how the pulse is accented and can be clearly seen in the following illustration:

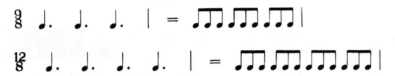

Simple meter: eighth notes (and accents) grouped in twos

Compound meter: eighth notes (and accents) grouped in threes

In a similar way to $\frac{6}{8}$ meter being compound duple, $\frac{9}{8}$ meter is *compound triple* and $\frac{12}{8}$ meter is *compound quadruple*:

The common compound meters are:

compound duple	$\frac{6}{16}$ ($\frac{2}{}$)	$\frac{6}{8}$ ($\frac{2}{}$)	$\frac{6}{4}$ ($\frac{2}{}$)
compound triple	$\frac{9}{16}$ ($\frac{3}{}$)	$\frac{9}{8}$ ($\frac{3}{}$)	$\frac{9}{4}$ ($\frac{3}{}$)
compound quadruple	$\frac{12}{16}$ ($\frac{4}{}$)	$\frac{12}{8}$ ($\frac{4}{}$)	$\frac{12}{4}$ ($\frac{4}{}$)

The interesting thing about compound meter, of course, is that it contains two different pulses simultaneously going at different speeds. For example, there is the faster secondary pulse of six eighth notes, but there is also a bigger, slower pulse of two dotted quarter notes in a measure. This primary pulse combines the eighth notes into two groups of three.

Although this may be a difficult concept to understand initially, most people can hear it very easily. Look at the rhythm to "For He's a Jolly Good Fellow," which follows. Have some class members who know it sing the melody while others clap either the secondary eighth-note pulse or the primary dotted-quarter pulse. Notice how everything fits together. In most musical situations, the slower dotted-quarter pulse is usually considered primary.

"For He's a Jolly Good Fellow"

Compound Meter

The following melodies are in compound meter:

"Down in the Valley"
"Eency, Weency Spider"
"Over the River and Through the Woods"
"Three Blind Mice"
"When Johnny Comes Marching Home"

Choose one or two that most of the class know and try to sing the melody while tapping the eighth notes on your desk with one hand and the dotted quarter notes with the other. This is not easy at first, but an understanding of these interlocking qualities of compound rhythm will make your performances smoother and more musical. ●

Class Practice

With the help of your teacher, identify the meter and indicate the note value that represents the primary pulse for each of the following compound meter signatures.

EXAMPLE: 6/8   duple meter
                    dotted quarter-note pulse

1. 6/4 _____   5. 9/8 _____

2. 12/4 _____   6. 9/4 _____

3. 6/16 _____   7. 12/8 _____

4. 12/16 _____   8. 9/16 _____

Additional practice with compound meter terminology can be found in Practice materials 4-3 at the end of this chapter.

In the same way that we made a rhythm tree for simple meters, we can make a rhythm tree for compound meters. Here it is for both notes and rests. As you can see, the division of the primary pulse into three parts is clearly visible.

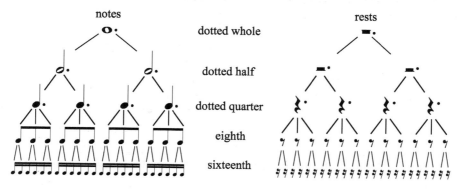

For each of the following compound meters, write one measure of notes representing the primary pulse and one measure of notes representing the division of the pulse. Follow the example.

EXAMPLE:

Pulse   *Division of the Pulse*

$\frac{6}{4}$ 𝅗𝅥.   𝅗𝅥.   ♩ ♩ ♩ ♩ ♩ ♩

Pulse   *Division of the Pulse*

1. $\frac{6}{16}$

2. $\frac{9}{4}$

3. $\frac{12}{16}$

4. $\frac{12}{4}$

5. $\frac{9}{16}$

Additional practice in identifying compound meters is available in Practice materials 4-1.

A Counting Method for Compound Meters

Remember from our discussion of simple meter that the basic pulse in either simple or compound meter is counted the same: "one, two, three, four."

The Primary Pulse

$\frac{6}{8}$ 𝅘𝅥.   𝅘𝅥. | 𝅘𝅥.   𝅘𝅥.   ‖
     ONE   two   ONE   two

$\frac{9}{4}$ 𝅗𝅥.   𝅗𝅥.   𝅗𝅥. | 𝅗𝅥.   𝅗𝅥.   𝅗𝅥.   ‖
     ONE   two   three   ONE   two   three

$\frac{12}{16}$ 𝅘𝅥𝅮.   𝅘𝅥𝅮.   𝅘𝅥𝅮.   𝅘𝅥𝅮. | 𝅘𝅥𝅮.   𝅘𝅥𝅮.   𝅘𝅥𝅮.   𝅘𝅥𝅮.   ‖
     ONE   two   three   four   ONE   two   three   four

Divisions of the Pulse

Because compound meters are divided into three equal parts rather than two, a different set of syllables is used: *la* and *le*. Practice counting the following examples in compound meter until you feel comfortable with them. Remember that this is a different system from the one used to count simple meters. It may be confusing at first, but it will become easier with practice.

ONE-la-le two-la-le ONE-la-le two

ONE le two le ONE la two

ONE la le two le three le ONE le two la three

Some people prefer to count the eighth notes (or other pulse value) in compound meter. In this system, for instance, in $\frac{6}{8}$ you would say 1–2–3–4–5–6, emphasizing the 1 and 4.

1 2 3 4 5 6 1 3 4

We will continue to use *la* and *le*, but either system works equally well, and you should use the one that your teacher prefers.

When a further subdivision of the beat in compound meter is required—that is, when you need to indicate one-sixth of the primary pulse—the syllable *ta* is used.

The following examples can be tongue twisters at first, but will grow easier as you practice them.

ONE-ta-la-ta-le-ta two la-ta-le-ta ONE-la-le two

ONE la-ta le two - ta-le three-la-le ONE

As a class, clap and count the following rhythmic examples in compound meter. You probably know these pieces and that should help you decide whether you are performing them correctly or not. Begin by saying two measures of the divided primary pulse (1-la-le 2-la-le or 1-2-3 4-5-6) aloud before clapping. When you are comfortable with the counting system, also try playing the rhythms on an instrument or keyboard while counting mentally. Remember always to keep the basic pulse steady.

"For He's a Jolly Good Fellow"

(continued)

"Down in the Valley"

2. 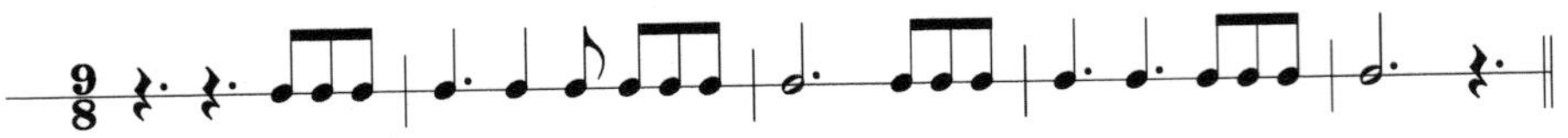

Additional work with counting syllables in compound meter may be found in Practice materials 3-2.

Beams in Compound Meter

The practice of combining basic beats under individual beams that we learned in Chapter 3 is employed in compound meter, with one major difference: The basic beat is divided into three pulses rather than two. In a compound meter such as $\frac{6}{8}$, the basic beat is normally felt as two pulses per measure, and the note representing this beat, the dotted quarter note, is divisible into three eighth notes or six sixteenth notes.

As in simple meter, any combination of eighth notes and sixteenth notes that adds up to a complete beat should be beamed together. The following are some of the more common combinations.

Similarly, dotted rhythms in compound meter are also grouped by beat. The common dotted rhythm pattern in compound meter is:

The following two patterns also occur from time to time, but less frequently.

In all cases, whether in simple or compound meter, it is important to keep the beginning of each beat clearly visible by beaming together all the notes that occur within that beat.

Class Practice

As a class, clap and count each of the rhythms given below. Then, rewrite them by beaming the eighth notes and sixteenth notes together, taking care not to place beams across beats. Clap the patterns you have written. Does being able to see the beginning of each beat clearly make it easier to read the patterns?

1. 

2. 

Music in Action

Counting Compound Meters

Clap and count the following rhythmic examples in compound meter. Begin by saying two measures of the divided beat (1-la-le 2-la-le) aloud before clapping. Experiment with a variety of speeds. When you are comfortable with this counting system, also try playing these rhythms on an instrument or keyboard while counting mentally.

1. 

2. 

3. 

4. 

Music in Action

Rhythmic Dictation

Your instructor will choose two rhythmic passages in compound meter from Appendix A and play them for you several times. You will be told the meter of each example. Listen carefully to each passage, and try to notate it in the space provided below. If the passages seem too long, your instructor can divide them into shorter segments. Use the counting method to help clarify the rhythmic patterns you hear.

1. ______________________________

____

2. ______________________________

____

Conducting Compound Meters

When conducting in compound meter, the basic beat patterns for 2, 3, or 4 beats per measure that we learned in Chapter 3 don't change. They remain the same for both simple and compound meter. The subdivisions of the pulse, however, change from two to three, and conductors must take this change into account. There is, after all, a fundamental difference in the rhythmic *feel* of simple as opposed to compound meter. Good conductors make this distinction clear with their body language to get the best musical results.

Music in Action

Conducting

The following melodies are in compound meter. Practice conducting each of them while you sing them on *la*. Keep practicing until you are comfortable singing and conducting simultaneously.

"Oh Dear, What Can the Matter Be"

"Wayfaring Stranger"

Music in Action

Compound Meters

As a class, clap the following two-part examples in compound meter. Half the class should clap the top part and half the bottom part. Then, by yourself, try tapping the examples on a desk or tabletop, one part per hand.

Andante

3.

Ties

Often, a composer will want to hold a note beyond the end of a measure in a particular meter. Suppose, for example, we want a note to last four pulses in ¾ meter. Obviously, four pulses will not fit into a single three-pulse measure. To permit the note to last four pulses, we use a **tie**, which extends the note into the next measure. As shown in the following example, the tie is a curved line connecting the notehead to be prolonged with the same pitch in the next measure.

In performance, the second note will not be sounded separately. Instead, the first note will be held through the time value of the second, producing a single sound, four pulses in duration.

Ties are not only useful for creating notes of longer duration than the number of pulses in a measure, they are sometimes also needed at the end of a measure. In the following illustration, for example, the tie is needed because a half note cannot occur on the last beat of the first measure.

Another use of ties is to help make clear metric groupings, both within the bar and over the bar line. In the following example, the normal grouping in ⅜ is maintained by the use of ties.

Ties are very similar in appearance to slurs, which are used to specify a smooth, connected style of playing. **Slurs**, however, always connect different pitches and may extend over several pitches at once, whereas ties always connect two notes of the same pitch.

Repeat Signs

Occasionally, composers want several measures in a composition to repeat immediately. They can indicate this either by writing all of the measures again or by using **repeat signs**. Although it is easy enough to rewrite a few measures, repeat signs are more convenient for longer passages.

Repeat signs are two large dots, one above the other, that appear at the beginning and the end of the measures to be repeated. Double bar lines generally accompany the repeat signs at the beginning and the end of the repeated measures to call attention to the repeat signs.

This example, when performed, will sound like this:

If the repeated measures include the first measure of the composition, the repeat sign occurs only at the end of the section to be repeated and is omitted from the beginning. For example,

when performed, will sound like:

Class Practice

As a class, clap and count the following rhythms. Pay particular attention to the repeat signs and ties. It will also be helpful if you sing the rhythms or perform them on an instrument. Be sure to hold each note for its full value.

1.

2.

3.

4.

5.

Additional practice with compound meter, including proper beaming and the use of ties, may be found in Practice materials 4-4 and 4-5.

Triplets and Duplets

Sometimes, a note in simple meter is subdivided as if it were in compound meter. That is, a note normally subdivided into two equal parts is now momentarily subdivided into three equal parts. This is called *borrowed division*.

    normal subdivision

    borrowed division

The *3* above the beam indicates that three even eighth notes occur within the time normally taken by two. When a borrowed division of this type occurs, it is called a **triplet**. A note of any value may be subdivided into a triplet. The three most common are:

♩ = ♫♪ eighth-note triplet

𝅗𝅥 = ♪♪♪ quarter-note triplet

𝅝 = 𝅗𝅥𝅗𝅥𝅗𝅥 half-note triplet

Less frequently, a note in compound meter is subdivided as if it were in simple meter:

♩. = ♫♪ normal subdivision

♩. = ♫ borrowed division

When this occurs, it is called a **duplet**. The two most common duplets are:

♩. = ♫ eighth-note duplet

𝅗𝅥. = ♪♪ quarter-note duplet

Notice that (1) in both duplets and triplets, a numeral is used to alert the performer to an unusual subdivision, and (2) where no beam exists, a bracket indicates exactly which notes belong to the triplet or duplet figure.

Triplets and duplets are best employed as rhythmic exceptions, to be used sparingly in a particular piece of music. If more frequent use is necessary, it makes more sense for the entire piece to be written in the corresponding compound or simple meter.

A Counting Method for Triplets and Duplets

The way most people count triplets is to momentarily shift their thinking from simple meter into compound meter. Notice in the following example that the syllables change from those of simple meter to those for compound meter at the point where the triplet occurs.

ONE two-and three ONE two-la-le three

ONE two-and ONE-la-le ONE

Duple rhythms work the same way, only in reverse. Duple rhythms normally occur in compound meters. So at the point where they occur, the thinking (and the syllables) changes from those for compound meter to those for simple meter.

ONE - la - le two   ONE - la - le two - and   ONE

Class Practice

Clap and count the following rhythmic examples. Pay particular attention to the triplet or duplet, and be sure to switch syllables for it. Remember, always keep the basic beat steady.

Henry Tucker: "Sweet Genevieve"

1.

"Havah Nagilah"

2.

Class Practice

As a class, clap or perform on instruments the following two-part rhythmic examples in compound meter. If necessary, you may wish to practice some of the simpler exercises in Appendix B first. Then, experiment with tapping out the examples on a desk or tabletop, one part per hand.

Music in Action

Composing

Melodies from a guitar piece by Ferdinando Carulli and a keyboard piece by the Renaissance composer Giles Farnaby follow. Both are in compound meter. You may have heard one or both of these pieces before. Clap the rhythm of each melody several times. Then, in the space provided, write a second rhythmic part that, when clapped with the rhythm of the melody, will complement it and create a two-part clapping piece. Your teacher may wish to work on this as a class or assign it as homework. If used as homework, perform these clapping pieces in class and discuss their strengths and weaknesses.

As a class, choose several songs that everyone knows. These may be folk songs, popular songs, or the theme songs from your favorite movies. For each song, say the words aloud several times until you have the rhythm created by these words clearly in mind. Then, decide the meter of this rhythm. Is it simple or compound? Finally, determine where the downbeat occurs. To do this, begin by deciding whether the *first* word begins on the downbeat or on some other part of the measure. After you have done this, try writing the rhythm suggested by the words. Here, there is no one absolutely correct way of doing things, although your rhythms should always sound natural, not awkward. ●

A Final Note

Chapter 1 posed the following question: What is musical rhythm? Are we now ready to begin formulating an answer to that question? So far, we have discussed the individual rhythmic elements, but not how these parts interact within an actual composition. It is this interaction that gives a piece of music its unique rhythmic character. On one level, this interaction is relatively easy to describe: Musical rhythm is the inherent flow and tension between the steady pulse of a particular meter and the irregular note values that occur within that meter. Unfortunately, this simplistic definition, while true, ignores the more subtle and complex aspects of the rhythm of most pieces of music.

In an actual composition, a number of factors always work together to produce its characteristic rhythm: tempo, accents, and the interaction of rhythm with melody and harmony, to name a few. Also, because the subtle rhythmic qualities of every style of music differ from each other, musicians learn to make slight adjustments when performing, to accommodate the specific rhythmic demands of a particular style.

Although we have completed a second chapter on rhythm, it doesn't mean we can forget about it and move on to other elements of music. Rhythm is too important and too fundamental to music to learn superficially and settle for less than the best we can do. The best we can do, as we all know, comes from repeated practice. Look at the average college student's skills with video games, skateboards, and cell phones to see the results of continued concentrated practice. Becoming a better musician works the same way. For the vast majority of us, it's the only way. Continuing to develop our skills with rhythm requires our continued attention.

Music in Action   Applying Your Skills
The following three-part rhythms are taken from Appendix B. As a class, clap and count these rhythms. Then, divide into small groups and clap and count them again.

Moderate   **South America**

2.

Music in Action

Listening

Listen once again to the works you chose for the first Music in Action in Chapter 1. This time, try to explain in more musical terms what is taking place rhythmically. Be specific when talking about the pulse, meter, and tempo. Discuss in a general way the interaction of the various rhythmic elements. For each piece, in one or more paragraphs, describe your experience of the rhythm. Does this new description show that you now have a better understanding of musical rhythm in general? ●

Practice

Practice 4-1

In each of the following sequences, identify the meter name and the note value that represents the pulse. Then, indicate measures by placing bar lines in the appropriate places in each example. Begin by looking at the time signature and deciding the number of beats each measure will contain. Then, determine the note value that represents one beat. When you have finished, either play each rhythmic pattern on an instrument or sing it.

	Meter Name	Note Value
1. $\frac{6}{4}$	_____	_____
2. $\frac{6}{16}$	_____	_____
3. $\frac{12}{8}$	_____	_____

Practice 4-2

Write in the counting syllables for each of the following rhythms. Begin by deciding whether the example is in simple or compound meter. Then, practice clapping the rhythms and saying the syllables aloud. Be sure to keep the pulse steady.

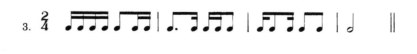

Practice 4-3

Give the correct terminology for each of the following meter signatures. Remember that the top number indicates the beats per measure, while the lower number tells us the kind of note that gets the beat.

EXAMPLE: $\frac{3}{2}$ simple triple

1. $\frac{6}{8}$ _____

2. $\frac{12}{16}$ _____

3. $\frac{6}{4}$ _____

4. $\frac{12}{4}$ _____

5. $\frac{9}{4}$ _____

Practice 4-4

Rewrite each of the following rhythmic patterns in the meter indicated. To do this, you will have to divide some notes (for instance, ♩ into ♪♪) and use ties. Keep in mind that simple and compound meters divide the beat in different ways.

EXAMPLE:

Practice 4-5

Rewrite the following rhythmic patterns by beaming the eighth notes and sixteenth notes together. Remember not to place beams across beats.

Focus on Skills 2: **Rhythm**

 Visit Music Fundamentals in Action, at CourseMate, for interactive Focus on Fundamentals exercises.

The questions in this Focus on Skills section cover simple and compound meters from Chapters 3 and 4. If you have difficulty with any of them, be sure to review the relevant sections of those chapters before beginning Chapter 5.

1. From the time signature, identify the meter and the note value that represents the pulse of each example. Then mark off measures by placing bar lines in the appropriate places.

    a.

    b.

    c.

    d.

    e.

2. The following rhythmic passages are notated and barred correctly. Write the meter signature for each in the appropriate place.

    a.

    b.

    c.

    d.

3. Rewrite the following rhythmic patterns by beaming the eighth notes and sixteenth notes appropriately.

a.  (musical notation in 2/4)

(blank 2/4 staff)

b.  (musical notation in 6/8)

(blank 6/8 staff)

c.  (musical notation in 9/8)

(blank 9/8 staff)

4. Rewrite each of the following rhythmic patterns in the meter indicated. To do this correctly, you may need to divide some of the notes and use ties.

a.  (musical notation) = 6/8

b.  (musical notation) = 6/4

c. (musical notation) = 4/4

Pitch

Visit Music Fundamentals in Action, at CourseMate, to:

- Take a Pretest on pitch
- Hear the author's Let's Talk About Music podcast on pitch notation
- Find many more practice exercises to help you succeed in this course
- See Tips&Tools for each chapter

Introduction

Not all musicians read music. Neither does music have to be written on paper to exist. Most of the world's folk music traditions are oral, with pieces passing by rote from one generation to the next. Even the classical music of some cultures, much of it of great complexity, is maintained by an oral tradition. Moreover, some styles of music—jazz and rock in America or the raga tradition in India, for example—require improvising: written arrangements in these styles are little more than skeletons or outlines, reminding us of the actual performance when the "real" music appears.

Even though many musical traditions have existed for centuries without a highly organized notational system, European and American art music of the past 500 years cannot. To play the music of Bach, Chopin, Mahler, or Gershwin, for example, we need a precise set of plans—a blueprint or road map telling us in specific terms not only what pitches and rhythms to perform, but also the manner, or style, in which to play them.

There are, of course, obvious advantages to being able to write down your musical ideas. First, they can be preserved exactly and not altered, particularly from generation to generation. Second, complicated musical structures can be built in a standard manner easily understood by all. Third, the music can be accurately and efficiently transmitted to other musicians, both immediately and hundreds of years later. Furthermore, we can assume that it will always sound the same. This is no small accomplishment, when you think about it.

Consider the great operas, string quartets, and symphonies of the past. Could they ever have been performed in the first place, much less saved for centuries, without a system of notation? What about the music played by the swing-era bands of Count Basie or Duke Ellington? Although there was a great deal of solo improvising, the arrangements themselves were tightly organized and carefully written out.

As you continue the process of learning to read musical notation, remember that you are, in essence, learning a new language—the language of music. This language will allow you to communicate with other musicians, both those of today and those of the past.

Listening

Listen to a recording of a short orchestral work by a classical composer such as Mozart or Beethoven. As you listen, consider that this music was written more than 200 years ago. It can still be performed today because the notational system conveys information to contemporary performers that allows them to re-create the music accurately. As a class, discuss the kinds of musical information a notational system for this style of music would need to contain. You may wish to look at a score, either during or after the discussion.

In contrast, today most rock and rap music is not notated, at least not when it was originally performed. (Some solos by great performers are transcribed later for study purposes.) Although the arrangements may be played virtually the same way each time, they are seldom written on paper and read during the performance in the manner of classical music. As a class, listen to a current rock or rap piece and discuss what kinds of information a notational system for this style of music would need, so that someone who has never heard this music could play it in a recognizable way two centuries from now. ●

Enharmonic Pitches

We will begin this chapter by expanding on the information about pitch that we learned in Chapters 1 and 2. Our work will begin with enharmonic pitches, ledger lines, and the octave sign, but by the end of the chapter our goal is to be able to understand and read a musical score. You may remember from Chapter 2 that the black keys of the piano can have more than one name. (This is even true for the white keys when double sharps and double flats are used.) The fact that F sharp and G flat or C sharp and D flat are the same note on the keyboard may be momentarily confusing. When two different letter names identify the same pitch, we call them **enharmonic pitches**. The term means that the two pitches, while written differently, actually sound the same tone. At this point, the best way of dealing with enharmonic pitches is to remember that sharped notes sound above the pitches they relate to, while flatted notes sound below. The reason for this duality in labeling will become clear when we discuss scales in a later chapter.

Every pitch can be raised (sharped) or lowered (flatted). Because there is no black key between E and F or B and C, it is possible to have two instances of white key enharmonic sharps and flats. We can, for example, identify the pitch *E sharp* as the key directly above E, which is white and more frequently called *F*. In the same way, *C flat* is the key directly below C, which is white and also called *B*.

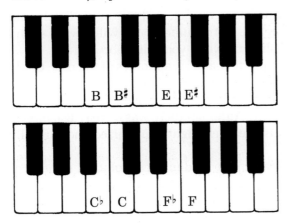

Notice the enharmonic qualities of these four white keys when they are combined on one keyboard.

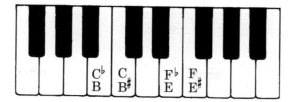

Practice for locating pitches on the keyboard can be found in Practice materials 5-1 at the end of this chapter.

Ledger Lines

So far, almost all the written pitches we have encountered have been located on the staff. Often, however, pitches higher or lower than the range limitations of the five-line staff need to be indicated. This is done with the use of ledger lines. **Ledger lines** are short, individual lines added above or below the staff, having the effect of extending the staff. Notice that ledger lines are the same distance apart as the lines of the staff and that the ledger lines for one note do *not* connect to the ledger lines for another note:

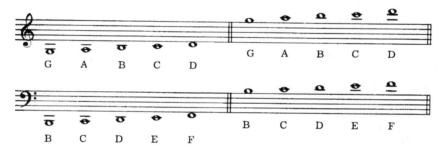

Notice also that you should never enclose a pitch with ledger lines.

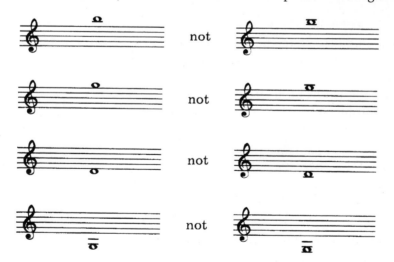

The use of ledger lines within the great staff can be momentarily confusing. In the following example, both notes in each vertically aligned pair represent exactly the same pitch. This notational overlap within the great staff is useful because it allows pitches to be clearly grouped with the musical line to which they belong.

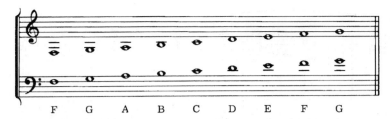

F   G   A   B   C   D   E   F   G

In the following piano music example, the left hand plays pitches located above middle C. To avoid confusion, however, these pitches are written with ledger lines in the bass clef.

Allegretto   Mozart: Sonata in B♭ Major, K. 570, III

Practice for naming pitches that use ledger lines in both treble and bass clef may be found in Practice materials 5-2 and 5-3.

The Octave Sign

Musicians are most comfortable reading music that is written on the staff or close to it. The excessive use of ledger lines makes music difficult to read and should be avoided. The **octave sign**, *8va* ⁻⁻⁻⁻ ⌝ or *8* ⁻⁻⁻⁻ ⌝, is another notational device that helps overcome this problem.

An octave is the distance between any note and the next note of the same name, either higher or lower. The octave sign *above* a group of notes, then, indicates that the notes under the sign are to be played one octave *higher* than written.

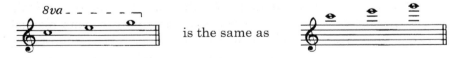

is the same as

The following example shows how the octave sign can be used to keep the ascending-scale passage on or close to the staff.

Kuhlau: Rondo from Sonatina, Op. 20, No. 1

p dolce

When the octave sign appears *below* a group of notes, it indicates that those notes are to be played one octave *lower* than written. Sometimes the word *bassa* is added to the octave sign.

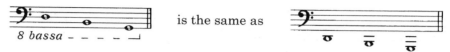

The following example by Debussy uses octave signs above and below pitches to explore the extremes of the piano range.

Debussy: "Brouillards" from Preludes, Book II

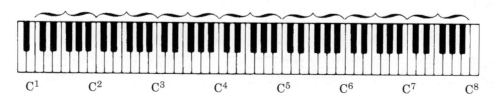

Practice for using the octave sign to avoid ledger lines may be found in Practice materials 5-4.

Octave Identification

It is often useful to be able to refer to a pitch in a particular octave. To identify each octave separately, a special system is used. Unfortunately, more than one system is used today. The one shown here is for the piano and refers to middle C as C4. If you own a synthesizer or electronic keyboard, however, your manual may refer to middle C as C3. This is confusing, but it happens because most electronic keyboards don't have all eighty-eight keys, and middle C on them is the third, not the fourth, C from the left.

C^1 C^2 C^3 C^4 C^5 C^6 C^7 C^8

We will use the system that spans the entire piano keyboard. Here, the octave beginning on middle C is labeled as follows:

C^4 B^4

Any pitch within this range can be identified by a letter name with a superscript numeral 4.

D^4 A^4 E^4 $G^4_\natural$ F^4 B^4

The following illustration shows how the octaves above middle C are identified.

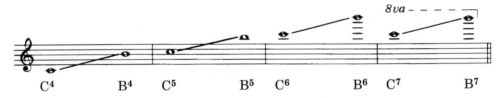

C^4 B^4 C^5 B^5 C^6 B^6 C^7 B^7

Any pitch within these ranges can be identified by a letter name and the appropriate superscript.

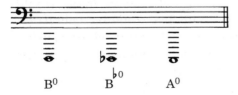

G^5 B^4 D^6 E^7 F^5 C^6

The octaves below middle C are labeled with descending numerals in a similar way.

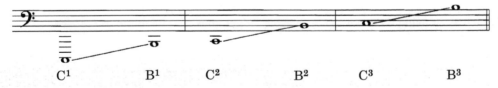

C^1 B^1 C^2 B^2 C^3 B^3

The lowest three pitches on the piano, which are below C^1, are identified by their letter name and a superscript numeral 0.

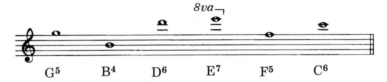

B^0 $B^{\flat 0}$ A^0

Notice how so many ledger lines make identification of these pitches difficult. Practice for using octave identification may be found in Practice materials 5-5, 5-6, and 5-7.

Dynamics

Composers indicate degrees of loudness and softness (called **dynamics**) by annotating their music with specific words and abbreviations, most often in Italian, occasionally in French or German.

Volume in music is usually either maintained at steady levels or gradually changed. The standard words and symbols for a *steady volume* are:

English	Italian	Abbreviation
very soft	**pianissimo**	*pp*
soft	**piano**	*p*
moderately soft	**mezzo piano**	*mp*
moderately loud	**mezzo forte**	*mf*
loud	**forte**	*f*
very loud	**fortissimo**	*ff*

Occasionally, extremes in volume are desired, particularly in contemporary music. In such cases, the symbols *ppp*, *pppp*, *fff*, and *ffff* are used.

Gradual changes in volume are indicated by the following words and symbols:

English	Italian	Abbreviation	Symbol
become softer	**diminuendo**	*dim.*	▷
	decrescendo	*decresc.*	
become louder	**crescendo**	*cresc.*	◁

Where the symbols for *diminuendo* or *crescendo* are used, the length of the symbol indicates the relative length of time in which the volume change is to occur. For example, *p* ———————— *f* indicates a gradual change from *piano* to *forte* that takes approximately twice as long as *p* ——— *f*. Furthermore, the change in the latter example will sound more obvious to the listener, because it will move through *mezzo piano* to *mezzo forte* more quickly than the first example.

Whereas the symbols that dictate gradual volume changes suggest the time in which the change is to occur, the Italian terms or abbreviations are less specific unless the Italian terms **subito** (suddenly) or **poco a poco** (little by little) are added to the volume indicator. *Subito f*, for example, means suddenly loud, while *dim. poco a poco* means gradually softer.

How to Read a Musical Map

Many pieces of written music, when performed, are played straight through. That is, you begin at the top and play to the end, in the same way as you would read a newspaper column or a paragraph on a page. But not all pieces are this straightforward. Some contain notational shortcuts—space-saving devices indicated by a variety of symbols and abbreviations. If you understand the code (recognize the symbols and abbreviations), then reading the musical map is easy. But if you don't, you can become hopelessly confused.

Let's begin by looking at a piece of piano music by Muzio Clementi, a composer who was a contemporary of Beethoven. This sonatina may, at first, appear to be thirty-eight measures long, but that is not the case. In fact, when performed correctly, it actually consists of seventy-six measures. Clementi is able, in performance, to double the amount of music contained on the printed page by using the device of repetition, a device he uses not once, but twice.

Clementi's first repetition occurs at the end of measure 15. The double bar with two dots before it is a repeat sign that should be familiar to you from your work in Chapter 4. It indicates that the first fifteen measures are to be repeated before continuing. The second repeat occurs in measure 38, at the very end. Here, as before, a repeat sign sends us back into the piece. This time, however, we do not go back to the beginning, but only back to measure 16, where a repeat sign (with the two dots now to the right of the double bar) brackets the 23 measures Clementi wants repeated.

Now, let's look at "Siciliana" from Robert Schumann's *Album for the Young*.

This example, which represents a more complicated musical map, contains three different kinds of repetition. The first kind occurs at the end of measure 8 and is similar to the ones we saw in the Clementi sonatina. The second device, however, is new. It occurs at measure 16 and is called the *1st and 2nd endings*. This device is in some ways similar to the repeat sign for the first eight measures. Notice that the double bar and the two dots in measures 8 and 16 indicate that the musical material between measures 9 and 16 is to be repeated. In this case, however, there are two *different* final measures. The first time the passage is performed the first ending is played, but on the repetition, only the second ending is used. That is, measures 9 to 15 are played, measure 16A is omitted, and measure 16B is played in its place.

Clementi: Sonatina, Op. 36, No. 1

The third device is even more complicated. Notice the Italian phrase *Da capo al fine senza repetizione* below measures 35 and 36. This phrase indicates that the performer is to return to the beginning of the piece (*da capo* = the head, the beginning) and play to the end (*fine* = the end) without repeating either measures 1 to 8 or 9 to 16 (*senza repetizone* = without repetition). The actual end of the piece, therefore, is at measure 25, not at measure 36 as it may have appeared originally.

These devices may at first seem to be extremely confusing ways to organize a score, but if you perform very much music, you will quickly grow used to them. In fact, this example contains all the commonly used devices except one: *Dal segno al fine.* This phrase, which is similar to *Da capo al fine*, is used when the composer wishes to return to the middle of the piece rather than to the very beginning. In this case, the symbol 𝄋 is placed at the point where the repetition is to begin, and the performer is expected to return to the sign (*Dal segno*) and play to the end (*al fine*).

Schumann: "Siciliana" from *Album for the Young*

Da capo al fine senza repetizione

Not all pieces of music use devices of repetition, and even those that do can vary in slightly different ways. But if you study the following chart carefully, you should be able to find your way through almost any piece of music without too much difficulty.

Device of Repetition	Abbreviation	Meaning
Repeat signs	‖: :‖	Perform the measures located within these signs twice.
1st and 2nd endings	1. 2.	Perform the indicated measures twice—the first time using the first ending, the second time using only the second ending.
Da capo al fine	D.C. al fine	Return to the beginning and play to the indicated end.
Dal segno al fine	D.S. al fine	Return to the sign and play to the indicated end.

Music in Action

Score Reading

Ask several members of the class who perform to locate one or more scores that use various devices of repetition. As a group, discuss these pieces. Can you identify the devices and what they mean? Can you work your way through the score successfully? ●

A Final Note

Feeling secure with pitch is of major importance to all musicians. So far you have been introduced to and given practical experience with pitch notation in the treble and bass clefs, as well as on the great staff. You should continue this work until you feel comfortable. It is important that you become familiar with pitch notation as quickly as possible, because the rest of the book is based on knowing this information. One of the easiest ways to fall behind at this point is to remain uncertain of and too slow at pitch identification. Steady consistent practice is the key.

Musical sound has four characteristics—duration, pitch, timbre, and volume. Although this book concentrates on developing your skills with duration and pitch, timbre and volume should not be ignored. At this point, you may wish to look at Appendix I, A Brief Introduction to Timbre. Later, you may want to study this section in more detail. For now, keep in mind that being musical involves more than just playing the right notes in the correct rhythms.

Practice 5-1

Locate the indicated pitches on the following keyboards and write each pitch in the correct place. If the pitch is a white key, write it directly on the keyboard. If it is a black key, use the answer line given above the keyboard. Then, practice finding and playing each of the pitches at the piano. If necessary, begin by locating the C and G landmarks.

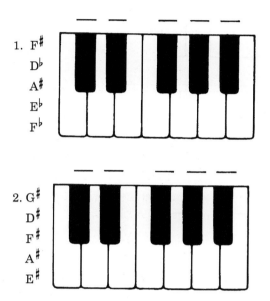

1. F♯
   D♭
   A♯
   E♭
   F♭

2. G♯
   D♯
   F♯
   A♯
   E♯

Practice 5-2

Identify the following pitches by letter name. Remember that ledger lines work like extensions of the staff. Before you begin, make sure that you are thinking in the correct clef.

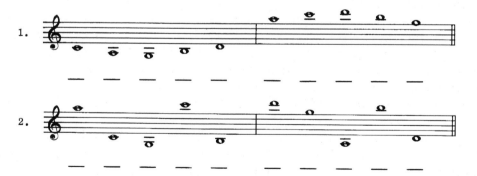

Practice 5-3

In the exercises below, identify each given pitch. Then, rewrite that same pitch, but in the other clef. A keyboard is provided to help you visualize the pitches. Remember that each group of two pitches should sound the same tone.

EXAMPLE:

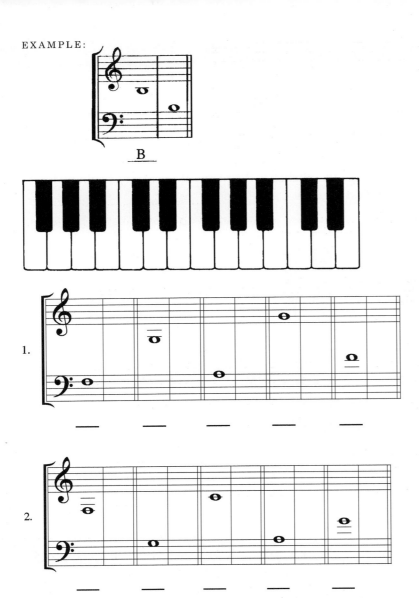

B

1.

_____ _____ _____ _____ _____

2.

_____ _____ _____ _____ _____

Practice 5-4

Name the pitches given below. Then, rewrite the passages using the octave sign to avoid the use of ledger lines.

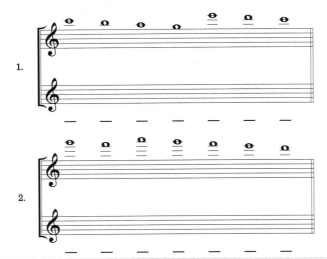

1.

_____ _____ _____ _____ _____ _____ _____

2.

_____ _____ _____ _____ _____ _____ _____

3.

Practice 5-5

Give the correct name and octave identification for the following pitches. Remember that middle C is labeled C4.

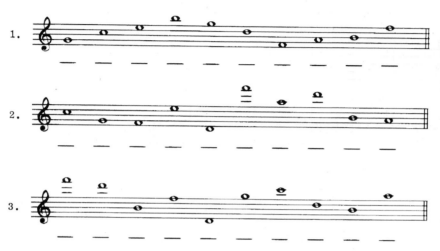

1.

2.

3.

Practice 5-6

Give the correct octave identification for the following pitches in the bass clef. Remember that the C in the second space of the bass clef is labeled C3.

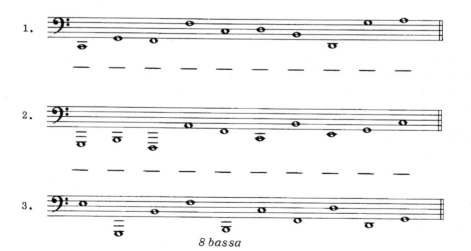

1.

2.

3.

8 bassa

Practice 5-7

Write each indicated pitch in the correct octave. The octave sign may be used where necessary. Remember that middle C is C4.

1.

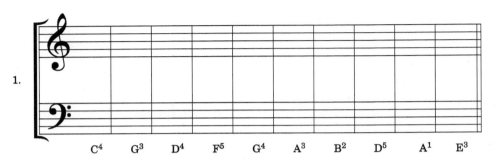

C⁴   G³   D⁴   F⁵   G⁴   A³   B²   D⁵   A¹   E³

2.

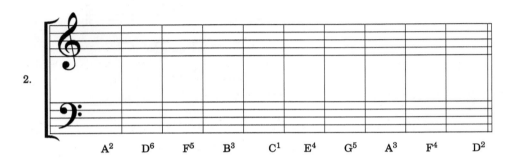

A²   D⁶   F⁵   B³   C¹   E⁴   G⁵   A³   F⁴   D²

Focus on Skills 3: **Pitch**

 Visit Music Fundamentals in Action, at CourseMate, for interactive Focus on Fundamentals exercises.

Feeling comfortable with pitch notation is of such importance that we need to check our understanding of it immediately. Consequently, this Focus on Skills comes after a single chapter. If you experience any difficulty, make sure to review the relevant sections before beginning Chapter 6.

1. Locate the specified pitches on the following keyboards, and write each pitch in the correct place. If the pitch is a white key, write it directly on the keyboard. If it is a black key, use the answer line given above the keyboard.

   a.

   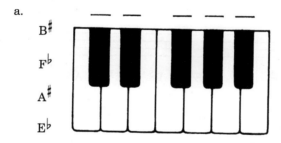

   b.

   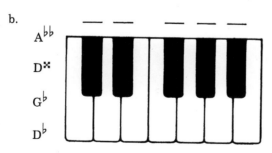

2. Identify the following pitches by letter name and octave designation.

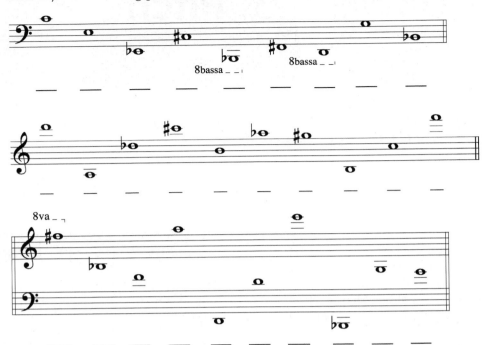

3. Write each indicated pitch in the correct octave. Use half notes and make sure that each stem is going in the proper direction. The octave sign may be used where necessary.

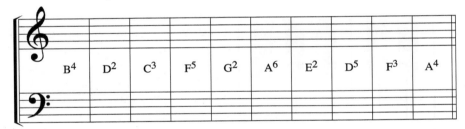

| B^4 | D^2 | C^3 | F^5 | G^2 | A^6 | E^2 | D^5 | F^3 | A^4 |

Major Scales

𝄐 Visit Music Fundamentals in Action, at CourseMate, to:

- Take a Pretest on major scales
- View a Hands On Music video demo of major scales
- Find many more practice exercises to help you succeed in this course
- See Tips&Tools for each chapter

Introduction

All the world's melodies are made from *scales*. In the West, a **scale** is a group of pitches—usually five to eight—that are arranged in ascending or descending patterns of whole steps and half steps. The scale is a fundamental building block of music, much as the skeleton is the foundation of the human body. The fact that music of one culture often sounds unfamiliar to people of another culture begins with the scale.

Many different scales are used around the world. Most of them date from antiquity, and we don't really know how they came into being. But these scales all have in common the ability to define and color music that is made from them.

Today, the two most important scales of Western music are the **major scale** and the **minor scale**. Both of them are built from different combinations of whole steps and half steps. The music written with these two scales is called **tonal music**.

Scales as Interval Patterns

Western music divides the octave into twelve equal half steps. A scale formed by dividing the octave in this way is called a **chromatic scale**.

Ascending chromatic scale (usually written with sharps):

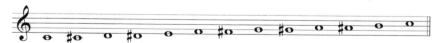

Descending chromatic scale (usually written with flats):

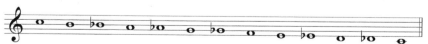

Notice that these are all the notes on the keyboard—black and white—within one octave.

Because the chromatic scale consists entirely of half steps, it seldom functions as a musical scale. Rather, it is the source from which a huge variety of other scales are drawn. Most scales are made of a combination of whole and half steps, although some scales use one or more intervals larger than the whole step. This variation in interval size gives each scale, and the music in that scale, a particular color or quality, because the unique interval patterns of a scale are transferred to the melody and the harmony.

The major scale and the natural minor scale (which will be discussed more fully later) are both seven-note scales having five whole steps and two half steps, yet they sound strikingly unlike each other because the pattern of whole steps and half steps is different. The concept of a scale as an interval pattern that reflects the interval patterns of melody and harmony is fundamental to understanding tonal music.

Class Practice

Write one-octave chromatic scales beginning on the pitches indicated. Remember to use sharps for the ascending scale and flats for the descending scale. Remember also to keep the notated pitch sequences B–C and E–F intact, because the interval between them is already a half step.

Ascending Scales

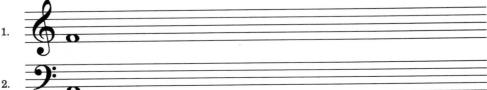

Descending Scales

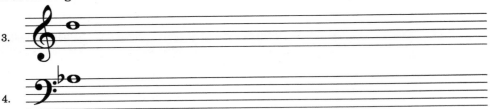

Elements of the Major Scale

The major scale is an interval pattern of five whole steps and two diatonic half steps. The half steps always occur between the third and fourth tones and the seventh and first tones of the scale. On the keyboard, the major scale falls on all white keys when it begins on the pitch C.

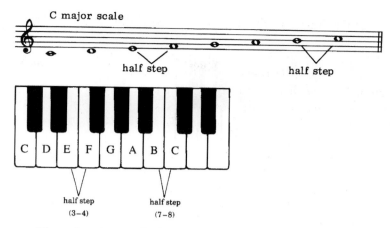

C major scale

half step   half step

C D E F G A B C

half step   half step
(3–4)   (7–8)

The other intervals (remember that an interval is the distance between two pitches) are all whole steps. This creates a pattern for the major scale of W W H W W W H.

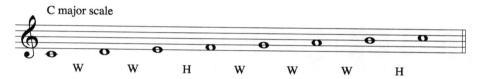

C major scale

W   W   H   W   W   W   H

Remember that as long as you reproduce this whole step/half step pattern you can create a major scale from any pitch.

Here is how this pattern of whole steps and half steps gives the major scale its characteristic quality. The half step between the seventh and first tones creates a strong pull toward the first tone. This first tone is called a **tonic**. The tonic, sometimes also called the home note, is the pitch to which the other tones of the scale seem to be related. As you sing or play a major scale, notice how the tonic becomes the focus for a group of seemingly related pitches, similar to a center of gravity.

Music in Action

Finding the Tonic

As a group, make a list of three melodies that most class members know well. These can be themes from your favorite television shows or songs from the movies, as well as melodies from classical, popular, or folk music. Two things are important in making your choices. The first is to choose only songs in major keys (your teacher will help you if necessary). The second is to choose melodies that the class knows well and can sing.

1. _____
2. _____
3. _____

As a group, sing the melodies you have chosen and identify the tonic of each by sound. Notice how often and in what places the tonic occurs. Are these places restful or active?

After you have sung each melody and located the tonic, sing a major scale beginning on the tonic of that melody. Do you notice the relationship between the scale and the melody? ●

The pattern of whole steps and half steps that produces a major scale can be moved to any other beginning pitch and, if the pattern is kept intact, will form a different major scale. In all, there are fifteen different major scales—seven that use flatted notes, seven that use sharped notes, and one natural scale. In the G major scale, for instance, an F♯ is needed to produce the whole step between the sixth and seventh degrees and the half step between the seventh and first degrees:

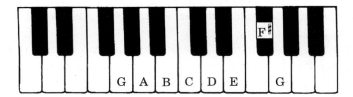

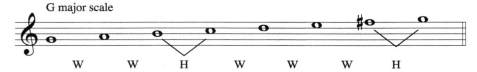

Similarly, the major scale beginning on A requires three sharps (F♯, C♯, G♯) to produce the correct pattern:

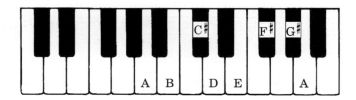

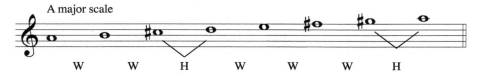

In the following example, five flats are required to produce the correct pattern of whole steps and half steps.

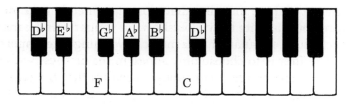

As you practice writing scales, remember that as long as you reproduce the pattern of whole steps and half steps exactly, the result will be a major scale, regardless of the pitch you begin on. Remember, also, that major scales are alphabetical sequences of pitches. All major and minor scales use only diatonic, not chromatic, half steps.

Practice for spelling major scales, in both ascending and descending versions, can be found in Practice materials 6-1, 6-2, 6-3, 6-4, and 6-5 at the end of this chapter.

Keyboard

The keyboard can be a valuable aid in helping you understand scale construction. The whole-step and half-step patterns and the scales that these patterns form can be visualized and recalled more easily when practiced on the keyboard.

Practice playing and singing one-octave, ascending major scales starting from the following pitches. It is not necessary to use the proper scale fingering at this time; however, you should not use just one finger. A good rule is to avoid using a thumb on a black key. (If you prefer to learn the correct fingerings now, they are given in Appendix E.)

1. G major
2. D major
3. G♭ major
4. C♯ major
5. E♭ major

6. B♭ major
7. D♭ major
8. F major
9. B major
10. A major ●

Keyboard

Practice playing and singing one-octave, descending major scales from each of the following pitches. It is not necessary to pay attention to the correct fingerings at this time, but they are given in Appendix E if you wish to use them.

1. F major
2. G major
3. D major
4. B major
5. A major
6. E major
7. C major

8. G♭ major
9. C♯ major
10. F♯ major
11. D♭ major
12. E♭ major
13. A♭ major
14. B♭ major ●

The ability to sing melodies at sight is a valuable tool. A number of methods exist that help develop this ability. Probably the most common system, called **movable** *do*, assigns a specific syllable to each pitch of the scale. In this system, the tonic of a scale is always *do*. Study the following illustration and practice singing the major scale, both ascending and descending, using the syllables. Then, practice singing the exercises that follow the illustration. These exercises may seem difficult at first, but stick with them—they are intended to help you become familiar with the syllables in various combinations.

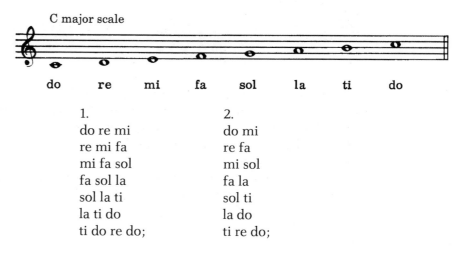

C major scale

do   re   mi   fa   sol   la   ti   do

1.	2.
do re mi	do mi
re mi fa	re fa
mi fa sol	mi sol
fa sol la	fa la
sol la ti	sol ti
la ti do	la do
ti do re do;	ti re do;

*	*
do ti la	do la
ti la sol	ti sol
la sol fa	la fa
sol fa mi	sol mi
fa mi re	fa re
mi re do	mi do
re do ti do	re ti do

Although *movable do* is perhaps the most commonly used sight-singing system, it is not the only one in use today. Others include substituting the numbers 1 to 7 for the scale degrees or using the actual pitch names. In fact, many schools teach a form of sight singing called **fixed *do***. In this system, C is always *do*, D is always *re*, and so forth. Consequently, your teacher may prefer that you use an alternative system from the one recommended here. ●

Music in Action ◉ Sight Singing

Sing each of the following melodies, using a neutral syllable like *la*, the letter names of the pitches, or the scale-degree numbers. Locate the tonic by sound. Then write the sight-singing syllables below each note. Finally, notate the major scale on which each melody is built.

"Michael, Row the Boat Ashore"

"Sur le Pont d'Avignon"

Scale

Mozart: "Eine Kleine Nachtmusik"

3.

Scale

Naming Scale Degrees

Each scale degree has a specific name. The scale degrees, in ascending order, are: **tonic**, **supertonic**, **mediant**, **subdominant**, **dominant**, **submediant**, **leading tone**, and **tonic**. These scale-degree names always remain the same regardless of the octave in which the pitch of that name appears.

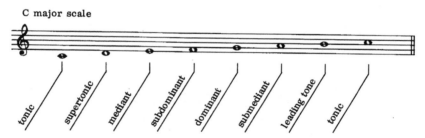

At first, these names might appear arbitrary. If, however, you consider the tonic as the tonal center of gravity, then the names logically describe the relationship between the scale degrees. Notice how the tonic becomes the central pitch when the scale degrees are arranged in the following way:

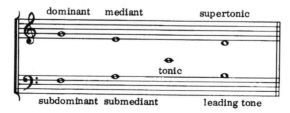

Name the following scale degrees.

1. third degree _____
2. fifth degree _____
3. sixth degree _____
4. first degree _____

5. seventh degree _____
6. second degree _____
7. fourth degree _____

Additional practice identifying scale degree names may be found in Practice materials 6-6 and 6-7.

It may seem momentarily confusing to you that the individual pitches of a scale may be referred to in more than one way. The following chart may be helpful in clearing up the confusion. The pitch names on the far left are a descending C major scale; the terms to the right indicate three different ways each particular scale degree can be referred to or labeled. Although the third option (numbers) has not been previously discussed in this book (the concept is easily understood), it is used frequently in written analytical discussions of music, and all musicians should become familiar with it.

C	do	tonic	$\hat{1}$
D	re	supertonic	$\hat{2}$
E	mi	mediant	$\hat{3}$
F	fa	subdominant	$\hat{4}$
G	sol	dominant	$\hat{5}$
A	la	submediant	$\hat{6}$
B	ti	leading tone	$\hat{7}$

Music in Action   Playing Scales

Instrumentalists should be able to play one- and two-octave major scales, both ascending and descending. If you cannot do this, you should begin at once to develop this facility. Improving your ability to play scales will be of immediate benefit, because many of the patterns of tonal music are directly related to the scales on which they are based. To begin, practice the easier scales slowly and evenly, concentrating on accuracy and quality of tone. After you have mastered these, move on to more difficult scales. ●

Music in Action 🔊 Ear Training

Sing in your mind any of the following melodies that you know. Put a check mark by the ones that are based on a major scale. Then, as a class, sing aloud all the melodies you can. If you don't know a particular melody, listen as it is sung and decide if it is in a major key.

1. "The Simpsons" TV show theme _____
2. "Titanic" theme _____
3. "Two and a Half Men" TV show theme _____
4. "Star Wars" theme _____
5. "James Bond" theme _____
6. "Moon River" _____ ●

All musicians need to *hear* music as completely as they can. This involves listening not to the emotional content but to the actual mechanics of the music. Identifying the instruments, distinguishing the number of lines or voices, and accurately notating rhythms are all part of developing your ear. But when most people think of training themselves to hear better, they think first of pitch.

Some people have excellent ears. That is, they have an astonishing ability to make extremely fine aural discriminations. Some people can even name pitches as they hear them played or sung. This ability to recognize pitches is often called **perfect pitch**. However, there is nothing inherently "perfect" about it because the pitch standard has varied from century to century and from place to place over time. Furthermore, there are degrees of ability within perfect pitch—some people can name all the pitches in a cluster of notes played on the piano, others can only name the notes when played individually or on a particular instrument.

Although perfect pitch cannot be learned, a similar ability can be developed with practice. This ability is called **relative pitch**. Relative pitch involves learning the sounds of the various intervals and applying this knowledge when listening and performing. People with highly developed relative pitch can also name notes that they hear, if they are given a beginning pitch. If you improvise or play jazz, rock, or pop music by ear, you may already have good relative pitch. But it can be made even better with practice. If you want to play by ear, write music, or just better understand the music you like to listen to, remember that these abilities can be developed and expanded with practice.

Ear training is the term musicians give to the process of developing their ability to hear better. We have already done some of this in the Music in Action sections, and we will do more from time to time. Keep in mind that progress may be slow at first, and success may, as with most skills, seem to come in plateaus. Keep in mind too that everyone begins at a different level of ability. You should not be discouraged by other people's abilities. If you work consistently, you will see your own abilities grow and develop.

Music in Action 🔊 Ear Training

Your teacher or another member of the class will play a major scale. Then he or she will play one pitch that will be either the tonic or the dominant from that scale. In the spaces below, indicate which pitch is being played.

1. _____
2. _____
3. _____
4. _____

Now try the same thing using three pitches—tonic, dominant, and submediant.

1. _____
2. _____
3. _____
4. _____

(continued)

Finally, see if you can identify one of four different pitches—
tonic, dominant, submediant, or subdominant.

1. _____

2. _____

3. _____

4. _____ ●

A Final Note

The major scale is known to all of us. In fact, it may be too familiar. Most people can sing a major scale, complete with the correct syllables, thanks to the musical *The Sound of Music*. But this very familiarity may be a problem for beginning music students, who may believe that the major scale is a simple entity—a stepping-stone to more interesting musical material.

You should not allow yourself to become complacent about scales, however. A thorough knowledge of scales is basic to understanding and performing music. The major scale seems familiar because so many of the melodies and so much of the harmony you have heard throughout your life are based on it. To deal *theoretically* with music based on major scales, you must both understand the major scale as an interval pattern and acquire skill and facility in writing, playing, and singing this common pattern. Scales are basic. There is no substitute for knowing them.

Music in Action ◉ **Sight Singing**

Below are three melodies in major keys from Appendix D. Practice singing these melodies, both on *la* and with movable *do*. Once you are familiar with the melodies, practice playing them at the keyboard.

Practice

Practice 6-1

Write ascending and descending major scales, in both treble clef and bass clef, from each starting pitch. When writing major scales, there should be only one pitch of each letter name. For example, it is incorrect to have both G♭ and G♮ in the same scale. The correct sequence is F♯–G. (The sequence of scales in this exercise is arranged so that each succeeding scale requires only one additional sharp.)

When you have written the scales, check that the half steps occur between the third and fourth degrees and between the seventh and first degrees. Indicate the half steps for each scale. A keyboard is given to help you visualize the whole steps and half steps.

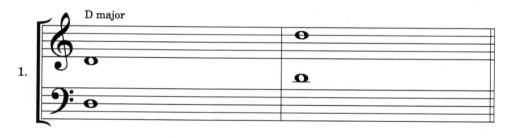

EXAMPLE:

G major

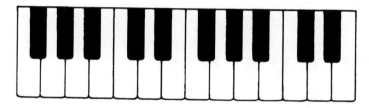

1. D major

2. E major

(continued)

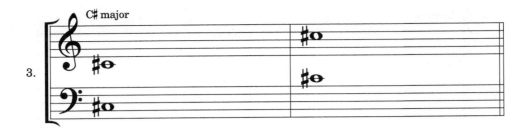

C♯ major

3.

Practice 6-2

Write ascending and descending major scales from each starting pitch. (The sequence of scales in this exercise is arranged so that each succeeding scale requires one additional flat.)

When you have written the scales, check that the half steps occur between the third and fourth degrees and between the seventh and first degrees. Indicate the half steps for each scale. A keyboard is given to help you visualize the intervals.

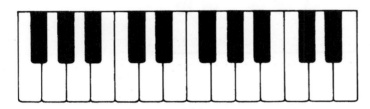

EXAMPLE:

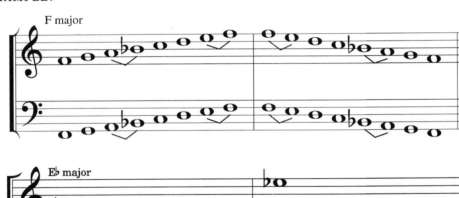

F major

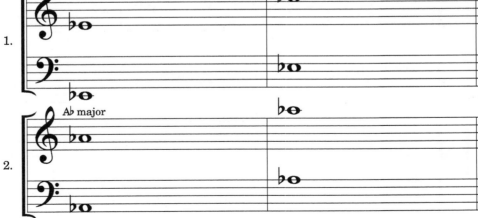

E♭ major

1.

A♭ major

2.

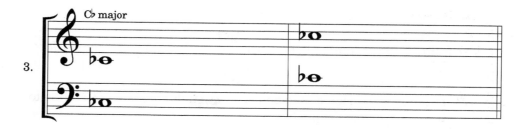

3.

Practice 6-3

Write ascending major scales starting from the given tonic pitches. These are the same scales as in Practice materials 6-1 and 6-2, but here they are in no particular order. Remember to use only one pitch of each letter name. When you have written each scale, bracket the third and fourth scale degrees and the seventh and first degrees and write their names in the chart to the left. Are both intervals half steps?

EXAMPLE:

Half steps

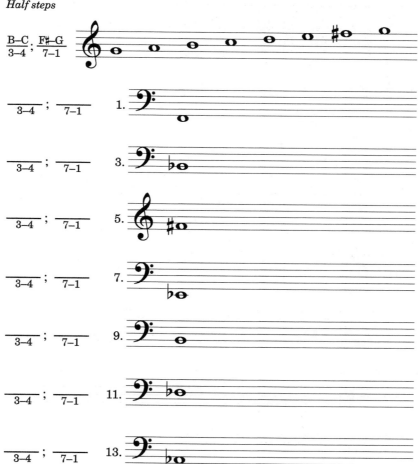

$\dfrac{\text{B–C}}{3\text{–}4}$; $\dfrac{\text{F}\sharp\text{–G}}{7\text{–}1}$

$\overline{\phantom{3\text{–}4}}$; $\overline{\phantom{7\text{–}1}}$ 1.

$\overline{\phantom{3\text{–}4}}$; $\overline{\phantom{7\text{–}1}}$ 3.

$\overline{\phantom{3\text{–}4}}$; $\overline{\phantom{7\text{–}1}}$ 5.

$\overline{\phantom{3\text{–}4}}$; $\overline{\phantom{7\text{–}1}}$ 7.

$\overline{\phantom{3\text{–}4}}$; $\overline{\phantom{7\text{–}1}}$ 9.

$\overline{\phantom{3\text{–}4}}$; $\overline{\phantom{7\text{–}1}}$ 11.

$\overline{\phantom{3\text{–}4}}$; $\overline{\phantom{7\text{–}1}}$ 13.

Practice 6-4

Starting from the given tonic pitches, write major scales in descending form. This exercise is essentially the same as Practice materials 6-3, except it is in reverse—that is, you must start on the eighth scale degree and work down—7, 6, 5, 4, 3, 2—to the first degree. Remember to use only one pitch of each letter name. Remember also that the pitches of a major scale remain the same whether the scale is in ascending or descending form. When you have written each scale, bracket the half steps and write the names of the first and seventh scale degrees and the fourth and third degrees in the chart to the left.

EXAMPLE:

Half steps

Practice 6-5

Spell the following ascending major scales using letter names and any necessary accidentals. Remember that, when written, accidentals follow the letter name.

EXAMPLE: A   B   C♯   D   E   F♯   G♯   A

1. A♭ ___ ___ ___ ___ ___ ___ ___
2. E♭ ___ ___ ___ ___ ___ ___ ___
3. C♯ ___ ___ ___ ___ ___ ___ ___
4. C♭ ___ ___ ___ ___ ___ ___ ___
5. D♭ ___ ___ ___ ___ ___ ___ ___
6. G♭ ___ ___ ___ ___ ___ ___ ___
7. E ___ ___ ___ ___ ___ ___ ___

Practice 6-6

Identify by letter name the following scale degrees:

1. leading tone of the G major scale   _____
2. mediant of the D♭ major scale   _____
3. subdominant of the A♭ major scale   _____
4. mediant of the C major scale   _____
5. subdominant of the C♯ major scale   _____
6. submediant of the C♭ major scale   _____

Practice 6-7

Complete the following:

1. C is the submediant of the _____ major scale.
2. E♭ is the subdominant of the _____ major scale.
3. B♭ is the subdominant of the _____ major scale.
4. F♯ is the dominant of the _____ major scale.
5. G is the mediant of the _____ major scale.
6. C is the leading tone of the _____ major scale.

Major Key Signatures

🎼 **Visit Music Fundamentals in Action, at CourseMate, to:**

• Take a Pretest on major scales
• View a Hands On Music video demo of major scales
• Find many more practice exercises to help you succeed in this course
• See Tips&Tools for each chapter

Introduction

So far, we have used individual accidentals when writing scales. This is useful when first learning them, but to continue to do this makes performing, particularly sight-reading, extremely complicated. Consider, for example, the difficulty of reading a piece of music in a key in which every pitch has a sharp sign, as in the following example by Bach.

Bach: "Preludio III" from *Well-Tempered Clavier,* Book I (key of C♯ major written without key signature)

Fortunately, there is an easier way.

The Key Signature

Because every scale has the same consistent interval structure, a musical short-hand has been developed to indicate, just once for an entire composition, the pitches requiring accidentals. It is called the **key signature**. The key signature is a grouping, at the beginning of each staff, of all the accidentals found in the scale on which the piece is based. Here is how a key signature would look with the previous example.

An important point to remember is that an accidental appearing in the key signature applies to that note in all octaves. For instance, an F♯ in the key signature indicates that all Fs encountered in the piece are to be played or sung as F♯s. A similar rule holds for chromatic alterations *within* a measure. That is, once an accidental is introduced in a measure, it remains in force for the entire measure unless canceled by a natural sign. But unlike an accidental in the key signature, an accidental within a measure affects only the same note in the same register and in the same voice. This is an important distinction between the sharps or flats of a key signature and those introduced as accidentals.

Sharp Keys

The number and placement of sharps and flats in a key signature is not arbitrary; there is a definite order that makes key signatures easy to read and remember. The following shows the order for the sharp major keys.

Key Signatures: Sharp Major Keys

Notice the invariable pattern for sharp key signatures: If there is only one sharp, that sharp is always F♯; if two sharps, they are always F♯ and C♯, and so on. The complete order of sharps is F♯–C♯–G♯–D♯–A♯–E♯–B♯. You should learn both the order and the location of the sharps in both the treble and bass clefs. Fortunately, once you've learned them, you know them; they never change.

On the staves provided, copy the pattern of sharps for the sharp major keys. Make sure that the sharps are clearly centered, either on a line or in a space. Also make sure that you are placing each of them in the right octave.

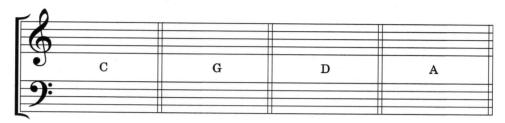

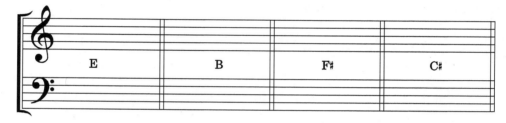

In identifying major key signatures that use sharps, the key is always the pitch a half step above the last sharp indicated in the signature. This is because the last added sharp is always the *leading tone* of that key.

This method of identifying sharp keys is useful, but you should also memorize the number of sharps associated with each major key—information that is given in the following chart. Study the chart carefully until you can identify the sharp key signatures using either method.

Major key	Number of sharps	Major key	Number of sharps
C	0	E	4
G	1	B	5
D	2	F♯	6
A	3	C♯	7

For practice identifying sharp major key signatures, see Practice materials 7-1 at the end of this chapter.

Flat Keys

The order of flats in major key signatures is as follows:

Key Signatures: Flat Major Keys

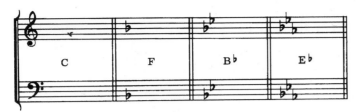

Flat key signatures, like sharp key signatures, have a consistent order and location on the staff. Notice that the last added flat is always the subdominant of that key. The complete order of flats is B♭–E♭–A♭–D♭–G♭–C♭–F♭. Both the order and the location of the flats should be learned for both the treble and bass clefs.

Class Practice

On the staves provided, copy the pattern of flats for the flat major keys. Make certain that the flats are clearly centered on a line or in a space, and that they are in the correct octave.

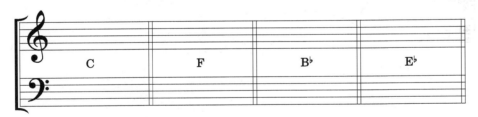

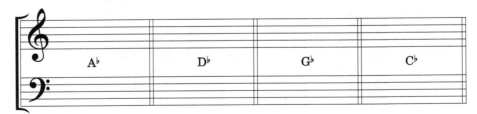

When identifying major key signatures that use flats, we cannot use the system that we learned for major keys that use sharps. Instead, with the flat key signatures, the name of the key is the same as the name of the next-to-last flat. (Obviously, this does not apply to the key of F major, because F major has only one flat.)

As with the sharp key signatures, this method of identification should merely supplement the information contained in the following chart.

Major key	Number of flats		Major key	Number of flats
C	0		A♭	4
F	1		D♭	5
B♭	2		G♭	6
E♭	3		C♭	7

For practice identifying flat major key signatures, see Practice materials 7-2.

The Circle of Fifths: Major Keys

The circle of fifths is a useful visual tool that allows us to grasp key relationships among diatonic scales.

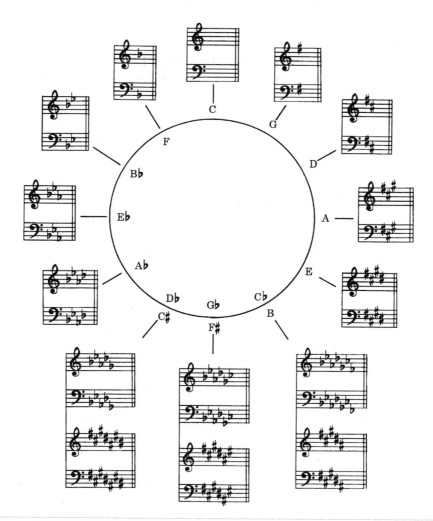

Based on the perfect fifth—an interval of seven half steps that we will study in the next chapter—the circle of fifths goes clockwise adding sharps and counterclockwise adding flats. That is, if the major key signatures are arranged in order of increasing number of sharps, they progress, one to the next, by a perfect fifth. Thus, C major has no sharps (or flats), G major (a perfect fifth higher) has one sharp, D major (a perfect fifth above G) has two sharps, and so on. With the flat keys, the progression of perfect fifths works in reverse order, by the number of flats.

Notice, incidentally, that adjacent scales on the circle of fifths share six of their seven notes. This means that modulations, or key changes, between these closely related keys will go smoothly, because they have so many notes in common.

The value of the circle of fifths when first studying music is that it helps us maneuver through the keys in our minds. It's a way to visualize relationships in sound, whether scales or chord progressions and modulations.

Additional practice with writing and recognizing major key signatures may be found in Practice materials 7-3, 7-4, and 7-5.

A Final Note

If you play an instrument, you have undoubtedly had the experience of playing a wrong note when you momentarily forgot the key signature. This happens to everyone. At such a time, you might have felt that key signatures are a nuisance, and that music would be easier to play without them. But this is *not* the case. Without key signatures, most music would be sprinkled with an incredible number of accidentals, and the resulting clutter would make the music more difficult to read and perform, not easier. Although key signatures are often perplexing at the beginning, they never change, and they are quickly mastered with practice. As you become comfortable with the shorthand of key signatures, you will begin to find them a help rather than a hindrance, and it will become impossible to imagine reading tonal music without them.

Practice 7-1

Name the major key represented by each of the following sharp key signatures. Begin by drawing a circle around the sharp that represents the leading tone of that key. Then, remember that the leading tone is a half step below the tonic and name the key.

1.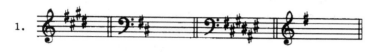

_____   _____   _____   _____

2.

_____   _____   _____   _____

Practice 7-2

Identify the major key represented by each of the following flat key signatures. Remember that the name of the key is the same as the name of the next-to-last flat.

1.

_____   _____   _____   _____

2.

_____   _____   _____   _____

Practice 7-3

Write out the indicated major key signatures, using either sharps or flats as required. When attempting to keep all the sharps and flats in order in your mind, it is helpful to remember that the order of flats—B–E–A–D–G–C–F—is the reverse of the order of sharps—F–C–G–D–A–E–B.

1.
   A Major

2.
   E Major

3.
   B♭ Major

4.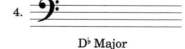
   D♭ Major

5.
   F♯ Major

6.
   A♭ Major

(continued)

7. F Major

8. C♯ Major

9. G♭ Major

10. E♭ Major

11. G Major

12. C♭ Major

13. D Major

14. C♭ Major

15. B Major

Practice 7-4

Identify the correct major key, based on the number of sharps or flats indicated.

1. three sharps _____
2. one sharp _____
3. three flats _____
4. two sharps _____

5. two flats _____
6. five flats _____
7. seven sharps _____

Practice 7-5

Appendix D contains 56 melodies in major keys. Look at each of the following melodies in Appendix D and decide what major key each is in.

1. No. 5 _____
2. No. 13 _____

3. No. 19 _____
4. No. 31 _____

Focus on Skills 4: **Scales 1**

 Visit Music Fundamentals in Action, at CourseMate, for interactive Focus on Fundamentals exercises.

The following questions cover Chapters 6 and 7: Major Scales and Major Key Signatures. If you have difficulty with any of them, be sure to review the relevant sections before beginning Chapter 8.

1. Write a one-octave chromatic scale, ascending and descending, starting from the following pitch.

2. Write ascending major scales starting from the following pitches.

a.

b.

c.

3. Write descending major scales starting from the following pitches.

a.

b.

c.

4. Complete the following sentences.

    a. The dominant of the B♭ major scale is _____.

    b. The supertonic of the G♭ major scale is _____.

    c. The supertonic of the G major scale is _____.

    d. The leading tone of the F major scale is _____.

    e. The subdominant of the C♯ major scale is _____.

    f. A is the mediant of the _____ major scale.

    g. E is the dominant of the _____ major scale.

    h. B♭ is the subdominant of the _____ major scale.

5. Write out the following major key signatures.

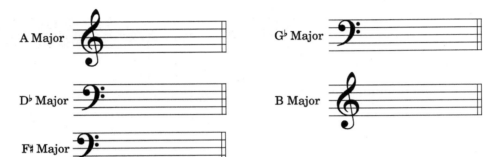

A Major

D♭ Major

F♯ Major

G♭ Major

B Major

8

Intervals

Visit Music Fundamentals in Action, at CourseMate, to:

- Take a Pretest on intervals
- Hear the author's Let's Talk About Music podcast on intervals
- View a Hands On Music video on intervals
- Find many more practice exercises to help you succeed in this course
- See Tips&Tools for each chapter

Introduction

Intervals measure musical distances. All musicians need the ability to do that, so think of your work with intervals as learning the basic language skills of tonal music. It's a step you can't afford to slight. Intervals are fundamental. Here is something else to consider: perhaps you know someone who studies piano. If so, the chances are good that they spend a lot of time playing scales. Many students don't understand why this is important, so consider this: scales contain the fundamental patterns upon which tonal music is built. By practicing these patterns—in the form of scales—performers become musically acquainted with material that will appear repeatedly in the music itself.

But what, exactly, are these patterns contained in scales? They are *interval patterns*. The interval patterns of scales become the interval patterns of melody and harmony, and what we hear as music is actually combinations of these patterns. The interval, therefore, is one of *the* basic units of tonal music. In this chapter, we will learn a way to recognize and identify intervals that will also be used in future chapters concerned with triads and harmony.

Interval Identification

As we learned earlier, an interval is the musical distance between two pitches. If the two pitches are sounded simultaneously, the interval is called a **harmonic interval**.

Harmonic intervals

If the two pitches are sounded in succession, like two tones of a melody, the interval is called a **melodic interval**.

Melodic intervals

In either case, it is the distance between the two pitches that is identified and measured. Two elements are considered in identifying intervals: size and quality.

Interval Size

The first step in identifying an interval is to determine the size of the interval. This is done by counting the letter names of the two pitches whose interval we are trying to determine plus the letter names of all the pitches in between.

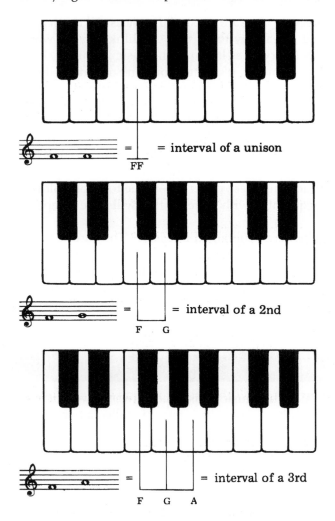

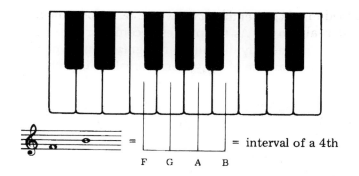

= = interval of a 4th

F   G   A   B

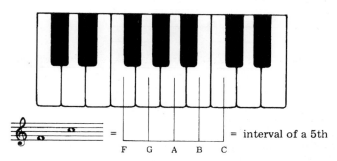

= = interval of a 5th

F   G   A   B   C

As the preceding illustration shows, each letter name is counted only once. Thus, in the second example, the enharmonic pitch between F and G (F♯ or G♭) was not counted in determining the size of the interval. For this reason, it is easier to measure interval size on the staff than on the keyboard. Furthermore, the staff facilitates interval recognition because of the following rules concerning the position of intervals on the staff:

The notes of a *second* always appear on adjacent lines and spaces.

The notes of a *third* always appear on consecutive lines or spaces.

Fourths always have one pitch on a line and the other in a space, with a space and a line between.

Fifths always have either (1) both pitches on lines, with one line between or (2) both pitches in spaces, with one space between.

This pattern continues for sixths, sevenths, octaves (the term for the arithmetic distance of an eighth), and so on. As the pitches become farther apart, however, the pattern becomes increasingly difficult to recognize. Until you become familiar with the overall appearance of the wider intervals, it is probably wise to count the lines and spaces between the pitches of the interval.

Identify the following intervals by interval size.

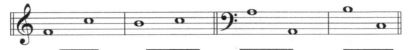

_____   _____ _____   _____ _____   _____

Complete the indicated intervals by writing the pitch that is the correct interval size above the given pitch.

Additional practice identifying and writing interval sizes is available in Practice materials 8-1, 8-2, 8-3, and 8-4 at the end of this chapter.

Interval Quality

The second step in recognizing an interval is to identify the sound *quality* or *color* of the interval. The quality or color of an interval is related to the number of half steps contained between the two pitches. In the following example, all four intervals are thirds. But if you play them on a keyboard or sing them, you will find that each has a distinctly different quality or color. This is because they are different kinds of thirds.

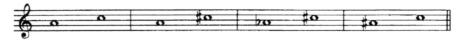

The following terms are used to describe the quality of intervals:

Interval	Abbreviation
Perfect	P
Major	M
Minor	m
Augmented	A or +
Diminished	d or °

Determining the quality of an interval may be done in one of two ways. One way is to memorize the number of half steps contained in the various kinds of intervals, and then to use this information when confronted with a new interval. The problem with this method is that it involves both a lot of memorizing and a lot of counting half steps.

The other way to determine interval quality is to remember the types of intervals that occur between the first note of a major scale and each of the other notes in the scale, and then to gauge new intervals against this information.

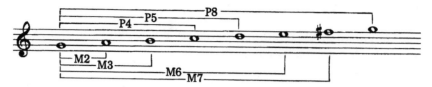

Although both ways of identifying intervals work equally well, the major-scale method (when you know your scales well) is probably faster and more accurate. Counting half steps can involve too much rote learning and is subject to error.

Perfect Intervals

Only four kinds of intervals are called *perfect intervals*: the unison, the fourth, the fifth, and the octave. They are labeled *perfect* because in Medieval and Renaissance music they were considered the only intervals suitable for momentary or permanent stopping places (called cadences) in a piece. The following illustration shows (1) the number of half steps in each type of perfect interval and (2) the standard way of identifying intervals, using letters for quality and numbers for size.

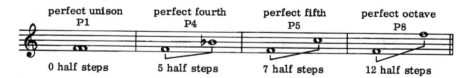

For any particular interval, both the size and the quality must be correct for the interval itself to be correct. Remember that the size is the total count of letter names included in the interval, while the quality is determined by counting half steps. In the case of a perfect fifth, for example, the size must be a fifth, and the interval must contain exactly seven half steps.

In a major scale, the quality of the intervals between the tonic and the subdominant, dominant, or octave is always perfect.

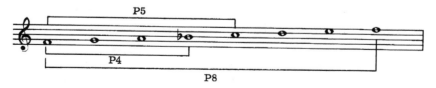

Therefore, you can quickly check the quality of any of these intervals by assuming that the lower pitch of the interval is the tonic, and asking yourself if the upper pitch is in the scale of the lower pitch. If it is, and if the **interval size** is a fourth, fifth, or octave, the interval is perfect in quality.

Consider the following example:

The interval size is a fourth. To determine the quality, we assume that the E♭ is the tonic of a major scale. Is A♭ in the E♭ major scale? Because the answer is yes, this is a perfect fourth. If the upper pitch were not in the scale, then the quality of the interval would be something other than perfect.

Perfect intervals can also be **augmented** or **diminished in quality**. A perfect interval is made augmented by retaining the interval size while, at the same time, expanding the interval by a half step.

perfect fourth
P4

5 half steps

augmented fourth
A4

6 half steps

A perfect interval is made diminished by retaining the interval size while decreasing the interval by a half step.

perfect fifth
P5

7 half steps

diminished fifth
d5

6 half steps

Notice that although the augmented fourth and the diminished fifth both contain six half steps, one is identified as a fourth and the other as a fifth. This is because the interval size of the two is not the same. Another point to remember is that although a unison can be augmented by adding a half step, it cannot be made diminished.

Practice for working with perfect intervals is available in Practice materials 8-5, 8-6, and 8-7.

Music in Action   Recognizing Perfect Intervals
Locate and identify all the perfect intervals in the following piece.

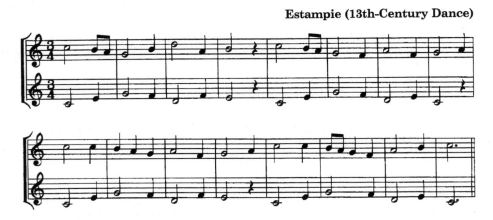

Estampie (13th-Century Dance)

When you have identified the perfect intervals, play the piece or sing it with the class. Discuss where the perfect intervals occur and the type of sound they contribute to the piece. ●

Although any interval can be augmented or diminished in quality, perfect intervals can never be major or minor in quality. The intervals of major and minor quality are the second, the third, the sixth, and the seventh. The following illustration shows the number of half steps contained in each of the four types of major intervals.

In a major scale, the quality of the intervals between the tonic and the supertonic, mediant, submediant, and leading tone is always major.

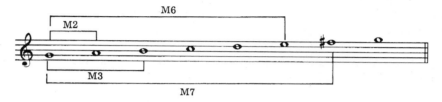

The same procedure for identifying perfect intervals can be applied to seconds, thirds, sixths, and sevenths as well. We simply assume that the lower pitch is the tonic; if the upper pitch is in the major scale of the lower pitch, the interval is major.

Another good way to learn this information is contained in the following chart. It lists the intervals found within a major scale and the number of half steps in each interval. Although you should be familiar with both ways of identifying and writing intervals, you can use whichever way seems easiest to you.

Intervals of the Major Scale

Interval	Number of half steps
Perfect unison	0
Major 2nd	2
Major 3rd	4
Perfect 4th	5
Perfect 5th	7
Major 6th	9
Major 7th	11
Perfect 8ve	12

The number of half steps in each of the major intervals should be memorized. It then becomes simple to change the quality of major intervals to minor, augmented, or diminished. For example, a major interval decreased by a half step becomes minor in quality.

A minor interval further decreased by a half step becomes diminished. A major interval can be diminished by decreasing it a whole step (two half steps) while maintaining the correct interval size.

A major interval increased by a half step becomes augmented.

Notice that both the augmented third and the perfect fourth contain five half steps. Even though they have the same sound, they are not written the same because of their different sizes. The augmented third must *look* like a third, and the perfect fourth must *look* like a fourth.

Class Practice

Complete the indicated intervals by writing the correct pitch above each given pitch.

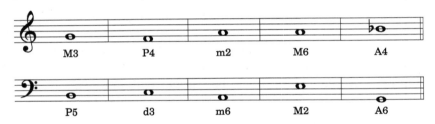

Practice for working with major and minor intervals may be found in Practice materials 8-8, 8-9, 8-10, and 8-11.

Music in Action

Recognizing Intervals
In the following two excerpts, identify the harmonic intervals created between the upper and lower voices. Write your answers in the spaces provided. Remember that the interval changes when one voice moves while the other voice remains stationary.

"Nowel syng we" (Medieval English Carol)

As a class, sing or play each excerpt; then discuss the following questions:

1. What is the largest interval and how frequently does it occur?

2. What is the smallest interval and how frequently does it occur?

3. How are the perfect intervals used? How important are they?

4. Are there any repetitions of interval patterns?

5. Did you have trouble performing the figure ♫♫ at the end of the Landini excerpt? It is a borrowed division. Do you remember what these are and how they are to be counted? If not, refer back to the Triplets and Duplets section of Chapter 4. ●

Music in Action

Singing Intervals

It is important that you practice singing intervals. Keep in mind that a few minutes' practice each day is far more beneficial than a lengthy session once or twice a week. You can practice interval skills any number of ways, but keep your exercises simple so that you can build on your successes. Use the following as a sample from which to develop your own. Perhaps each member of the class could design a singing exercise for class use. These could then be shared so that every class member would have a sizable collection of practice exercises.

Begin by singing these ascending and descending intervals in the major scale.

do re	do ti	do la	do mi
do mi	do la	do ti	do re
do fa	do sol	do do	do do
do sol	do fa		

Here is another useful ascending and descending exercise:

do mi sol	mi do la	sol ti re	la fa re
re fa la	re ti sol	la do mi	sol mi do
mi sol ti	do la fa	ti re fa	fa re ti
fa la do	ti sol mi	mi	do

These exercises can also be sung using scale-degree numbers. Doing this will give you a slightly different perspective on the major scale and the intervals that it contains. ●

Intervals that are one octave or smaller in size are called **simple intervals**, while intervals larger than an octave are known as **compound intervals**. The following example illustrates a major ninth, a major tenth, and a perfect eleventh:

Of course, the larger the interval, the more difficult it can be to read and identify correctly. For the purposes of identification it is easier to reduce the compound interval by one octave. Thus, a major ninth becomes a compound major second; a major tenth, a compound major third; and a perfect eleventh, a compound perfect fourth.

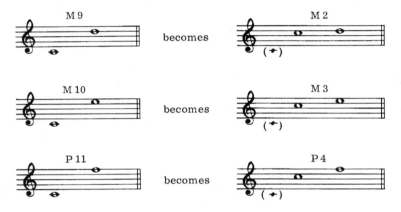

Compound intervals are major, minor, augmented, diminished, or perfect, depending on the quality of the corresponding simple interval. Remember that the quality always stays the same because all you are doing when you reduce a compound interval to a simple interval is subtracting one octave.

Class Practice

Identify the following compound intervals by reducing them by one octave and labeling the simple interval that results.

Additional practice with compound intervals is available in Practice materials 8-12 and 8-13.

Harmonic Inversion of Intervals

Intervals are inverted harmonically by reversing the pitches from top to bottom. That is, *the higher pitch is moved one octave lower* so it is below the other pitch. The same interval results if *the lower pitch is moved one octave higher*. The point to remember when inverting intervals is that one pitch remains stationary and the other moves an octave.

inverts to

The interval size always changes when an interval is inverted. A fifth inverts to a fourth, a sixth to a third, and a seventh to a second. Notice also that *the sum of the interval plus its inversion always equals nine.*

The quality of inverted intervals changes in the following ways:

Perfect intervals always invert to perfect intervals.

P4   becomes   P5

Major intervals always invert to minor intervals; minor intervals always invert to major intervals.

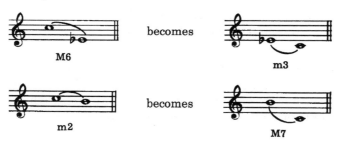

M6   becomes   m3

m2   becomes   M7

Augmented intervals always invert to diminished intervals; diminished intervals always invert to augmented intervals.

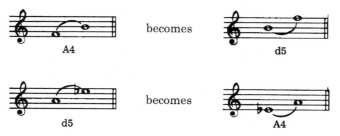

A4   becomes   d5

d5   becomes   A4

Another important point to remember is that inverted intervals can, in some ways, be considered to belong to the same interval family. That is, although the two pitches have changed location, and the interval between them has changed, the pitches themselves have not changed.

Practice for working with the harmonic inversion of intervals may be found in Practice materials 8-14.

Music in Action 🔊 Ear Training

Your teacher or another student from the class will play various intervals, beginning on different pitches, for you to recognize by ear. These will be played as either harmonic (sounding simultaneously) or melodic (sounding in succession) intervals. The intervals have been grouped in limited combinations according to size and quality to make your beginning work easier.

As you practice, remember that ear training is a continuous process; it grows easier as you continue. If time permits, your teacher may wish to return to this exercise several times in the future. An alternative to this would be for you and a friend from the class to practice on your own.

Major 2nds and Major 3rds

1. _____   4. _____
2. _____   5. _____
3. _____

Major 3rds and Perfect 5ths

1. _____   4. _____
2. _____   5. _____
3. _____

Perfect 4ths and Perfect 5ths

1. _____   4. _____
2. _____   5. _____
3. _____

Major 2nds, Perfect 4ths, and Major 6ths

1. _____   4. _____
2. _____   5. _____
3. _____

All intervals from the major scale, including the Major 7th

1. _____   4. _____
2. _____   5. _____ ●
3. _____

A Final Note

In this chapter, we have concentrated on identifying and writing musical intervals. This work can, at times, seem both mathematical and time-consuming, but it is absolutely necessary for you to be familiar with intervals. Intervals are a fundamental element of music; interval patterns are the building blocks of tonal music.

Even if the mechanics of writing and recognizing intervals becomes tedious, as it can at times, keep in mind that acquiring these skills is essential in advancing your understanding of tonal music. In the same way that musicians practice scales to acquaint themselves with scale patterns, they work with intervals to become familiar with interval patterns. Perhaps the following Music in Action will help to illustrate that melodies are patterns of intervals.

Music in Action 🔊 Ear Training

In your mind, sing the beginning of any of the following songs that you know. Beside the name of each, write the interval that occurs between the first and second notes of the song. This may seem difficult at first, but two hints may help: (1) Only the intervals found in a major scale are used—P1, M2, M3, P4, P5, M6, M7, P8. (2) Songs that don't begin on the tonic quite often begin on the dominant. If you continue to have trouble, try singing up or down the scale from the tonic to the other note.

1. "Be Prepared" from *The Lion King* _____
2. "Titanic" theme _____
3. "Will the Circle Be Unbroken?" _____
4. "Star Wars" theme _____
5. "Over the Rainbow" from *The Wizard of Oz* _____
6. "Moon River" _____ ●

Music in Action 🎵 Song Building

Create a small band of four or five people from among the members of the class and write a short "sound" score for this group. Use hand claps and a variety of everyday objects found in the classroom to make percussive sounds. In your score, use examples of repeated measures, 1st and 2nd endings, and either *D.C. al fine* or *D.S. al fine*. If necessary, review these scoring devices in the How to Read a Musical Map section of Chapter 5. When completed, perform the various pieces for the class. ●

Practice 8-1

Identify the interval size of these melodic intervals. Use the appropriate numeral, as shown in the example, to indicate the interval size. Begin by noticing the clef that is being used. Then, name both notes in your mind.

EXAMPLE:

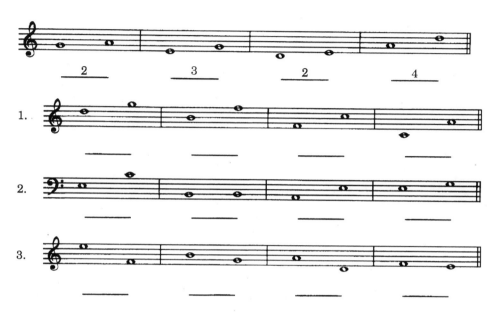

Practice 8-2

Complete the following harmonic intervals by writing in the pitch that is the correct interval size *above* the given pitch.

EXAMPLE:

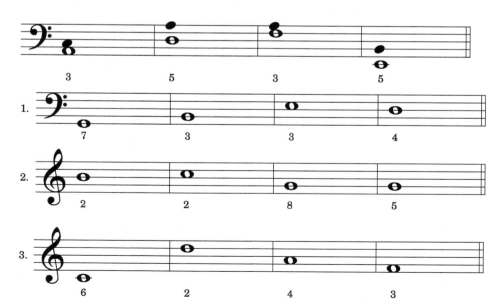

Practice 8-3

Complete the following harmonic intervals by writing in the pitch that is the correct interval size *below* the given pitch.

EXAMPLE:

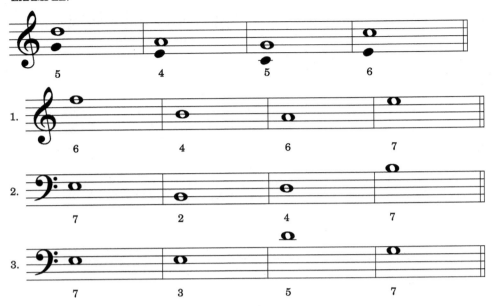

In lines 1 to 3:

1. 6   4   6   7
2. 7   2   4   7
3. 7   3   5   7

Practice 8-4

Identify the interval size between the pitches in each of the following sets. In lines 1 to 3, consider the second pitch to be *above* the first pitch.

1. E–F   D–A   G–B   F–E

   ____   ____   ____   ____

2. F–A   F–B   A–B   C–B

   ____   ____   ____   ____

In lines 4 to 6, consider the second pitch to be *below* the first pitch.

3. E–A   G–B   F–G   F–A

   ____   ____   ____   ____

4. G–C   G–F   A–D   A–F

   ____   ____   ____   ____

Practice 8-5

In the following harmonic intervals, circle the perfect unisons, fourths, fifths, and octaves. Begin by observing the clef and naming the two pitches. Remember to ask yourself if the upper pitch is in the major scale of the lower pitch.

Practice 8-6

Identify each of the following melodic intervals as either a unison, a fourth, a fifth, or an octave, and as either perfect (P), augmented (A), or diminished (d). A keyboard is provided to help you visualize the half steps. Remember that the major scale contains perfect fourths, fifths, and octaves, and that augmented intervals will be a half step larger than these and diminished intervals a half step smaller, except for the unison, which cannot be diminished.

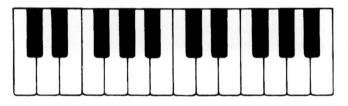

EXAMPLE:

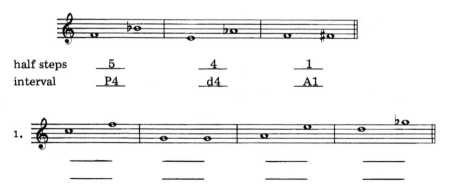

| half steps | 5 | 4 | 1 |
| interval | P4 | d4 | A1 |

(continued)

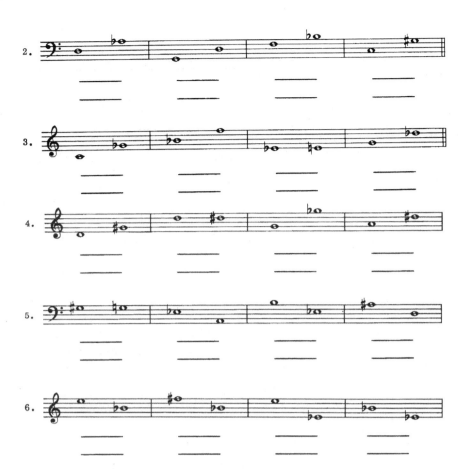

Practice 8-7

Complete each of the indicated intervals by notating the correct *higher* pitch. You may write them as either melodic or harmonic intervals. This exercise deals with unisons, fourths, fifths, and octaves only. Use the keyboard to help you visualize the half steps. Remember to maintain the correct interval size. Begin by thinking of the major scale for each given pitch; this will give you the perfect interval.

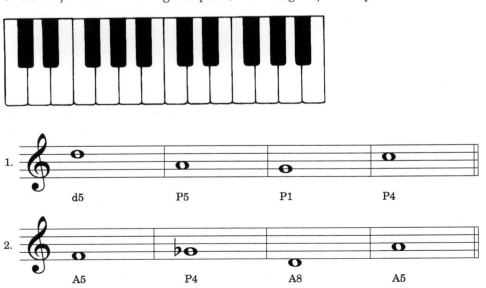

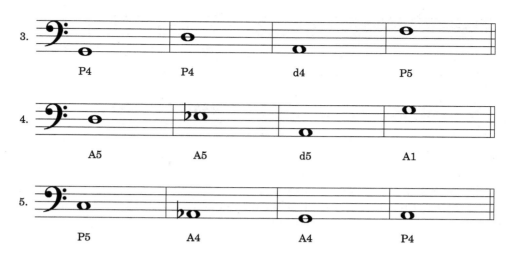

Practice 8-8

Identify and circle the major seconds, thirds, sixths, and sevenths in the following set of harmonic intervals. Remember to ask yourself if the upper pitch is in the major scale of the lower pitch, or to use the chart of half steps.

Practice 8-9

Construct the indicated major interval, either harmonic or melodic, by writing the correct *higher* notehead. Begin by thinking of the major scale for each given pitch.

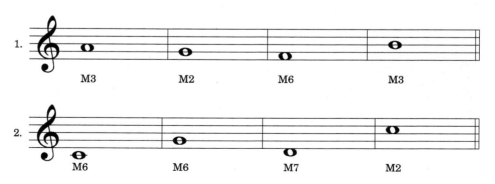

(continued)

3. M3 M2 M7 M7

Practice 8-10

Identify the following melodic intervals as either a second, a third, a sixth, or a seventh, and as either augmented (A), major (M), minor (m), or diminished (d) in quality. (Capital and lowercase Ms can often be confused unless you print them carefully. For this reason, your teacher may prefer that you use MA for major and MI for minor.) Use the keyboard to help visualize the half steps. Remember that the major scale produces major seconds, thirds, sixths, and sevenths above the tonic.

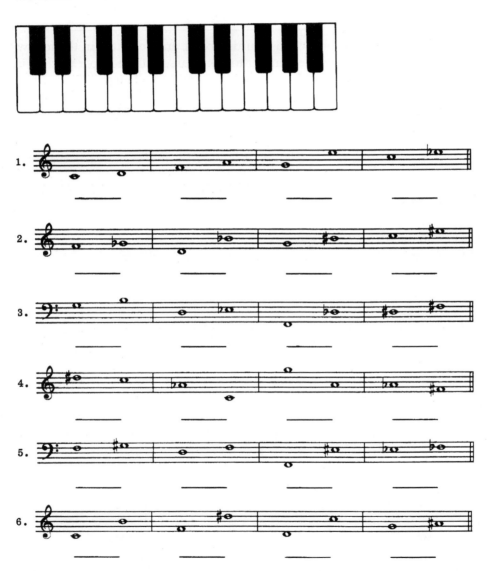

Practice 8-11

Construct the indicated harmonic or melodic intervals by writing the correct *higher* notehead. This exercise deals only with seconds, thirds, sixths, and sevenths. Remember to keep the correct interval size. Use the keyboard to visualize the intervals. Begin by thinking of the major scale that starts on each given pitch.

Practice 8-12

Identify the following compound harmonic intervals by reducing them by one octave and labeling the simple interval that results:

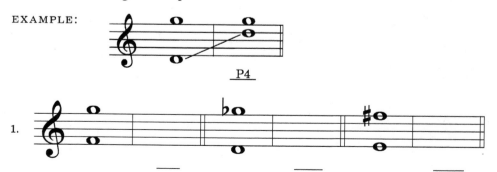

(continued)

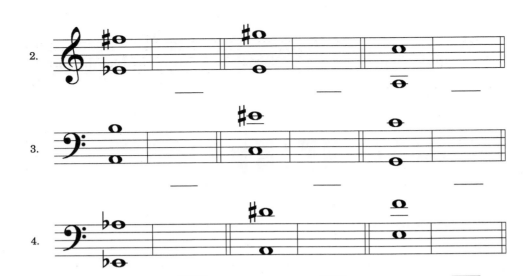

Practice 8-13

Identify the following compound harmonic intervals. Even though you are not asked to reduce each interval by an octave this time, you may find it helpful to do so mentally. Remember also that the quality of the compound interval is the same as the quality of the corresponding simple interval.

Practice 8-14

First, label each melodic interval, then invert it and identify the interval that results. Remember that the sum of any interval plus its inversion always equals nine.

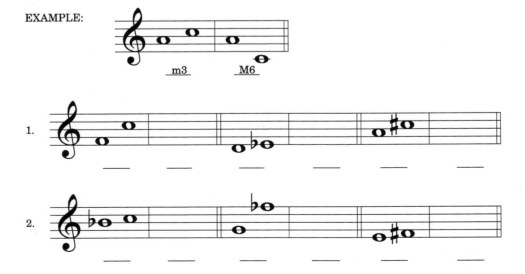

3.

4.

Practice 8-15

1. a. Think C4.
    b. Now name the pitch that is a P4 higher.
    c. From this new pitch, name the pitch that is an m2 lower.
    d. What is the name of the pitch you have reached? _____

2. a. Think D2.
    b. Now name the pitch that is an M6 higher.
    c. From this new pitch, name the pitch that is an m3 higher.
    d. From this new pitch, name the pitch that is an m7 lower.
    e. What is the name of the pitch you have reached? _____

3. a. Think F♯4.
    b. Now name the pitch that is a P4 higher.
    c. From this new pitch, name the pitch that is an M3 higher.
    d. From this new pitch, name the pitch that is a P5 lower.
    e. What is the name of the pitch you have reached? _____

Focus on Skills 5: **Intervals**

 Visit Music Fundamentals in Action, at CourseMate, for interactive Focus on Fundamentals exercises.

The following questions focus solely on Chapter 8: Intervals. If you have any difficulty, review the chapter before continuing. Intervals are too important to remain uncertain about them.

1. Identify each of these harmonic intervals.

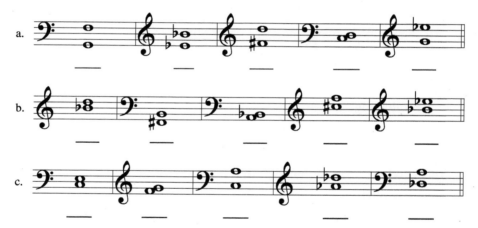

2. Write the pitch that completes the indicated interval *above* each given pitch.

3. Write the pitch that completes each interval *below* the indicated pitch.

a.

m3   P5   m6   M3   m7

b.

P4   M3   A5   M3   m2

4. Reduce each of these compound intervals by one octave and label the resulting simple interval.

a.

b.

5. Complete the following:

 a. Think G3.
 b. Now name the pitch that is an m7 lower.
 c. From this new pitch, name the pitch that is an M3 lower.
 d. From this new pitch, name the pitch that is a P5 higher.
 e. What is the name of the pitch you have reached? _____

6. Complete the following:

 a. Think B♭1.
 b. Now name the pitch that is an M6 higher.
 c. From this new pitch, name the pitch that is an m2 higher.
 d. From this new pitch, name the pitch that is a P4 higher.
 e. What is the name of the pitch you have reached? _____

Minor Key Signatures

Visit Music Fundamentals in Action, at CourseMate, to:

- Take a Pretest on minor scales
- View a Hands On Music video demo of minor scales
- Find many more practice exercises to help you succeed in this course
- See Tips&Tools for Each Chapter

Introduction

Learning the minor keys does not require learning a whole new set of key signatures because the minor keys are directly related to the major keys that you already know. This chapter presents the minor key signatures and explains how they are related to the major key signatures. In the next chapter we will study the minor scales themselves.

At this point, it is important to keep in mind that, although there is more than one form of the minor scale, there is only one set of minor key signatures. Learning the various forms of the minor scale, which are presented in Chapter 10, will be easier after you become familiar with the minor key signatures.

Related Keys

There is a simple and important relationship between major and minor keys. Notice, for instance, the relationship of accidentals between the following two scales.

F major scale

D natural minor scale

Both scales have one and the same accidental—B♭. In fact, if you begin on the sixth degree of *any* major scale and follow its note pattern for one octave, the result will always be a new, natural minor scale. Here's another example:

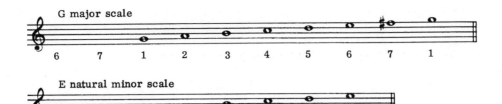

G major scale

E natural minor scale

This relationship, which is constant for all of the major keys, means that there are pairs of keys—one major, one minor—related by the same pitch content, hence by the same key signature. Such keys are called **related keys**. The term *relative minor* refers to the minor key or scale that is related to a particular major scale by having the same key signature. The term *relative major* refers to the major key or scale with the same key signature as a particular minor scale.

The relative minor-major relationship may be remembered in two ways: (1) The relative minor scale always begins on the sixth degree of the major scale. (2) The relative minor scale always begins three half steps (a minor third) below its related major scale. Most students find the second way easier. Either way, remember that related scales always have the *same* key signature but *different* tonics.

The major-minor relationship

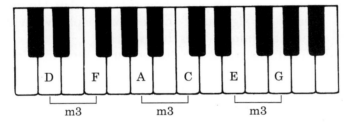

F Major/D minor   C Major/A minor   G Major/E minor

Key signature   Key signature   Key signature
of 1 flat   of no sharps   of 1 sharp
                     or flats

Class Practice

Identify the relative minor key for the following major keys:

1. B major _____   3. E♭ major _____
2. A major _____   4. D♭ major _____

Identify the relative major key for the following minor keys:

1. F minor _____   3. B♭ minor _____
2. A♭ minor _____   4. C♯ minor _____

Additional practice identifying related keys may be found in Practice materials 9-1, 9-2, and 9-3 at the end of this chapter.

Minor Key Signatures

The minor key signatures, for sharp keys and flat keys, are given below, followed by the number of accidentals associated with each key. Notice that lowercase letters are used to indicate minor keys. Notice also that the last sharp added to each sharp key is the supertonic, and the last flat added to each flat key is the submediant. As you study these minor key signatures, make a mental association with the relative major for each key.

Key signatures: sharp minor keys

Minor key	Number of sharps
a	0
e	1
b	2
f♯	3
c♯	4
g♯	5
d♯	6
a♯	7

Minor key	Number of flats
a	0
d	1
g	2
c	3
f	4
b♭	5
e♭	6
a♭	7

The primary concept to remember is that each key signature is shared by one major scale and one minor scale. Furthermore, because they share a key signature, the two scales are thought of as related to each other. The terms *relative major* and *relative minor* refer to this relationship. The following chart may help to make this point clearer:

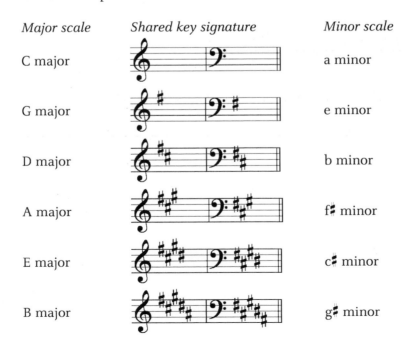

Major scale	Shared key signature	Minor scale
C major		a minor
G major		e minor
D major		b minor
A major		f♯ minor
E major		c♯ minor
B major		g♯ minor

Major scale	Shared key signature	Minor scale
F♯ major		d♯ minor
C♯ major		a♯ minor
F major		d minor
B♭ major		g minor
E♭ major		c minor
A♭ major		f minor
D♭ major		b♭ minor
G♭ major		e♭ minor
C♭ major		a♭ minor

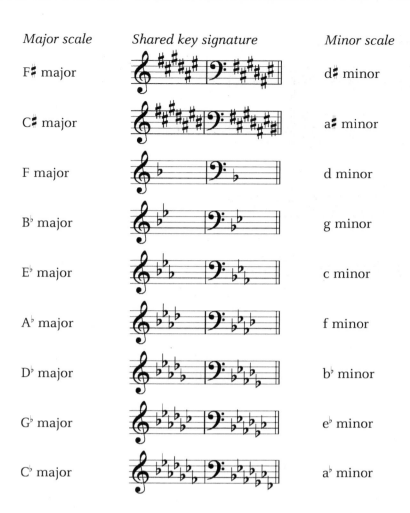

Class Practice

Identify the minor keys represented by the following key signature:

_____ _____ _____ _____

Additional practice recognizing minor key signatures may be found in Practice materials 9-4.

Write the following minor key signatures:

A♭ Minor   C♯ Minor   D Minor   E♭ Minor

Additional practice writing minor key signatures may be found in Practice materials 9-5.

Music in Action 🔊 Ear Training

Have your teacher or another student select and play on the keyboard several of the musical excerpts listed below (with their location in this book). After listening to each excerpt, decide whether it is in a major or minor key.

Composer	Title	Page(s)
1. Bach	Chorale from Cantata No. 180	22
2. Bach	Courante from French Suite No. 2	22, 207
3. Bach	Minuet in G Minor	56–57
4. Kuhlau	Rondo from Sonatina, Op. 20, No. 1	93
5. Mozart	Sonata in B♭ Major, K. 570, III	92
6. Scarlatti	Sonata in C Minor	203–204
7. Traditional	"St. James Infirmary"	265

Parallel Keys

In addition to the relative major–relative minor relationship between keys, in which two keys share the same key signature (but different tonics), there is also a parallel major–parallel minor relationship. This relationship between **parallel keys** occurs when two keys—one major and one minor—share the same tonic (but use different key signatures).

parallel keys

E major

e minor

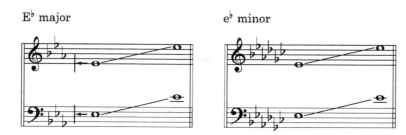

E♭ major   e♭ minor

Notice in these examples that the key signatures between parallel major and parallel minor vary by three accidentals, that is, E major has 4 sharps, e minor has 1 sharp; E♭ major has 3 flats, e♭ minor has 6 flats. This difference of 3 accidentals holds true for all of the parallel major–parallel minor relationships.

Both the parallel and the relative major/minor relationships are used frequently by composers, particularly in larger works such as sonatas and symphonies. The parallel relationship between keys allows the composer to switch a section of a work from major to minor (or vice versa) without changing the tonic note (called a change of mode), whereas the relative relationship allows them to keep the same key signature but use a different tonic (called a **modulation**).

Class Practice

Write the key signatures for the following parallel keys:

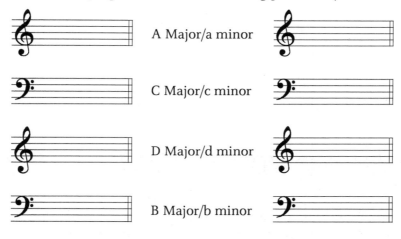

A Major/a minor

C Major/c minor

D Major/d minor

B Major/b minor

The Circle of Fifths: Minor Keys

For minor keys, as for major keys, a circle of fifths can be constructed. The same perfect-fifth relationship between adjacent keys exists, and again the enharmonic keys appear at the bottom of the circle. Notice also that the circle of fifths for major keys can be superimposed over the one for minor keys. This works because of the parallel relationship between major and minor keys discussed earlier.

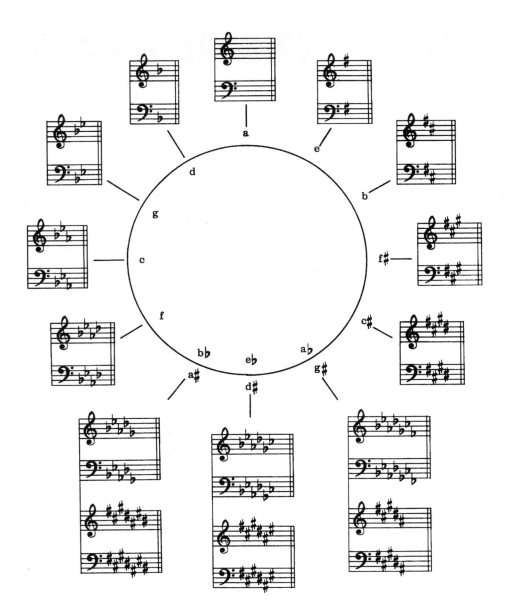

At this point it might be more useful to you to combine the two in your mind so that you remember one circle of fifths for both major and minor keys.

For practice combining the major and minor circle of fifths into one, see Practice materials 9-6.

Music in Action

Composing and Conducting

Write a short composition in compound meter for four percussionists. Use hand claps and find sounds available in the classroom. Create a score for your piece that clearly shows the four separate parts. Then, assign parts to various members of the class and give a performance, with you conducting, for the rest of the class. You may wish to rehearse once or twice before performing for the class. When conducting, remember to give a silent beat to prepare your performers to begin together. ●

A Final Note

Almost all beginning musicians have favorite keys. These are usually keys with no sharps or flats, or at most one or two, which seem easier. Sometimes, people study theory or take lessons for years and still find keys with more than four or five sharps or flats too difficult to negotiate successfully. Usually, the problem feeds on itself—some keys are initially easier, therefore we *choose* to work primarily in those keys. But this is a mistake; we don't learn by avoidance.

If you are going to be a good musician, even a good amateur musician, you need to be fluent in all keys—both major and minor. This ability won't come immediately, but it will develop slowly with practice. You can make working with minor scales easier by being certain that you understand the minor key signatures and how they relate to the major keys. If you need additional practice at recognizing or writing minor key signatures, do that now, before you begin the next chapter. You will find Chapter 10 much easier to understand once you are comfortable with the minor key signatures.

Practice 9-1

Identify the relative minor key for the following major keys:

1. E major _____
2. G♭ major _____
3. C♯ major _____
4. A major _____

5. C major _____
6. F♯ major _____
7. E♭ major _____

Practice 9-2

Identify the major key and the relative minor key that have the given number of sharps or flats.

	Major	*Relative minor*
1. two flats	_____	_____
2. two sharps	_____	_____
3. four flats	_____	_____
4. five flats	_____	_____
5. one sharp	_____	_____
6. five sharps	_____	_____
7. one flat	_____	_____

Practice 9-3

Identify the relative major key for the following minor keys:

1. F♯ minor _____
2. A♭ minor _____
3. A♯ minor _____
4. B♭ minor _____

5. D♯ minor _____
6. B minor _____
7. C minor _____

Practice 9-4

Identify the minor keys represented by the following key signatures:

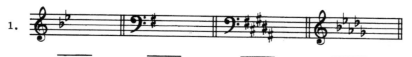

(continued)

3.

4.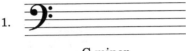

Practice 9-5

Write out the indicated minor key signatures, using sharps or flats as needed.

1.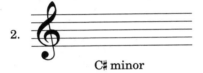

G minor

2.

C♯ minor

3.

D♯ minor

4.

G♯ minor

5.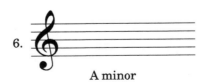

E♭ minor

6.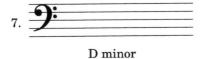

A minor

7.

D minor

8.

F minor

9.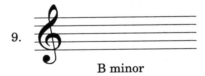

B minor

10.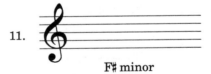

E minor

11.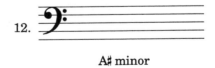

F♯ minor

12.

A♯ minor

13.

A♭ minor

Practice 9-6

In the blank circle of fifths below, combine the two versions you have studied—major and minor—into one. Use uppercase letters for major keys and lowercase letters for related minor keys, that is, C/a.

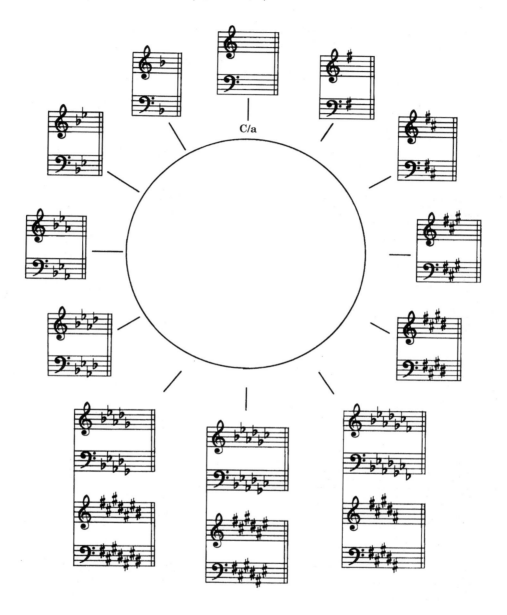

C/a

Minor Scales

Visit Music Fundamentals in Action, at CourseMate, to:

- Take a Pretest on minor scales
- View a Hands On Music video demo of minor scales
- Find many more practice exercises to help you succeed in this course
- See Tips&Tools for each chapter

Introduction

There is only one minor scale. But unlike the major scale, the minor scale comes in three forms. For convenience, they have been given the names *natural minor, harmonic minor,* and *melodic minor.* The reason there can be three forms of one scale is that the minor scale sounds less stable than the major scale. If you change a note of the major scale you destroy it; it doesn't sound the same anymore. But if you change a note in the minor scale it can sound more interesting; it offers more variety without seeming to destroy the basic characteristics of the scale.

Class Practice

Here are the three forms of the minor scale. Begin by singing through each of them and deciding what you hear in the three different forms.

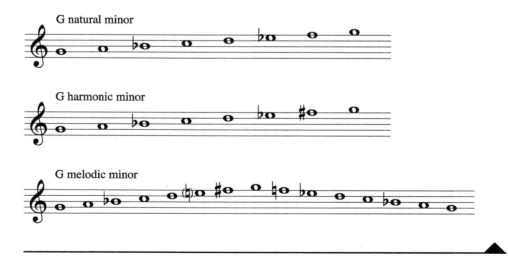

Hearing Major and Minor

The following excerpts are from two folk songs. You may already know one or both of them. The first one is in the key of D major, the second is in D minor. Ask someone to play both examples in class. Remember that the difference in sound or feeling that you hear between major keys and minor keys is a result of two different interval patterns of whole steps and half steps.

"Molly Malone"

"Joshua Fit the Battle of Jericho"

Like the major scale, the **natural minor scale** contains five whole steps and two half steps. The half steps, however, do not occur in the same place. This reordering of the interval pattern gives the natural minor scale its unique quality.

In the natural minor scale, the two half steps occur between the second and third degrees and the fifth and sixth degrees. The following illustration shows a natural minor scale beginning on the pitch A.

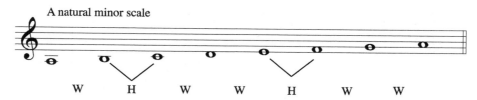

A natural minor scale

W   H   W   W   H   W   W

Notice that the pattern of whole and half steps switches to W H W W H W W for the natural minor scale.

Notice also that the natural minor scale beginning on A has no sharps or flats—that is, on the keyboard the pattern falls on all white keys.

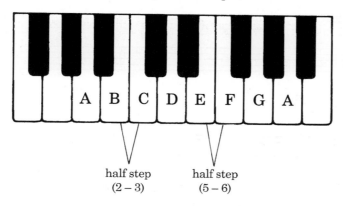

half step (2 – 3)   half step (5 – 6)

Also notice that, as in the major scale, the intervals between the tonic and the fourth and fifth scale degrees of the natural minor scale remain perfect (P4 and P5), and the interval from the tonic to the second scale degree remains major (M2). But unlike the major scale, the intervals between the tonic and the third, sixth, and seventh scale degrees in natural minor are minor intervals (m3, m6, and m7), rather than major intervals as in the major scale.

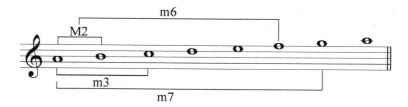

m6

M2

m3

m7

When the natural minor scale begins on any pitch other than A, one or more accidentals will be required to keep the interval pattern intact.

B natural minor scale

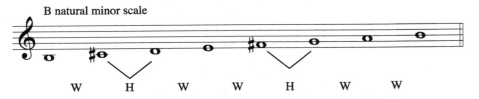

W   H   W   W   H   W   W

C natural minor scale

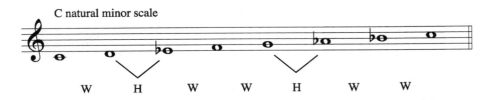

W   H   W   W   H   W   W

Class Practice

Write natural minor scales from the given pitches. Then, in the space to the right, write the key signature for each scale.

Practice for writing natural minor scales may be found in Practice materials 10-1, 10-2, and 10-3 at the end of this chapter.

Class Practice

Write the natural minor scale indicated by each of the following key signatures.

Additional practice with natural minor scales may be found in Practice materials 10-4 and 10-5.

Music in Action

Hearing Major and Minor

The American folk song "Erie Canal" is in the key of D natural minor In the space provided, rewrite this folk song in the parallel major key of D major. Then, sing or play both versions in class and discuss the differences between the two types of scales.

"Erie Canal"

Sing or play a natural minor scale. Then, sing or play a major scale. Do you notice a difference in the interval between the seventh and first degrees of the two scales? The seventh degree of the natural minor scale is not a half step below the tonic; it is a whole step away, and in this position is called a **subtonic** instead of a leading tone.

When the seventh degree of a scale is a whole step below the tonic, a somewhat ambiguous-sounding scale is created. Because of the whole step, the tonic does not seem to offer as strong a center of gravity as it does in the major scale. This weakening of the tonic's attraction is particularly striking in the harmony derived from the natural minor scale. This effect can be demonstrated by having someone in class play the following two versions of the opening measures of a "Praeludium" from *The Little Piano Book for Wilhelm Friedemann Bach* by J. S. Bach. The first version is based on the natural minor scale:

The second version is based on another form of minor scale known as the **harmonic minor scale**:

Notice how much stronger the harmony seems when chords are built from the harmonic minor version of the minor scale.

The difference between the natural minor scale and the harmonic minor is that the harmonic minor version *borrows* the leading tone of the parallel major scale (a pitch a half step below the tonic) to replace its own subtonic (a pitch a whole step below). In technical terms, the subtonic of the natural minor scale is raised a chromatic half step, thereby creating a real leading tone. Composers do this to create a stronger harmony, that is, a greater feeling of harmonic motion between chords.

A natural minor scale

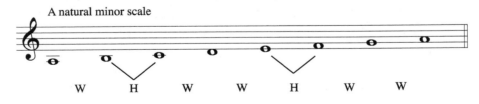

A harmonic minor scale

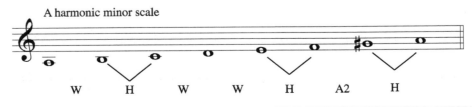

When the seventh degree is raised to create a leading tone, the resulting harmonic minor version of the scale has *three* half steps—between the second and third, fifth and sixth, and seventh and first degrees. Notice also that the interval between the sixth and seventh degrees is an augmented second (three half steps).

This interval is created by borrowing the leading tone from the parallel major. The augmented second is often difficult to sing or play in tune because although when written it looks like a second, it has the same number of half steps as a minor third and thus *sounds* wider than it *looks* on the staff.

To raise the seventh degree and still maintain the practice of having only one pitch of each letter name requires occasional double sharps. Remember: The double sharp sign raises the pitch of a note by two half steps.

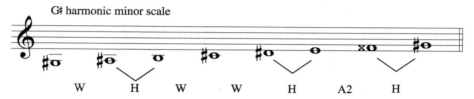

G♯ harmonic minor scale

W   H   W   W   H   A2   H

Class Practice

Write harmonic minor scales from the given pitches. To begin, write the natural minor scale and then borrow the leading tone from the parallel major to make it harmonic minor. Then, in the space to the right, write the key signature for each scale.

Practice for writing harmonic minor scales may be found in Practice materials 10-6, 10-7, and 10-8.

Class Practice

Write the harmonic minor scale indicated by each of the following key signatures.

Additional work with harmonic minor scales may be found in Practice materials 10-9, 10-10, and 10-11.

Hearing Major and Minor

Rewrite the following melody from the original key of G major to the key of G minor, using accidentals to create the harmonic minor version. Because the tonic note G does not change, this is known as a modal transformation or a change of mode, instead of a modulation. When you have finished, sing or play both versions in class and discuss the differences in sound between the major and harmonic minor versions of the same melody.

"The Wabash Cannon Ball"

Melodic Minor Scale

As mentioned earlier, the harmonic minor version of the minor scale strengthens the harmony by creating a leading tone that is a half step below the tonic. Doing this, however, causes a problem for the melody. The interval of the augmented second that is thus created between the sixth and seventh scale degrees of the harmonic minor scale can be difficult to sing or play. So the **melodic minor** version of the minor scale developed, in part, as a means of avoiding this augmented second. Notice that melodic minor is the only version of the minor scale that has one interval pattern when ascending and another when descending.

A melodic minor scale

6 7 1   1 7 6

W H W W W W H   W W H W W H W

In the ascending form of the melodic minor scale, both the sixth and seventh degrees are borrowed from the parallel major. Technically, the seventh degree, as in the harmonic minor version, is raised to create a half-step relationship between the seventh degree and the tonic, and the sixth degree is raised to avoid the augmented second. Notice, however, that these alterations create a scale in which only the third degree is different from the major scale.

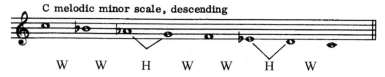

C melodic minor scale, ascending

W H W W W W H

This similarity to the major scale is so noticeable that it almost obscures the minor-sounding quality of this version of the minor scale. Since the leading tone is needed more often in ascending musical passages than in descending ones, the descending version of melodic minor lowers both the seventh and sixth degrees. This alteration, which actually produces a descending natural minor scale, balances the ascending version and helps restore a minor-sounding quality to the scale.

C melodic minor scale, descending

W W H W W H W

As in the harmonic minor, double sharp signs will occasionally be required to form the melodic minor.

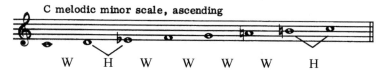

D♯ melodic minor scale

Class Practice

Write melodic minor scales from the given pitches. You may wish to begin by writing natural minor scales and then adding accidentals as necessary. When you have finished, write the key signature for each scale in the space to the right.

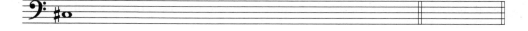

Practice for writing melodic minor scales may be found in Practice materials 10-12, 10-13, and 10-14.

Write the melodic minor scale indicated by each of the following key signatures.

Additional practice with harmonic minor scales is available in Practice materials 10-15.

Music in Action 🔊 Ear Training

Ask someone in class who plays an instrument or keyboard to prepare a well-known tune such as "The Star Spangled Banner" or "Three Blind Mice" so that he or she can play it in its original major key as well as in the three forms of the minor scale. As a class, discuss the differences between (1) the major and natural minor version and (2) the three forms of the minor versions. ●

Minor Scales in Actual Music

So far, this chapter has made it appear that there are three distinct forms of the minor scale, and that composers writing a piece of music in a minor key choose one of them to the exclusion of the other two. Although it is useful to think this way when you are first learning the three forms of the minor scale, this is not what really happens in the music. In actuality, composers view the sixth and seventh degrees of the minor scale as unstable (because these are also the scale degrees borrowed from the parallel major), and they often use all three forms of the scale within the same composition. This is why it is more accurate to say that the three forms of the minor scale are not really three different scales, but rather they represent three different solutions, or possible approaches, to various harmonic and melodic problems within a composition written in a minor key.

Consider for a moment the names *harmonic minor* and *melodic minor*. These names give us a clue as to why and how composers might use various versions of the minor scale within the same piece. Remember that the harmonic minor version creates a real leading tone a half step below the tonic, and that this, in turn, creates slightly different chords and stronger harmonies. The harmonic minor form of the minor scale, therefore, is used by composers primarily to create particular chords and harmonic progressions. The melodic minor version, on the other hand, deals with the difficult interval of the augmented second and is used mainly in melodic situations.

Although this may seem confusing at first, particularly when you look at new pieces in minor keys and try to decide which forms of the minor scale are being used at any particular point, it will become clearer with practice.

Just keep in mind that the sixth and seventh degrees of the minor scale are unstable, and you must look *inside* the music to be certain which form is being used.

The following example is a sonata in C minor by Scarlatti. As you know, the key signature always identifies the natural minor version of the scale. The appearance of both B natural and A natural within this excerpt indicates that the melodic minor form of the minor scale is the one being used at this point. Notice also that the ascending form of the melodic minor scale sometimes occurs in descending passages, as it does in measures 2, 3, and 4 of this example.

Scarlatti: Sonata in C Minor

How to Sing Minor Scales

There are conflicting opinions about the correct method of sight singing minor scales. One school argues that the syllables of the major scale from *la* to *la* should be used to show the inherent relationship between the major scale and the minor scale. The other school argues that retaining the sound of the tonic with the syllable *do* is more important. According to this view, all scales should be started on *do* and the remaining syllables altered when necessary:

C natural minor

do   re   me   fa   sol   le   te   do

As you can see in this example for natural minor, the syllable for the third scale degree is *me*, rather than *mi*, because the third degree is lowered. Also, the syllables for pitches 6 and 7 are *le* and *te*, rather than *la* and *ti*, because the sixth and seventh scale degrees are lowered. Similar alterations in syllables are necessary for the harmonic and melodic versions of the minor scale.

Music in Action ◉ **Sight Singing**

The two methods of sight singing minor scales are given below for each of the three forms of minor scales. Sing the scales both ways. Your teacher will decide which system is most advantageous for you. Then, practice that system until you can sing the minor scales easily and accurately.

C natural minor

1. la   ti   do   re   mi   fa   sol   la
2. do   re   me   fa   sol   le   te   do

C harmonic minor

1. la   ti   do   re   mi   fa   si   la
2. do   re   me   fa   sol   le   ti   do

C melodic minor

1. la   ti   do   re   mi   fi   si   la   sol   fa   me   re   do   ti   la
2. do   re   me   fa   sol   la   ti   do   te   le   sol   fa   me   re   do

---

Music in Action ◉ **Sight Singing**

Sing or play the following melodies. Locate the tonic for each melody, and identify the principal form of the minor scale on which each melody is based. Then, write the appropriate sight-singing syllables in the spaces provided, and learn to sing one or more of the melodies, using the sight-singing syllables.

"Johnny Has Gone for a Soldier"

Tonic _____   Form of minor scale _____

Tonic _____   Form of minor scale _____

Music in Action Ear Training

The excerpts below are all in minor keys. Ask someone from the class who plays piano to play them. As you listen, try to determine if each excerpt uses the natural, harmonic, or melodic version of the minor scale, or some combination of these versions. This can be difficult, and you might make mistakes at first, but keep trying—you will see improvement with practice.

Schumann: "The Wild Rider" from _Album for the Young_

Bach: "Minuet" from _The Little Piano Book for Wilhelm Friedemann Bach_

(continued)

Bach: Courante from French Suite No. 2

Schumann: "The Poor Orphan Child" from *Album for the Young*

A Final Note

The importance of scales to the process of becoming a better musician cannot be overemphasized. Scales contain the interval patterns of tonal music. All musicians, from concert pianists to jazz performers, recognize their importance and practice them regularly.

As a beginning music student, your first step is to learn the structure of the major and minor scales and the ways in which these scales influence melody and harmony. The next step is to begin regarding scales as *the* basic musical element. If you sing or play an instrument, you should devote some of your daily practice to scale work. It is only through this type of drill that you will become musically familiar with the tonal patterns of the music you wish to play. Practicing scales gives you this familiarity in a way that practicing pieces of music—no matter how difficult—does not.

Music in Action

Hearing Scales

As a musician, you should begin to notice the numerous ways in which scale passages appear in tonal music. In addition, you should develop the ability to identify various kinds of scales by their sound. To begin this process, your teacher will play ten scales. By sound, identify each scale as major, natural minor, harmonic minor, or melodic minor. With your teacher's or another student's help, repeat the process with different groups of scales until you are consistently successful in identifying them. ●

Music in Action

Listening

Many rock and popular songs are written in minor keys. Here are the names of several. As a class, listen to one or more of them. Is it obvious which of the forms of the minor scale is being used, or is it more ambiguous?

Santana: "Black Magic Woman"

The Eagles: "Hotel California"

The Animals: "House of the Rising Sun"

Dire Straits: "Sultans of Swing" ●

Music in Action 💿 Sight Singing

Below are several melodies in minor keys from Appendix D. First, determine the form of the minor scale that each is in. Then, practice singing these melodies, both on *la* and with movable *do*. Once you are familiar with the melodies, practice conducting them as you sing. It would also be helpful to practice playing them at the keyboard.

1.

2.

3.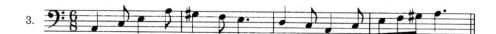

●

Practice 10-1

From each starting pitch, write ascending and descending natural minor scales in both treble clef and bass clef. The scales in this exercise are grouped in perfect fifths so that each successive scale requires one additional sharp. The new sharp is always the supertonic of that scale.

Remember that, like the major scale, the minor scale is composed of an alphabetical sequence of pitches, and thus no chromatic half steps are used. When you have written the scales, check that the half steps fall only between the second and third and the fifth and sixth degrees. Indicate the half steps in each scale. A keyboard is provided to help you visualize the intervals.

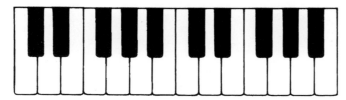

EXAMPLE:

E natural minor

B natural minor

1.

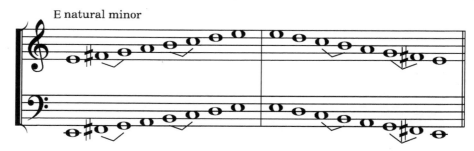

C♯ natural minor

2.

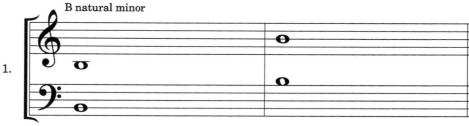

D♯ natural minor

3.

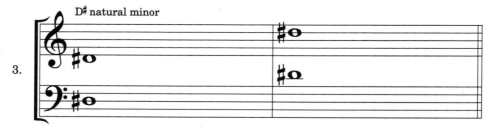

Practice 10-2

Write ascending and descending natural minor scales from each starting pitch. (The scales in this exercise are grouped so that each succeeding scale requires one additional flat—the submediant of that scale.) When you have written the scales, check that the half steps fall only between the second and third and the fifth and sixth degrees. Indicate the half steps in each scale. A keyboard is provided to help you visualize the intervals.

EXAMPLE:

D natural minor

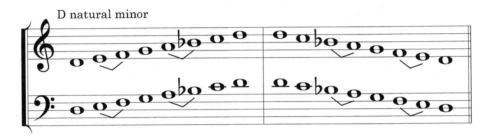

C natural minor

1.
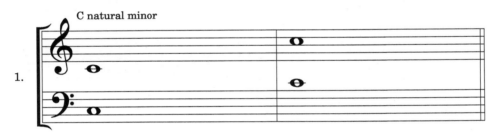

B♭ natural minor

2.
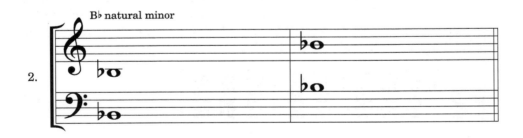

E♭ natural minor

3.
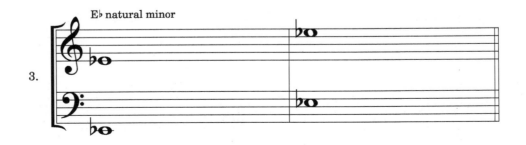

Practice 10-3

Write ascending natural minor scales beginning with the given tonic pitches. Then, in the space provided, write the key signature for each scale. This exercise and the one following use the same scales you wrote in the previous two exercises, but now they are out of sequence. A keyboard is provided to help you visualize the intervals.

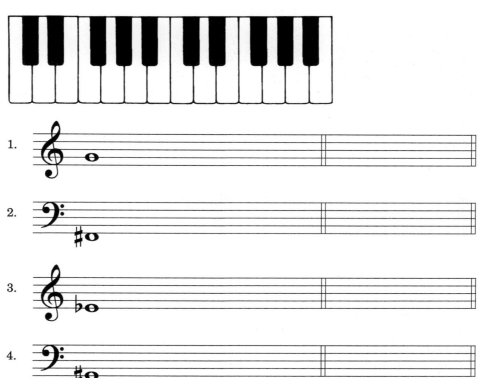

Practice 10-4

Write natural minor scales in descending form, beginning with the given tonic pitches. Indicate the half steps in each scale. Remember that the pitches of a descending scale are in reverse order, that is, 8–7–6–5–4–3–2–1. A keyboard is provided to help you visualize the intervals.

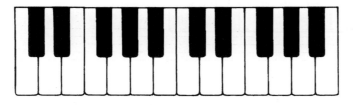

(continued)

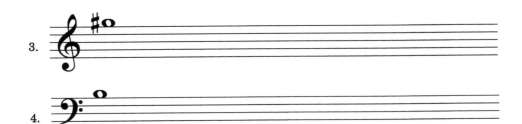

3.

4.

Practice 10-5

Spell the indicated natural minor scales using letter names and any necessary accidentals.

EXAMPLE: $\underline{\text{G}}$ $\underline{\text{A}}$ $\underline{\text{B}^\flat}$ $\underline{\text{C}}$ $\underline{\text{D}}$ $\underline{\text{E}^\flat}$ $\underline{\text{F}}$ $\underline{\text{G}}$

1. $\underline{\text{D}}$ __ __ __ __ __ __ __

2. $\underline{\text{E}}$ __ __ __ __ __ __ __

3. $\underline{\text{B}^\flat}$ __ __ __ __ __ __ __

4. $\underline{\text{G}^\sharp}$ __ __ __ __ __ __ __

Practice 10-6

Write the following harmonic minor scales, in ascending and descending forms, in both treble clef and bass clef. A simple way to begin is to write a natural minor scale and then borrow the leading tone from the parallel major. This, of course, is the same as raising the seventh degree of the natural minor scale by a half step. (Try to learn to think both ways; don't rely on either method exclusively.) To check your work, make sure that each scale has three half steps, and then mark them. This exercise deals with sharp scales only. If you have any difficulty, use the keyboard to visualize the scale.

EXAMPLE:

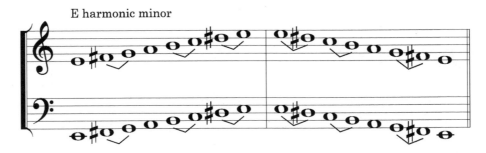

E harmonic minor

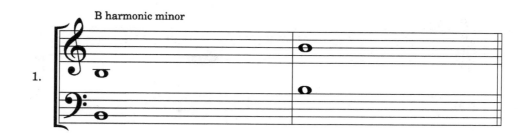

B harmonic minor

1.

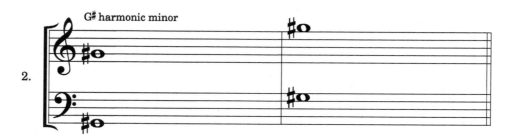

G# harmonic minor

2.

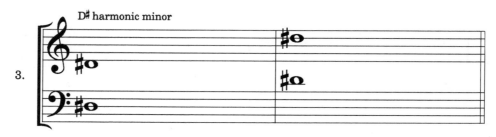

D# harmonic minor

3.

Practice 10-7

Write the following minor scale in the harmonic minor form, in both ascending and descending patterns, using both treble clef and bass clef. Even though this exercise deals with flat scales only, you will occasionally need to use a sharp sign to raise the seventh scale degree to the proper pitch. When you finish, check that each scale has three half steps, and mark them. Use the keyboard to help you visualize the scale.

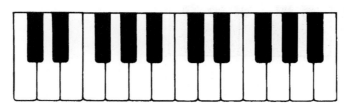

EXAMPLE:

D harmonic minor

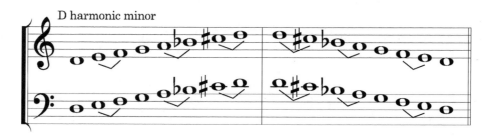

(continued)

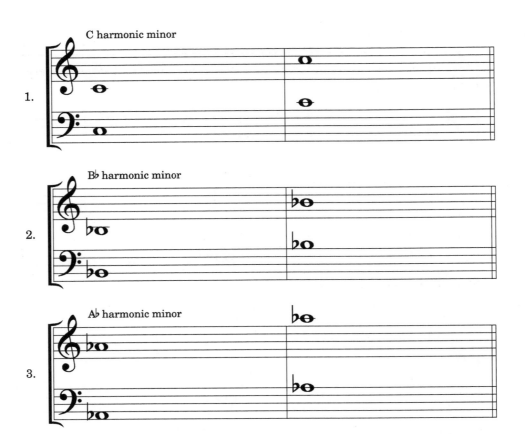

Practice 10-8

Write the following harmonic minor scales in ascending form. This exercise and the one following use the same scales as in the previous two exercises, but now out of sequence. Use the keyboard to help visualize the scale. Then, in the space provided, write the key signature for each scale.

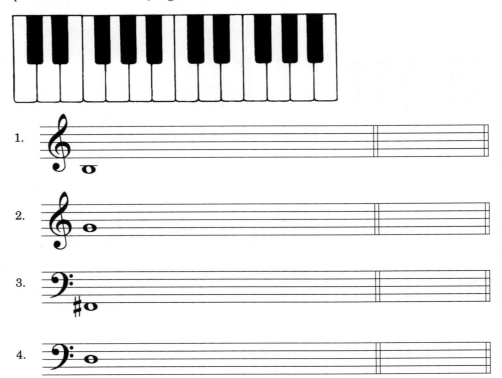

Practice 10-9

Spell the indicated harmonic minor scales using letter names and any necessary accidentals.

1. B __ __ __ __ __ __ __
2. E __ __ __ __ __ __ __
3. C♯ __ __ __ __ __ __ __
4. D♯ __ __ __ __ __ __ __

Practice 10-10

Identify by letter name the following scale degrees:

1. supertonic of C harmonic minor _____
2. leading tone of G harmonic minor _____
3. subdominant of B harmonic minor _____

Practice 10-11

Complete the following:

1. G is the dominant of the _____ harmonic minor scale.
2. G♯ is the leading tone of the _____ harmonic minor scale.
3. A is the leading tone of the _____ harmonic minor scale.

Practice 10-12

Write melodic minor scales, ascending and descending, in both treble clef and bass clef, beginning with the given tonic pitches. (This exercise deals with sharp scales only.) Mark the half steps in each scale. Use the keyboard to visualize the scale.

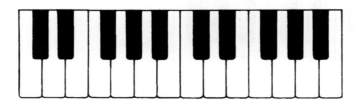

EXAMPLE:

E melodic minor

(continued)

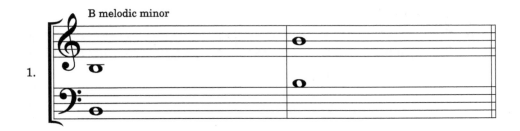

B melodic minor

1.

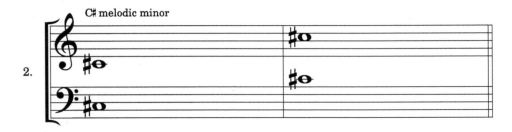

C# melodic minor

2.

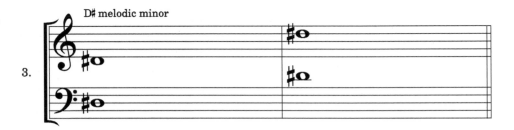

D# melodic minor

3.

Practice 10-13

Write melodic minor scales, ascending and descending, in both treble clef and bass clef, beginning with the given tonic pitches. Even though this exercise deals only with flat scales, you will need to use sharps occasionally to alter the seventh scale degree. Be sure to mark the half steps in each scale. Use the keyboard to visualize the scale.

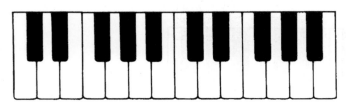

EXAMPLE:

D melodic minor

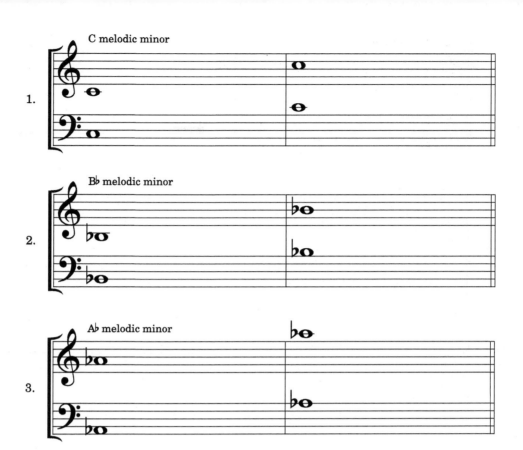

Practice 10-14

Write melodic minor scales, ascending version only, beginning with the given tonic pitches. Then, in the space provided, write the key signature for each scale. These are the same scales as in the two previous exercises, but now out of sequence. Use the keyboard to visualize each scale.

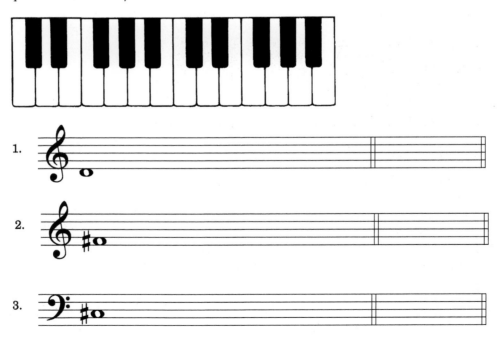

(continued)

4.

Practice 10-15

Spell the indicated melodic minor scales using letter names and any necessary accidentals.

1. E ___ ___ ___ ___ ___ ___ ___ ; ___ ___ ___ ___ ___ ___ ___

2. C♯ ___ ___ ___ ___ ___ ___ ___ ; ___ ___ ___ ___ ___ ___ ___

3. A ___ ___ ___ ___ ___ ___ ___ ; ___ ___ ___ ___ ___ ___ ___

4. C ___ ___ ___ ___ ___ ___ ___ ; ___ ___ ___ ___ ___ ___ ___

Pentatonic and Blues Scales

𝄞 **Visit Music Fundamentals in Action, at CourseMate, to:**
- Take a Pretest on minor scales
- View a Hands On Music video demo of minor scales
- Find many more practice exercises to help you succeed in this course
- See Tips&Tools for each chapter

Introduction

So far, we have learned the chromatic scale, the major scale, and the three forms of the minor scale. These important scales are used in most of the music we hear around us every day. But before we go further with tonal music, it is important to know that major and minor scales make up only a small portion of the hundreds of scales in use around the world from antiquity until now.

In this chapter, we are going to look at two other important scales in worldwide use today: the *pentatonic scale* and the *blues scale*. These scales are so widely used that you probably hear music based on one or both of them almost everyday.

These two scales are the most important for us because the pentatonic scale is the basis for most of the world's folk music and some of its classical music, while the blues scale is the basis, not only for the blues itself, but also for current American popular music, in particular, certain styles of rock and jazz. Although the ability to write, sing, and play these scales is not as essential as your abilities with major and minor scales, some degree of understanding is important. Additionally, Appendix G includes a discussion of the Medieval modes as well as the twentieth-century wholetone and *octatonic scales*. Your teacher may or may not have time to discuss these additional scales in class, but their continued use today makes it a good idea, at least, to read about them on your own.

The Pentatonic Scale

The **pentatonic scale** is a scale with five tones per octave (Greek *penta* means *five*). It may have been one of the first scales ever used, which might explain why it is the basis for much folk music throughout the world.

Major Pentatonic

There are a variety of pentatonic scales in use today, but the best-known version, the *major pentatonic*, contains no half steps. It also has two intervals greater than a whole step:

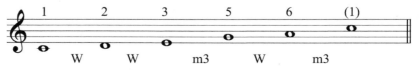

Without any half steps, the center of gravity (the tonic) of this pentatonic scale is extremely ambiguous. It may be helpful to think of it as a simpler version of the major scale with the half steps removed (scale degrees 4 and 7). This lack of a musical center of gravity is so pronounced that any one of the five pitches of the pentatonic scale can serve as the tonic. You can demonstrate this peculiarity by playing the pentatonic scale pictured here, beginning on each of its five different pitches.

"Auld Lang Syne" is one of many well-known pentatonic folk melodies. Even if you know this tune, you may never have thought of it as a pentatonic melody. But if you count the pitches, you will see that there are only five different ones and that they correspond to the pentatonic scale given above.

"Auld Lang Syne"

Folk music is not the only type of music that uses pentatonic scales, however. Here is a melody from Rossini's *William Tell*, Overture. Even though the center of gravity (the tonic) is G rather than C, as in "Auld Lang Syne," the structure of the scale is the same.

Rossini: *William Tell*, Overture

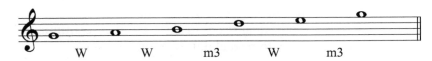

Pentatonic scale on G

The following version of the major pentatonic scale is also in common use. Notice that, in this version, the half steps have been eliminated by removing scale degrees 3 and 7 from a major scale. Notice also that this scale is a transposed version of the first pentatonic scale that we looked at. That is, if we begin the first scale on its fourth note (G), we would have a scale with the same interval pattern as this new version.

Pentatonic scale on C

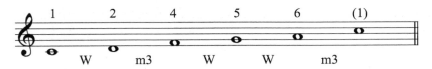

"I Gave My Love a Cherry" is a folk melody that uses this version of the major pentatonic scale.

"I Gave My Love a Cherry"

The following examples are drawn from Western music. Several of them could also be harmonized tonally, that is, with harmonies based on the major scale. This duality produces a most interesting musical combination: The character and ambiguity of the pentatonic scale are preserved in the pentatonic melody, while the harmony and musical center of gravity are tonal.

"Ol' Texas"

Debussy: "Nuages" from *Nocturnes*

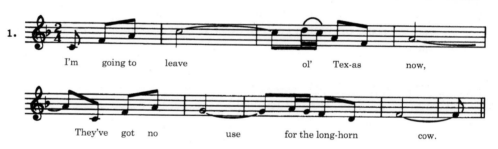

"Lonesome Valley"

(continued)

walk   it by Him - self,   O   no-bod-y else could walk it

for Him,   He had to   walk   it by Him - self.

"This Train"

4.

This train   is   bound for glo - ry,   this   train,

This train   is   bound for glo - ry, this train.

Practice for writing major pentatonic scales is available in Practice materials 11-1 at the end of this chapter.

Practice for writing major pentatonic scales is available in Practice materials 11-1 at the end of this chapter.

Music in Action

Locating the Tonic

Sing or play the pentatonic melodies of the preceding four examples. In each, locate and circle the tone that functions as the tonic. Beginning on the tonic, write the pentatonic scale on which each melody is based. Compare the forms of the scales you have written.

1.

2.

3.

4.

Music in Action ◀)) Ear Training

The major pentatonic scale can appear in places you would least expect, such as in the intros and solos of the following songs. As a class, listen to one or more of them and discuss how and why the pentatonic scale "works" within this context.

Jack Johnson: "Better Together" (guitar intro)

Joan Jett: "I Love Rock 'N' Roll" (guitar solo)

Pearl Jam: "Yellow Ledbetter" (guitar solo)
Rod Stewart: "Maggie May" (guitar solo)
The Rolling Stones: "Honky Tonk Woman" (guitar intro) ●

Music in Action ● Song Building

Write a short vocal melody based on a major pentatonic scale and learn to sing it. The length of your piece should be equivalent to a short poem or two to four sentences of prose. If you wish, also write a second part to accompany it. When you have finished (and practiced), perform your piece for the class. Then, experiment with performing two pieces by different members of the class simultaneously. This is possible because there are only five notes in the pentatonic scale so the more dissonant intervals found in a major or minor scale don't occur between voices written in pentatonic scales. Instead, interesting combinations will often occur. ●

Minor Pentatonic

Here is another version of the pentatonic scale, this one beginning on the fifth note of our original scale.

Pentatonic scale on A

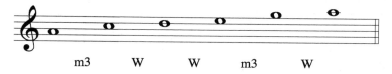

Notice that even though a melody written with this version has more of a minor sound to it, the scale is still a five-note scale with no half steps. It *sounds* minor because of the interval of a minor third between the first two notes of the scale.

"Wayfaring Stranger"

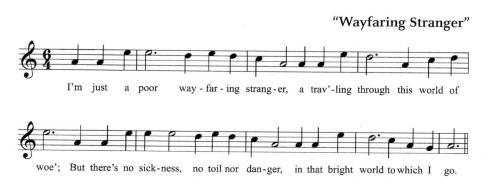

But not all minor pentatonic scales lack half steps. The following example contains two half steps:

Minor Pentatonic scale on A

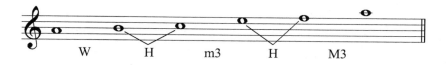

The Japanese folk melody "Sakura, Sakura" makes use of this minor version of the pentatonic scale.

"Sakura, Sakura"

Notice in this example that the piece ends on an E even though the center of gravity is clearly an A. This is possible because the minor pentatonic scale, like the major pentatonic scale, is more ambiguous than a major or a minor scale.

Practice for writing minor pentatonic scales may be found in Practice materials 11-2.

Music in Action 🎵 **Song Building**

Write a short vocal melody based on a minor pentatonic scale and learn to sing it. Then, as before, experiment with performing two pieces by different members of the class simultaneously. Does the minor pentatonic scale lend itself to this activity as readily as the major pentatonic scale did? In class, discuss the results of this experiment. ●

The Blues Scale

Originally, the blues was a type of black folk music created in America by African slaves and their descendents, sung unaccompanied or with a banjo or guitar. It is one of many ways in which African and European musical elements merged into new forms of music in America in the Eighteenth and Nineteenth centuries. Ragtime and New Orleans jazz represent two of the most prominent of these mergers.

One of the chief characteristics of the blues is the **blues scale**. This scale developed as black musicians tried to merge pentatonic African scales with European harmony based on major and minor scales. This merger was more difficult to accomplish than you might think, because the pentatonic scales of Africa have microtonal qualities that don't exactly match the pitches found on a piano. In fact, even today, jazz pianists sometimes speak of looking for the notes "between the cracks" of the piano, and when playing will often strike two pitches a minor second apart simultaneously because the sound they really want is somewhere in between.

The blues scale that resulted from this merger of African and European elements is a six-note scale:

Blues scale

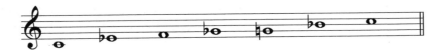

When compared to a major scale, it is missing the second and sixth scale degrees entirely, lowers the third and seventh degrees, and adds a flatted fifth scale degree to the existing fifth scale degree a perfect fifth above the tonic. These three notes, the lowered third, fifth, and seventh, are known as **blue notes**. Because they are chromatic to the major scale harmonies they are often played over, blue notes add a high degree of tension to the music.

Here is a melody based on the blues scale. Notice how frequently the lowered (or flatted) third, fifth, and seventh scale degrees occur.

Here is a traditional blues melody. Notice the lowered (or flatted) third (B♭) and seventh (F♮) scale degrees.

Traditional: "Behind Closed Doors"

Now, I don't want my ba - by ___ stand-in' be-hind a closed

door. ___ No, I don't want my ba - by ___

stand-in' be - hind a closed door. ___ Now

when the door is closed, no one but the Lord a-bove to know. ___

Music in Action Song Building

Write a melody for your instrument or voice based on the blues scale. Your piece should be 12 bars long and in either simple or compound quadruple meter. When you have finished (and practiced), perform your piece for the class. ●

As you can probably tell from listening to the previous example, the three blue notes are the most important notes of the blues scale. Not only do they define the character of the scale, but they also create the tension and drive associated with the blues.

Today, the six-note blues scale is often combined with the major scale, creating a ten-note scale:

Blues scale and major scale combined

In this version, the blue notes create even more tension because they often occur a half step away from the notes used for the harmony. In addition, jazz pianists, when playing the accompanying harmony, will often play the flatted third simultaneously with the regular third and the flatted seventh with the regular seventh, creating tension in the search for the untempered notes of the African pentatonic scale that "fall between the cracks."

Now look at another traditional blues tune. Notice that, although "Blues and Booze" has only two blue notes, it still feels similar in style to the previous example. This is because both examples use the same blues harmonic progression. (We will learn this blues progression in Chapter 14.)

Traditional: "Blues and Booze"

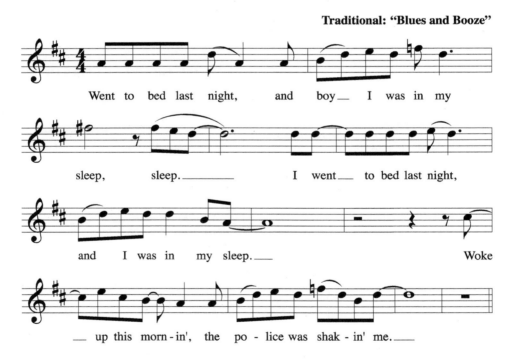

Music in Action   As a class, sing "Behind Closed Doors" and "Blues and Booze" several times. Discuss the use, or lack of use, of blue notes, and what this adds to the sound of the music. ●

Practice for writing the blues scale may be found in Practice materials 11-3.

A Final Note

Major and minor scales have been the most important scales of Western art music since the mid-1600s. They are still the most important today, although atonal, microtonal, and electronic music offer striking alternatives. But you would be wrong if you took this to mean that major and minor scales are the only ones that matter. As this chapter has shown, other types of scales can be found in the folk, popular, and classical music that you know. Keep in mind, too, that much of the world's music has *never* used major and minor scales.

The scales mentioned in this chapter represent only a small number of the many scales in use throughout the world today. For all musicians, and for anyone else interested in learning how music "works," some familiarity with these scales and the music they produce is essential. This chapter is only a beginning. Now that you know they exist, start listening for these scales in the music you hear every day. Before long, you'll find yourself recognizing them in the most unusual places.

Practice 11-1

Beginning on the indicated pitches, and using the following form as a model, write examples of the major pentatonic scale. Check your solutions by singing or playing the scales you have written.

Practice 11-2

Using the following form as a model, begin on each indicated pitch and write examples of the minor pentatonic scale. Check your answers by singing or playing the scales you have written.

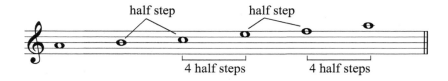

(continued)

1.

2.

3.

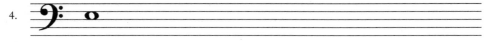

4.

5.

6.

7.

Practice 11-3

Write examples of the six-note blues scale from each given pitch. Use the following scale as a model. When you have finished, check your answers by singing or playing the scales you have written.

1.

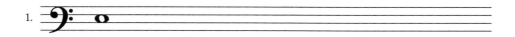

2.

Focus on Skills 6: **Scales 2**

 Visit Music Fundamentals in Action, at CourseMate, for interactive Focus on Fundamentals exercises.

These questions cover the material presented in Chapters 9, 10, and 11. (If your class did not cover Chapter 11, omit questions 7, 8, and 9.) If you have difficulty with any of these questions, review the relevant sections before beginning Chapter 12.

1. Write descending natural minor scales beginning with the pitches indicated.

   a.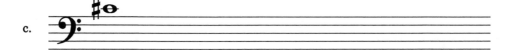

   b.

   c.

2. Write ascending harmonic minor scales beginning with the given pitches.

   a.

   b.

   c.

3. Write ascending and descending melodic minor scales beginning with the pitches indicated.

a.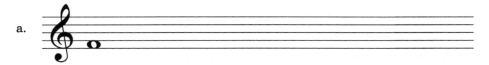

b.

c.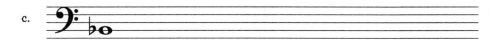

4. Complete the following sentences.

a. The mediant of A natural minor is _____.

b. The dominant of E harmonic minor is _____.

c. The supertonic of D natural minor is _____.

d. The leading tone of F harmonic minor is _____.

e. The subdominant of C♯ harmonic minor is _____.

f. G is the subdominant of the _____ harmonic minor scale.

g. B♭ is the submediant of the _____ harmonic minor scale.

h. A is the leading tone of the _____ harmonic minor scale.

5. Write out the following minor key signatures.

C minor

D minor

A minor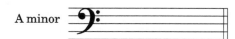

F♯ minor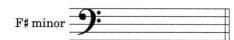

C♯ minor

6. Complete the following sentences.

    a. The relative minor of B major is _____.

    b. The relative minor of F major is _____.

    c. The parallel major of D minor is _____.

    d. The relative major of G minor is _____.

    e. The relative major of C♯ minor is _____.

7. Write a major pentatonic scale and a minor pentatonic scale beginning on the same pitch.

8. Write the blues scale beginning on each given pitch.

    a.
    b.

9. Write a major scale with added blue notes starting from the given pitch.

Triads

 Visit Music Fundamentals in Action, at CourseMate, to:

- Take a Pretest on triads and progressions
- Hear the author's Let's Talk About Music podcast on triads
- Find many more practice exercises to help you succeed in this course
- See Tips&Tools for each chapter

Introduction

In Western music, the major or minor scale on which a piece is based determines all the interval patterns of that music. This is true for both the horizontal intervals found in melody and the vertical intervals found in harmony. The fundamental component of harmony is the chord. A **chord** is the simultaneous sounding of three or more pitches. (Two pitches sounding simultaneously create an interval.) Harmony is the horizontal movement in time of a series of chords. In this chapter, we will concentrate on the most frequently used chord of tonal music—the three-note **triad**.

 **Music in Action** 🔊 **Ear Training**

The following simple musical example clearly demonstrates the distinction between the horizontal character of melody and the vertical character of harmony. Play it, or listen to it played, several times. Can you, in three or four sentences, describe the ways in which the vertical (harmonic) and horizontal (melodic) components each contribute to the piece as a whole?

"Lavender's Blue"

(continued)

Basic Structure of Triads

The triad is the basic chord of tonal music. Other chords—such as sevenths, ninths, and elevenths—are extensions of the triad. Four qualities of triads are possible: major, minor, augmented, and diminished. The quality of a triad is determined by the kinds of thirds it contains.

Triads are three-note chords built of two superimposed thirds. These two thirds, when stacked on top of each other, create the interval of a fifth between their two outside pitches. You will find that this interval of a fifth is as important to the harmony as it is to the melody. When the triad is written in *root position*—that is, as two superimposed thirds—we identify the three notes of the triad, from the lowest to the highest, as *the root, the third*, and *the fifth*. In the following example, notice that the third of the triad is an interval of a third above the root, and the fifth of the triad is an interval of a fifth above the root.

F Major triad, root position

If the triad appears in an altered form, the terms still apply to the pitches as if they were in root position, even though the intervals are no longer a third and a fifth:

F Major triad, altered forms

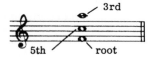 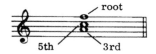

Triads take their name from the name of the root, that is, the lowest-sounding pitch when the triad is constructed as superimposed thirds. Notice that both examples above are F major triads, even though the second example does not have the F as the lowest-sounding pitch.

Most beginning musicians can spell scales more easily than triads. This is because scales are based on the interval of a second while triads are based on the interval of a third. Until you get used to it, it's harder to think in thirds. The following Class Practice exercise will help you begin to think in thirds. It deals only with the interval size of a third and not with the major, minor, augmented, or diminished qualities of triads.

Class Practice

As a class, practice reciting the following three-letter patterns until you can say them evenly.

ACE   CEG   EGB   GBD   BDF   DFA   FAC   ACE

After you can say them evenly, work for speed. These patterns of three will help you think of triads from the root up.

Major and Minor Triads

The *major triad* (in root position) is built from two superimposed thirds. The lower third is a major third; the upper one is a minor third. The interval between the two outside notes—in this case, F and C—is a perfect fifth.

F Major triad

The *minor triad* is also built of superimposed thirds, but the order is reversed: The lower third is minor and the upper third is major. The outside interval remains a perfect fifth.

F Minor triad

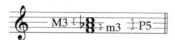

In both major and minor triads, the interval between the root and the fifth of the triad is always a perfect fifth. Some students find it easier to remember major triads as a major third plus a perfect fifth above the root, and minor triads as a minor third plus a perfect fifth.

F Major triad   F Minor triad

Class Practice

Practice writing major and minor triads in root position from the same given tonic note. Remember that major triads have a major third on the bottom while minor triads have a minor third as the lower third. Remember also that the interval between the root and the fifth must always be a perfect fifth.

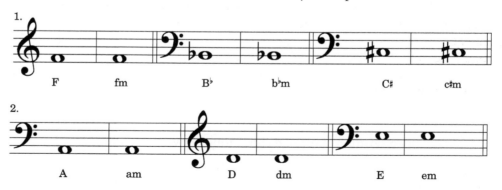

(continued)

3.

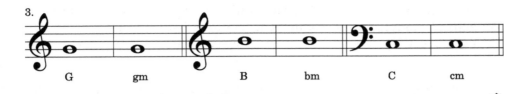

           G   gm   B   bm   C   cm

Music in Action

Playing and Hearing Major and Minor Triads

Practice playing the following triads on the piano. Play them with each hand separately, and then both hands together using the thumbs and third and fifth fingers. As you play, listen to the difference in sound between the major and minor triads. Then ask someone else to play the triads for you and see if you can identify their quality by ear.

1.

2.

3.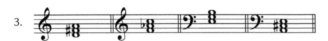

4.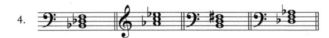

5.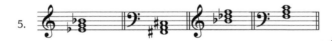

Close and Open Positions

When triads appear as two superimposed thirds, they are said to be in *close position*. That is, the three notes of the triad are all contained within an octave.

Close position

    When the notes of the triad are spaced farther apart than in close position, and the three notes are no longer contained within the octave, the triad is said to be in *open position*.

Open position

Notice how open position skips one chord tone between each note.

D Minor triad

Composers frequently employ open position to provide a change of musical color and for reasons of voice leading. The following Class Practice exercise will help you to recognize root-position triads in open position.

The following are root-position triads in open position. The lowest note is the root of the triad. In each case, label the triad as major (M) or minor (m) in quality and, in the space provided, rewrite it in close position.

EXAMPLE:

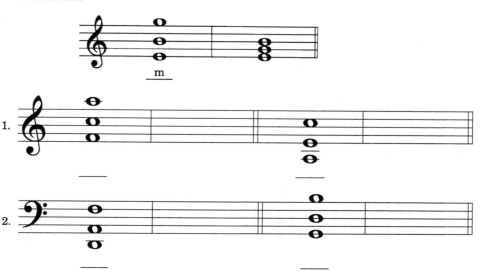

1.

2.

Practice for writing major and minor triads may be found in Practice materials 12-1, 12-2, 12-3, and 12-4 at the end of this chapter.

Augmented and Diminished Triads

The *augmented triad* consists of two superimposed major thirds. Notice that the resultant interval between the root and the fifth of the triad is an augmented fifth.

The *diminished triad* consists of two superimposed minor thirds, an arrangement that creates the interval of a diminished fifth between the root and the fifth of the triad.

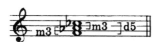

Although augmented and diminished triads are found less often in tonal music than are major and minor triads, they can contribute a unique color and tension. Overused, however, they can weaken the tonal center of a piece.

Practice writing augmented and diminished triads in root position from the same given tonic note. Remember that augmented triads consist of two major thirds with the interval of an augmented fifth between the root and the fifth, and diminished triads consist of two minor triads with the interval of a diminished fifth between the root and the fifth.

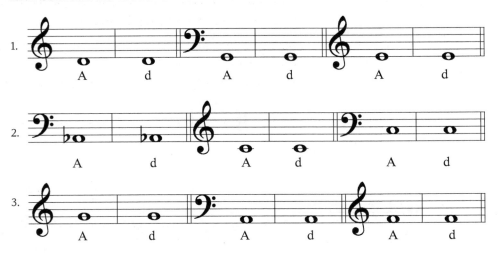

Practice for working with augmented and diminished triads may be found in Practice materials 12-5, 12-6, 12-7, 12-8, and 12-9.

Music in Action

Playing and Hearing Augmented and Diminished Triads

Practice playing the following augmented and diminished triads on the piano. Play them with each hand separately and then both hands together. Pay particular attention to the sound of each kind of triad. Then ask someone to play the triads and see if you can identify their quality by ear.

Music in Action   Listening

This piece is a traditional hymn tune called "Old Hundredth." Later in this chapter we will return to analyze the chords of this hymn, but for now, let's listen to it played several times. As you listen, try to identify the quality of each chord by its sound (major, minor, augmented, or diminished). A space is provided below each chord to record your answers. Some chords may be more difficult to identify because they are *inverted* (the lowest sounding note is not the root—see p. 251). Hearing chord qualities may seem difficult at first, but your ability will improve with subsequent hearings. Then, as a class, discuss the harmonic character of this piece using the following questions as a guide:

1. What is the percentage of major and minor traids to augmented and diminised ones, and what reasons can you give for this?

2. Does the hymn sound predominantly vertical (harmonic) or horizontal (melodic)?

3. Is the melody more important, equally important, or less important, than the harmony?

Hymn tune: "Old Hundredth"

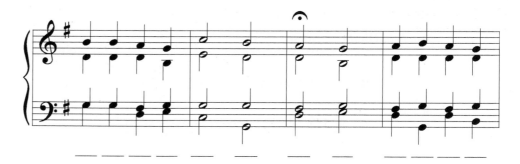

Triads and Scales

Triads can be built on any note of the major and minor scales. Musicians often identify triads built on scale degrees by the same terms as the pitches of the scale:

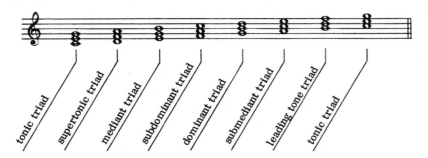

When triads are constructed on scale degrees, they must conform to the pitches of the scale. That is, if a scale has a B♭, all triads with a B will use a B♭.

Triads in F Major

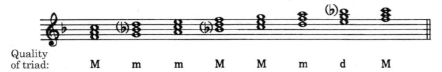

Quality of triad:	M	m	m	M	M	m	d	M

Notice that the major scale produces three major triads, three minor triads, and one diminished triad.

The triads associated with the minor scale, because of its several versions, are a bit more confusing. The natural minor scale produces the following triads:

Triads in D natural minor

Quality of triad:	m	d	M	m	m	M	M	m

But because the scale itself contains a subtonic, a whole step away, rather than a true leading tone only a half step below the tonic, the harmony it produces also lacks a leading tone. That, in turn, means that the dominant chord is minor rather than major in quality (because it contains a C natural rather than a raised C sharp). But by borrowing the leading tone from the parallel major, as the harmonic minor version of the scale does, we can raise the C to C sharp in the dominant (V) and leading-tone (vii°) chords, thus creating a stronger harmony. Notice that although true harmonic minor indicates that the mediant chord should also contain a C sharp, this would change the chord from a major triad to an augmented one, and composers do not always do that in actual music.

Triads in D harmonic minor

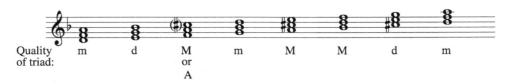

Quality of triad:	m	d	M or A	m	M	M	d	m

Although other alterations borrowed from major are possible, they are a little beyond the scope of this book. Here, we will limit ourselves to the leading-tone alterations discussed thus far.

Inversions of Triads

Triads do not always appear in root position. Quite often the third or the fifth of the triad is the lowest-sounding pitch. Nevertheless, the triad itself does not change; the root remains the root, and the quality remains the same.

Triads can appear in two positions other than root position: first inversion and second inversion. Triads in first and second inversions add variety to the harmony of a piece, and they also serve for voice leading.

In first inversion, the triad has the *third* of the root-position triad as the lowest-sounding pitch.

D Minor triad

Remember that a triad in root position appears on the staff as two superimposed thirds. In first inversion, the triad consists of the same three pitches, but now there is the interval of a fourth between the *upper* two pitches. Looked at another way, first inversion triads have a third on the bottom with a fourth stacked above it.

The triad in second inversion has the *fifth* as the lowest-sounding pitch.

D Minor triad, *second inversion*

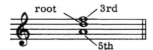

In second inversion, the triad has the interval of a fourth between the *lower* two pitches, that is, it has a fourth on the bottom with a third stacked on top.

In working with inversions, it is important to keep in mind that the triad does not change simply because its notes change position. This is because we hear the identifying interval of the triad in root position (the perfect fifth) differently from the way we hear the identifying interval of the triad in first or second inversion (the perfect fourth). The perfect fifth directs our ear to hear the lower pitch as the root, while the perfect fourth directs our ear to the upper pitch. Therefore, the pitch we hear as the root of the triad doesn't change with inversion.

In the study of harmony, it is essential that you be able to identify triads correctly in an inversion. This means that you must first recognize the *kind* of inversion (first or second); otherwise you will identify the wrong pitch as the root.

Labeling Inversions

To indicate whether a triad is in root position or in an inversion, a set of short-hand symbols has been developed. This shorthand system refers to the size of the intervals *above* the lowest-sounding pitch. Thus, a triad in *root position*, with intervals of a third and a fifth above the lowest-sounding pitch, could be shown as follows:

A triad in *first inversion*, with intervals of a third and a sixth above the lowest-sounding pitch, can be indicated by the following notation:

A triad in *second inversion*, containing intervals of a fourth and a sixth above the lowest-sounding note, can be shown as:

Notice that this shorthand system does *not* indicate the quality of the triad. Whether the triad is major, minor, augmented, or diminished is determined by how that triad functions in a particular key.

In practice, the shorthand system for labeling triad inversions has been abbreviated even further. For a triad in root position (the most common chord in tonal music), the numerals are omitted and the intervals of a fifth and a third are simply understood to be present.

Root position

For a first-inversion triad, whose characteristic interval is a sixth above the lowest-sounding note, a six is indicated while the third, being understood as present, is not marked.

First inversion

For a second-inversion triad, both numerals six and four are used to distinguish it from first inversion.

Second inversion

We'll look at labeling triads, with and without inversions, in more detail in the next chapter. But it won't hurt to begin our practice of labeling them now.

You'll find additional practice working with triads in inversion in Practice materials 12–10 and 12–11.

Music in Action

Naming Triads

Return to the hymn "Old Hundredth" (p. 250) and identify each triad by letter name. Then circle the inverted triads and identify the inversion and root of each of them. You will see that all of the triads in this hymn have one of their three pitches doubled; that is, the same letter name appears twice. This does not in any way change the nature of the basic triad. In fact, more often than not, the doubled pitch is the root of the chord.

Now listen to the hymn again, paying particular attention to the inverted triads. Remember that triads in inversion supply harmonic color as well as facilitate better voice leading. ●

A Final Note

Triads are among the primary building blocks of tonal music. If you intend to be a composer or a performer, you will need to *know* and *master* them. This mastery includes not only learning to write triads, as we have done in this chapter, but also learning to recognize them in musical situations, which we will do in the next chapter.

In studying triads, two things are important to keep in mind. First, there are only four types of triads—major, minor, augmented, and diminished. And while all triads in root position consist of two superimposed thirds, it is the *quality* of these thirds that determines the quality of the triad.

Second, it is important to remember that while root-position triads are the norm, triads may also be inverted, that is, the third or the fifth of the triad may appear as the lowest-sounding note. Because an inversion significantly changes the sound of a triad, we must also be able to write and recognize inversions.

Finally, keep in mind that if you are planning to be a professional or a good amateur musician, you will be dealing with triads for the remainder of your musical life. Before leaving this chapter, make sure that you have a solid, fundamental grounding in constructing and recognizing triads and their inversions.

Practice

Practice 12-1

Identify the root of each of the following triads, and label each as major (M) or minor (m) in quality. (Make sure that your instructor can distinguish between your uppercase and lowercase M.)

EXAMPLE:

root	G	C	A
quality	M	M	m

1.

___ ___ ___ ___

___ ___ ___ ___

2.

___ ___ ___ ___

___ ___ ___ ___

Practice 12-2

Complete the indicated major or minor triad in close position, beginning on the root given. Remember: The interval between the root and the fifth of the triad should be a perfect fifth; the interval between the root and the third of the triad will be a major third for major triads and a minor third for minor triads.

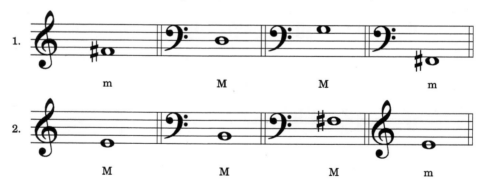

Practice 12-3

Complete the indicated close-position major or minor triads. In each case, the note given is the *third* of the triad.

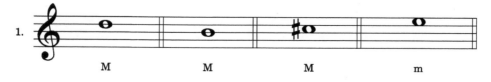

(continued)

2.

M   M   m   M

Practice 12-4

Complete the indicated close-position major or minor triads. In each case, the note given is the *fifth* of the triad.

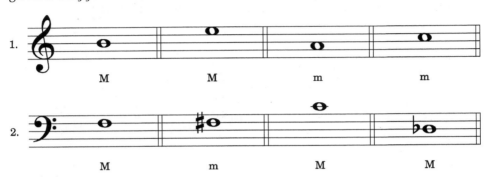

1.

M   M   m   m

2.

M   m   M   M

Practice 12-5

Identify the root of each of the following triads, and label the triads as augmented (A) or diminished (d) in quality.

EXAMPLE:

root   B   F

quality   d   A

1.

___   ___   ___   ___

___   ___   ___   ___

2.

___   ___   ___   ___

___   ___   ___   ___

Practice 12-6

The following are root-position triads in open position. In the space provided, label each as augmented (A) or diminished (d) in quality.

1.

___   ___   ___   ___

Practice 12-7

Complete the indicated augmented or diminished triad starting from the given root. Remember that the augmented triad is a major third above the root plus an augmented fifth above the root, and that the diminished triad is a minor third above the root plus a diminished fifth above the root.

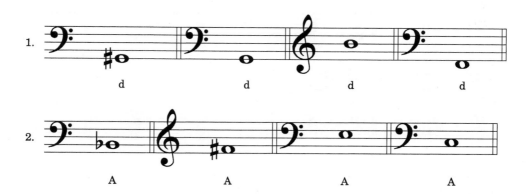

Practice 12-8

Complete the indicated close-position augmented or diminished triads. In each case, the note given is the *third* of the triad.

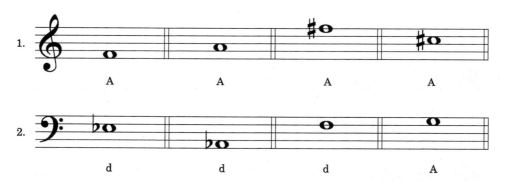

Practice 12-9

Complete the indicated close-position augmented or diminished triads. In each case, the note given is the *fifth* of the triad.

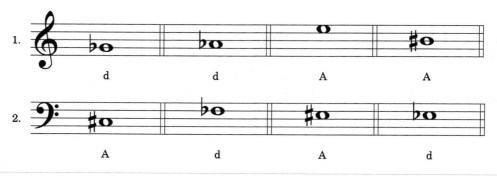

The following triads are in either first inversion or second inversion. Identify the inversion, the root of the triad, and the quality of the triad.

EXAMPLE:

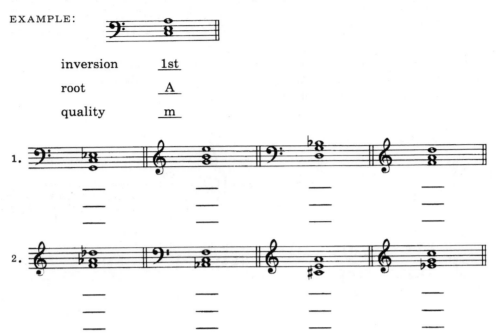

inversion   <u>1st</u>

root   <u>A</u>

quality   <u>m</u>

1.

____   ____   ____   ____

____   ____   ____   ____

2.

____   ____   ____   ____

____   ____   ____   ____

Practice 12-11

Write the indicated triad for each figured bass symbol. Remember that each given note is the lowest-sounding pitch of a major triad, and that the subscript numeral indicates whether the triad is in root position or in an inversion. When you have finished, write the letter name of the triad above it.

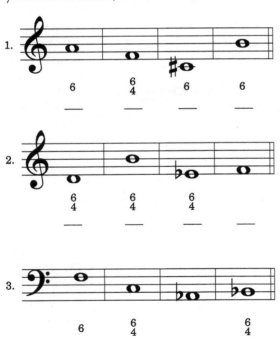

1.

6   6/4   6   6

____   ____   ____   ____

2.

6/4   6/4   6/4

____   ____   ____

3.

6   6/4   6/4

____   ____   ____

Triads in a Musical Context

𝄞 Visit Music Fundamentals in Action, at CourseMate, to:

- Take a Pretest on triads and progressions
- Hear the author's Let's Talk About Music podcast on triads
- Find many more practice exercises to help you succeed in this course
- See Tips&Tools for each chapter

Introduction

In the previous chapter, we learned the basics of triad recognition and construction. In this chapter, we will begin by looking at three different ways of identifying and labeling triads—roman numeral analysis, chord symbols, and guitar tablature. All three of these are in common use today. Then, we will briefly explore four-note chords, called seventh chords, before examining a few of the ways in which triads appear in actual pieces of music.

Three Ways to Label Triads

There are three different ways to label triads; because each way gives different information about the harmony, musicians need to be familiar with more than one. *Roman numeral analysis* is the preferred method for music theory, where an understanding of the relationship between the triads and the key is significant; if you continue to study music theory, you will use this way of labeling extensively. *Chord symbol identification* appears most frequently as a performing system in popular music, jazz, and rock. If you expect to develop your performing skills, from singing folk songs to playing with a jazz or rock group, you will need to understand this type of labeling. Finally, *guitar tablature* identifies triads for guitar players by creating a picture or diagram of the desired chord.

Roman Numeral Analysis

In roman numeral analysis, uppercase and lowercase roman numerals identify both the scale degree on which a triad is built as well as the quality of each particular triad. The uppercase roman numerals (I, IV, and V) identify the major triads; the lowercase roman numerals (ii, iii, and vi) identify the minor triads; and the symbol ° added to a lowercase number (vii°) identifies the diminished triad. A subscript 7 following the roman numeral means that the interval of a seventh has been added above the root. The key is indicated at the beginning of the analysis: an uppercase letter for a major key, a lowercase letter for a minor key.

C: I   ii   iii   IV   V   vi   vii°   I

Analyze the following triads with roman numeral analysis.

D: ___ ___ ___   G: ___ ___ ___   E♭: ___ ___ ___

The triads built from the harmonic minor version of the minor scale (with the raised leading tone borrowed from major) are labeled as follows:

d: i   ii°   III   iv   V   VI   vii°   i
             or
             III+

The symbol + beside an uppercase roman numeral (III+) indicates an augmented triad. Although we need practice in writing this triad, remember that the augmented triad is not used that frequently by composers.

Analyze the following triads in minor keys with roman numeral analysis.

e: ___ ___ ___   g: ___ ___ ___   f♯: ___ ___ ___

Practice for labeling triads in both major and minor keys may be found in Practice materials 13-1 and 13-2 at the end of this chapter.

Every major scale and every minor scale produce the same patterns of triads; that is, the quality of each triad remains constant no matter what the key. The information given in the following chart will prove extremely useful in writing triads. Study it carefully before continuing.

Major keys	Quality of triads	Natural minor keys	Changes to natural minor with a borrowed leading tone
I, IV, V	major	III, VI, VII	V
ii, iii, vi	minor	i, iv, v	
vii°	diminished	ii°	vii°
none	augmented		(possible III+ seldom replaces the major III)

Write the indicated triads in each key. Begin by supplying the correct key signature.

A: ii   vi   b: iv   V   c: ii°   VI   D: vii°   IV

Practice for writing triads in major and minor keys may be found in Practice materials 13-3 and 13-5.

Music in Action

Roman Numeral Analysis

The following two excerpts illustrate the roman numeral analysis of music. Pitches that are not part of the chord (that is, nonharmonic pitches) are circled. Notice also that the chords occasionally occur in an inversion rather than in root position, and they can take several beats or even a measure to reveal all their pitches.

Listen to each example several times and study the analysis. What kind of information does it give you about the individual chords? About the progression of chords? About how the chords relate to the melody? In class, discuss the information that roman numeral analysis does and does not provide. How is this information useful to a performer? ●

"Blow Ye Winds in the Morning"

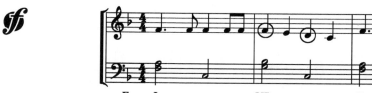

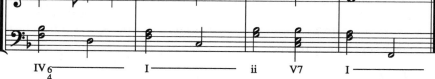

"Wayfaring Stranger"

Chord Symbols

In jazz, rock, and pop, the letter name of the triad (with an indication of both chord quality and inversion) replaces the roman numeral. While this chord symbol identification no longer indicates the relationship of the various triads to the key, it does convey triad information more directly. In performing situations, particularly when improvising, it is more useful.

This system of labeling supplies both the name of the triad and its quality. An uppercase letter indicates major triads (D, G, A); an uppercase letter plus a lowercase *m* indicates minor triads (E*m*, F#*m*, B*m*); an uppercase letter with a $^+$ or with the abbreviation *aug.* indicates augmented triads (G$^+$); and an uppercase letter with a ° or with *dim.* indicates diminished triads (C#°, F#°, D#°).

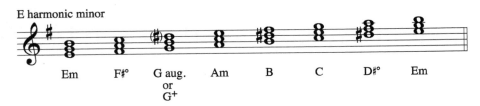

There are variations on this system, most of which can be figured out rather quickly with the possible exception of the minus sign (–), which is sometimes used to indicate a minor chord instead of a lowercase *m*. In this system, F#–, B–, and A– are minor triads.

Finally, if a triad is in an inversion, the name of the lowest-sounding note is indicated along with the name of the chord. For example, F/A indicates an F major triad with an A in the bass.

Write each indicated triad in root position.

Additional practice for labeling triads with pitch names is available in Practice materials 13-4.

Music in Action

Recognizing Chord Symbols

The following composition has been analyzed with the pitch name identification system. As a class, discuss the kinds of information this analytical system conveys to the performer.

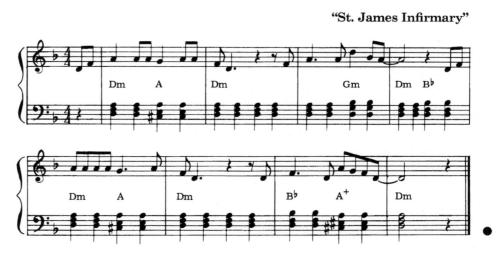

"St. James Infirmary"

Guitar Tablature

Guitar **tablature** does not serve quite the same function as roman numeral analysis and chord symbols. Unlike roman numeral analysis (which tells us how various triads function within a key), or chord symbols (which tell us the root and quality of a chord), guitar tablature tells the guitar player what physical action to make to produce the desired triad. This is because unlike musical staff notation, which is a visual representation of the actual sound, tablature is a picture of how to go about making that sound.

Guitar tablature usually appears above the melody line of a song and uses small diagrams such as the following to indicate the appropriate chords for the music.

These diagrams are pictures of the six strings and several of the *frets* (small metal bars spaced evenly across the length of the fingerboard) on the neck of the guitar nearest the tuning pegs. In the following diagram the vertical lines represent the six guitar strings and the horizontal lines represent the frets.

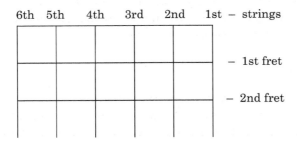

If a guitar player were to play this example of tablature, he or she would strum the open strings. (The first string is the highest-sounding string.)

Guitar tuning, open strings

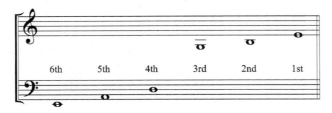

To indicate triads, small black dots are placed on the appropriate strings at the appropriate fret. These dots tell the guitar player where to place his or her fingers to create the desired triad. Any string without a dot is to be played as an open string unless there is an "x" above or below it. This "x" means that particular string is not to be played at all.

The following is the melody to "Worried Man Blues" with the guitar tablature indicated above it. Notice that this is extremely useful information to a guitar player trying to accompany this song.

Traditional, "Worried Man Blues"

It may interest you to learn, incidentally, that tablature is not a recent innovation. It was commonly used in Europe during the Renaissance (1450–1600) and Baroque (1600–1750) periods, and other systems of tablature existed in Asia long before that. Today, tablature (usually shortened to "tab") is used by folk, rock, pop, and jazz musicians worldwide. Although tablature does not replace the greater sophistication of standard notation, it does offer a way to make music that is both quick to learn and elegant in its concept and design.

Music in Action   Guitar Tablature

Ask several people in the class who play guitar to prepare accompaniments to "Worried Man Blues." Then, as a class sing the song to each of these different accompaniments. Afterward, discuss with the guitar players what role the tablature played in their preparation of their accompaniment. ●

Seventh Chords

So far we have dealt only with the triad—a three-note chord. The triad is, after all, the fundamental structure of tonal harmony. But music is not made up exclusively of triads. Past and present composers sometimes add a fourth pitch, and occasionally even a fifth and sixth pitch, to the triad. And while some styles of music, such as folk music or early rock 'n' roll, function primarily with triads, other styles, such as recent jazz or the Romantic compositions of Chopin and Liszt, use four-, five-, and six-note chords extensively. But no matter what the style, adding extra pitches to the triad is always for the purpose of increasing the harmonic tension.

Even though the study of chords more complex than the triad is beyond the scope of this book, seventh chords occur so frequently that we need to take a brief look at them. The dominant seventh chord, for example, is used so extensively that it is sometimes difficult to find an example of tonal music that *doesn't* contain at least one.

All seventh chords are so called because the fourth note creates the interval of a seventh above the root of the chord.

 interval of a seventh

Although seventh chords can be built on any degree of the scale, the one built on the dominant, that is, the dominant seventh chord, is used more frequently than any of the other possibilities. This is because the additional note enhances the harmonic tension already inherent in the dominant triad.

Dominant Seventh Chords

The **dominant seventh chord** is *always* a major triad with an added minor seventh above the root. This is true for both major and minor keys. This constant structure—a major triad with an added minor seventh—is what gives the dominant seventh chord its characteristic sound. Notice in the following example that when working in a minor key, the leading tone must always be raised to create a major triad on the dominant.

Dominant seventh chord in B♭ Major

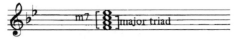

Dominant seventh chord in b♭ minor

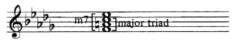

The dominant seventh chord is identified by the notation V_7, in which the roman numeral V indicates the triad built on the fifth, or dominant, note of the scale, and the subscript seven indicates the interval of a seventh. In harmonic analysis, both symbols are necessary to correctly identify the dominant seventh chord. With chord symbols and guitar tablature, the symbol F7 would be used for both of the previous examples.

To understand the difference between the dominant triad and the dominant seventh chord, play the following two patterns on the piano. Notice how the dominant seventh chord (V_7) produces an increase in harmonic tension. Listen to the difference between the V and V_7 several times. The dominant seventh sound is an extremely common sound in all styles of tonal music and one that you should begin to listen for and recognize.

Music in Action 🔊 Ear Training

You should learn to hear the difference between a seventh chord and a triad. Your instructor will play various chords. Some chords will be played as seventh chords, others as triads. In the following space, indicate whether you hear a seventh chord or a triad.

1. _____ _____ _____ _____

2. _____ _____ _____ _____

3. _____ _____ _____ _____

Inversions of Seventh Chords

Although it is really beyond the scope of this book, you should be aware that dominant seventh chords can be inverted just as triads can. Knowing this will enable you to recognize these chords more easily in musical situations.

Remember that triads have two possible inversions beyond root position. But, because the dominant seventh chord has four notes, there are three possible inversions of it beyond root position. Notice in the following diagram that the name of the inversion is determined by the lowest-sounding note just as in the inversion of triads. First inversion has the third of the chord as the lowest-sounding note, second inversion has the fifth as the lowest-sounding note, and third inversion has the seventh of the chord as the lowest-sounding note. Notice also that the numbers refer to the intervals above the lowest note, as they do with triads.

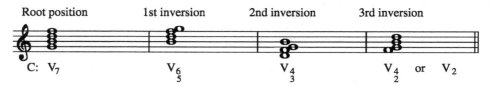

And just as with triads, a shorthand system of labeling has developed that indicates only the essential intervals above the lowest note. In the actual analysis of music, or in figured bass, these are the numbers that you will see.

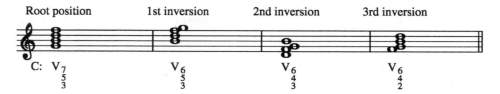

Practice for writing dominant seventh chords, in both root position and inversions, is available in Practice materials 13-6 and 13-7.

Recognizing Triads in Actual Music

In actual pieces of music, triads don't always appear as vertical chords. Composers often choose other types of settings for triads, particularly when they want the harmony to make a strong contribution to the horizontal motion of the piece. So, it is important for you not only to be aware that triads can appear in music in a variety of settings but also to be able to recognize the more common types. To help you begin, we will look briefly at the two most important ways in which composers have traditionally set triads: block chords and arpeggiations.

Block Chords

The following is an example of a composition using triads as block chords.

Schubert: *Valses nobles*

Notice in this example how vertical the harmony looks on the page. When listening to it performed, notice how your attention is drawn to this vertical quality more than to any horizontal motion. We hear these chords almost as separate entities even though, simultaneously, we are aware of their linear relationship to each other.

This special quality of block chords, to emphasize both the vertical and the horizontal dimensions of the music, can be seen in the following pattern, a staple in popular music since the 1950s. Notice how the vertical, almost percussive, qualities of the music are enhanced by the repetition of each chord.

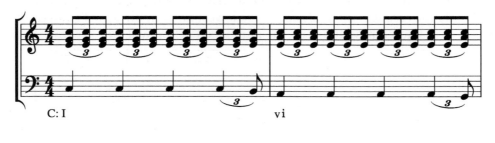

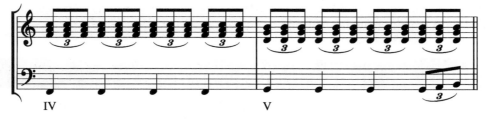

Music in Action — Block Chords in Popular Music

Make a list of five or six popular songs that use the block-chord style of accompaniment illustrated in the previous example. As a class, listen to two or three of them. Is your attention always drawn to the harmonic element in a similar way? How does the tempo affect the harmonic element, particularly its vertical qualities? ●

Arpeggiations

Often, composers choose arpeggiations rather than block chords to avoid directing the listener's attention too strongly toward the vertical aspects of the harmony. An arpeggiated accompaniment is an accompanying figure in which each chord is broken into a pattern of isolated notes that is generally repeated throughout much of the piece. These isolated notes have the effect of spreading the chord out over time, thus causing our attention to move linearly. Here are a few of the simpler arpeggiation patterns.

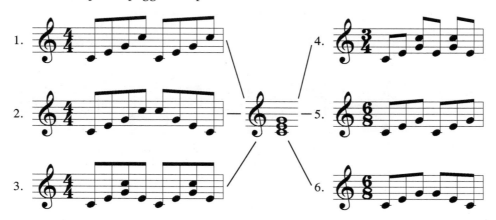

The following are several musical examples using some of these simple arpeggiations, or **broken chord patterns**, as they are sometimes called. The block chords on which these patterns are based are written below each line of music so that you can see more easily how each chord unfolds in time through the arpeggiations. Circled pitches are not a part of the chord.

Clementi: "Rondo" from *Sonatina in G Major,* Op. 36, No. 5

Beethoven: "Menuetto" from *Sonatina in D Major*

(continued)

I   I$^6_4$ V   I

Clementi: "Rondo" from *Sonatina in F Major,* Op. 36, No. 4

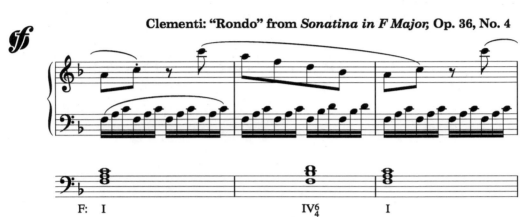

F: I   IV$^6_4$ I

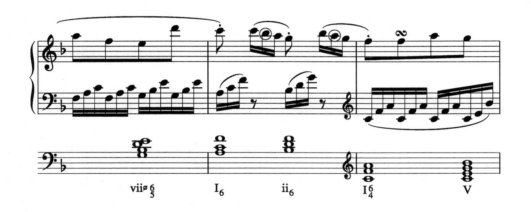

vii°$^6_5$ I$_6$ ii$_6$ I$^6_4$ V

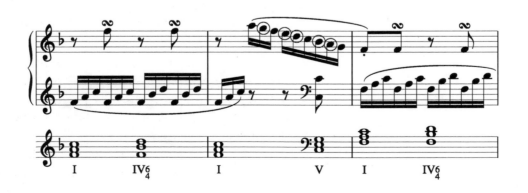

I   IV$^6_4$ I   V   I   IV$^6_4$

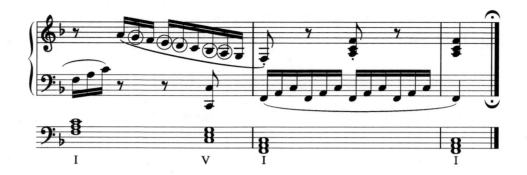

Music in Action · Arpeggiating Chords

The chord progression that follows is written in block chords. In the space provided, create an arpeggiated version of this pattern suitable for piano or guitar. You may invent your own or use one of the previous examples as a model. If you don't play piano or guitar, ask someone who does to play your pattern for you.

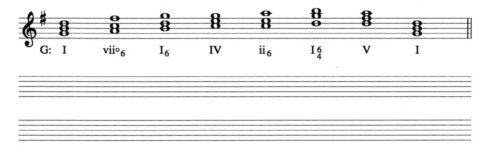

Both classical and popular composers throughout the centuries have used arpeggiated chords—and almost always for the same reason: It weakens the vertical qualities of the harmony and replaces them with a linear quality that helps to move the music forward. This contribution is so important that chord arpeggiations appear in almost all musical styles and at almost any tempo. ●

Music in Action ◄)) Ear Training

The ability to identify chord progressions or even individual chords by ear is extremely useful. But for people with little background or practice this can be extremely frustrating, particularly at first. Unless your ear is unusually well developed, it is unreasonable to expect that you could begin by taking the chords off a recording of your favorite piece. This is an extremely sophisticated skill that only comes to most people with consistent practice. Although this may be one of your goals, it is not where you begin.

If you are just beginning, keep in mind these three points as you practice.

1. You must practice consistently to improve. Ear training is not unlike preparing for an athletic event.

2. Success seems to come in plateaus; don't be overly concerned if you don't appear to show improvement every day or even every week.

3. It is better, and easier, to build on success. Ideally, your success rate should be in the area of 80 to 85 percent. If it is much lower, you are probably attempting material that is too difficult for you. This can actually slow your progress.

With this in mind, try the following: Your teacher or another student from the class will play a major or minor scale as a reference. Then he or she will play a triad that is either the tonic or the dominant triad of that key. In the spaces provided, indicate which triad is being played.

1. _____
2. _____
3. _____
4. _____

Now try this using three triads—the tonic, dominant, and submediant. It helps to remember which triads are major and which are minor.

1. _____
2. _____
3. _____
4. _____

Finally, see if you can correctly identify one of four different triads—tonic, dominant, submediant, and subdominant.

1. _____
2. _____
3. _____
4. _____

A Final Note

Triads are basic to tonal music. It is important that you not only be able to construct triads but that you be able to label them correctly, as well as recognize them within a wide variety of musical contexts. In this chapter we have looked at three distinct ways of labeling triads. Depending on the type of music that interests you most, one of these labeling systems may seem more useful to you than the others. However, you should become familiar with all three, because each offers unique musical information. If you plan to continue with music theory, roman numeral analysis will certainly become increasingly important. Make sure that you understand the basics of this system before going on to the next chapter.

It is also important that you have a beginning understanding of seventh chords, in particular the dominant seventh, because these chords appear frequently in both popular and classical music. Although extensive work with seventh chords is beyond the scope of this book, a general understanding of them will make the music you listen to and perform more meaningful.

Finally, keep in mind that triads are simple musical structures that create subtle and complicated musical patterns. It is important that you be able to recognize triads and seventh chords when they appear other than as block chords. Broken-chord arpeggiated figures are one such way they frequently occur. There are also many other ways that chords unfold over time that we have not considered. If, however, you keep in mind that all tonal music is based on triads and seventh chords, you should, with practice, be able to figure out how the chords are unfolding, no matter how unique the actual musical situation.

Practice

Practice 13-1

Use roman numerals to label the triads in the following major keys.

F: ___ ___ ___ ___ ___ ___ ___ ___

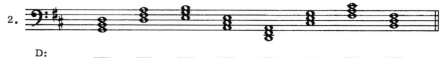

D: ___ ___ ___ ___ ___ ___ ___ ___

E: ___ ___ ___ ___ ___ ___ ___ ___

Practice 13-2

Use roman numerals to label the triads in the following minor keys.

f#: ___ ___ ___ ___ ___ ___ ___ ___

d: ___ ___ ___ ___ ___ ___ ___ ___

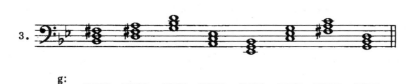

g: ___ ___ ___ ___ ___ ___ ___ ___

Practice 13-3

Write the indicated triads for each given key. Begin by writing in the correct key signature.

G: I   V₆   iii   vii°   IV

(continued)

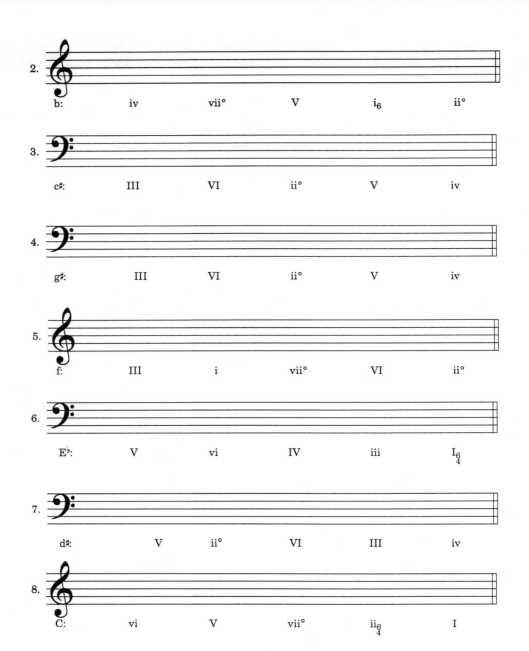

2.
b: iv   vii°   V   i₆   ii°

3.
c♯:   III   VI   ii°   V   iv

4.
g♯:   III   VI   ii°   V   iv

5.
f: III   i   vii°   VI   ii°

6.
E♭:   V   vi   IV   iii   I₆₄

7.
d♯:   V   ii°   VI   III   iv

8.
C: vi   V   vii°   ii₆₄   I

Practice 13-4

Label the following triads using pitch name identification.

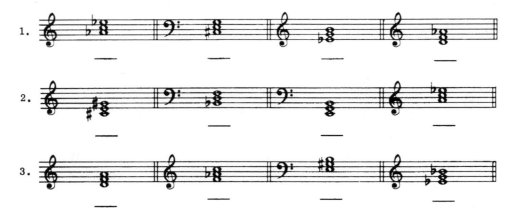

Practice 13-5

Write the triads indicated below. All triads should be in root position.

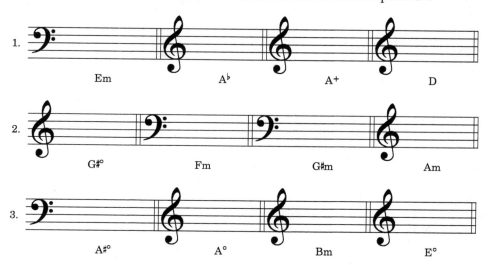

Practice 13-6

Practice writing dominant seventh chords in root position in the keys indicated. When dealing with a minor key, remember to use the harmonic minor version. Remember also that the dominant seventh chord is always a major triad with an added minor seventh.

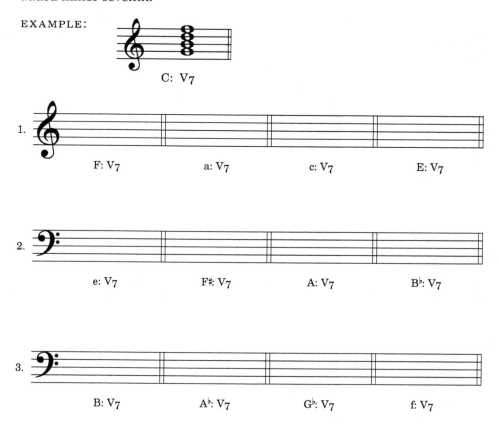

Practice writing inversions of the following dominant seventh chords. Remember that the dominant seventh chord is always a major triad with an added minor seventh. When working in minor keys, this means you must use the harmonic minor version of the scale.

EXAMPLE:

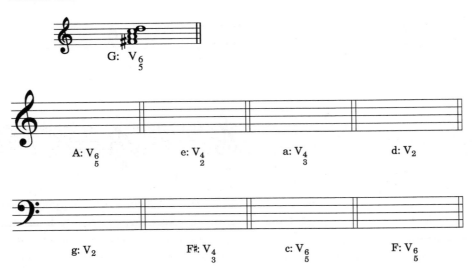

G: V_6^5 ... A: V_6^5 ... e: V_4^2 ... a: V_4^3 ... d: V_2

g: V_2 ... F#: V_4^3 ... c: V_6^5 ... F: V_6^5

Chord Progressions

Introduction

The material covered in this and the next chapter deals with *tonality*, a somewhat elusive concept whose definition most Western musicians take for granted. In its simplest sense, tonality is tonal music, that is, music in which both the melody and the harmony come from major and minor scales. But in a more subjective, personal sense, tonality is also that unique ability of musical tones, in both the scale and the music itself, to seem to relate to one another. To our ears, these "tonal" pitches establish a hierarchy in which one tone becomes the focal point—the point of rest, the tonic—around which the other scale degrees rotate and interact, each with varying degrees of tension and importance. This interrelationship of tonal scale degrees regulates not only the details of music—consonance and dissonance, phrase structure, and cadences—but also the overall form, or musical shape, of each work, as well. In this chapter we will concentrate on three of the most basic aspects of tonality: the dominant/tonic relationship, cadences, and simple chord progressions. We will then look at how all these factors come together in the 12-bar blues.

Of course, we can only begin to explore these topics. The material covered in this chapter generally requires quite a bit more time to work through and absorb than that in any of the previous chapters. But if this is your *only* class in music theory, these last two chapters will show you some practical applications for the information you have gained. If you plan further study of theory, these chapters will introduce many of the concepts you will encounter in your later studies. Either way, it is important to remember that this is only the beginning.

The Dominant/Tonic Relationship

Beyond the tension and release inherent in the movement of all tonal melodies, a sense of forward motion and resolution also exists in tonal harmony. Nowhere is this more evident than in the simplest of chord progressions—the dominant to tonic relationship. This relationship (the dominant triad moving to the tonic triad) is without doubt the most frequently used progression in tonal music. This is true because of the strong gravitational attraction established between

V and I. This relationship is so strong that these two triads, by themselves, can clearly establish the tonal center, or key, of a work.

To understand this, it is important to consider the dominant triad for a moment. It includes not only the fifth degree of the scale, but also the leading tone and the supertonic. These are all active scale degrees that, to our ears need to resolve. Remember also from our work with triads that a fourth pitch (a minor seventh above the root) is often added to the dominant triad to make it sound even more active. Therefore, both the dominant triad and the dominant seventh chord are active sounds, full of tension. However, all this tension is released, or resolved, when the dominant triad (or dominant seventh chord) moves to the tonic triad, the point of rest in tonal music. This movement between tension and resolution gives the harmony and the melody a feeling of forward motion and a sense of centering within the key.

In the following example, a French folk song, notice that the entire melody can be accompanied by only tonic and dominant harmonies.

"Sur le Pont d'Avignon"

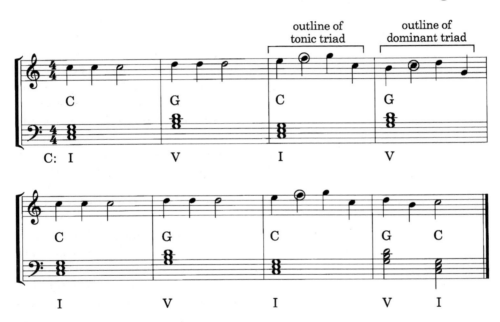

Notice also that both the melody and the harmony parallel each other. That is, when the triad changes, the melody also moves primarily to pitches that make up the triad (measures 3 and 4, for example). This movement between tonic and dominant in both the melody and the harmony, along with the tension and resolution that are generated, is fundamental to the establishment of tonality and is the basis for all harmonic movement in tonal music, no matter how complicated.

Music in Action

Hearing V to I

Ask someone in class to play or sing the melody of the previous example while you sing the root of each tonic or dominant triad. Can you feel the tension of the V chord resolve to the I?

Now try the opposite, with you singing the melody while someone else plays the I and V triads on the piano. Can you feel how the melody and harmony support each other?

Remember that this is a simple example with only one level of tension: the dominant triad. More complicated pieces of music will have many more subtle levels of tension, made possible by the availability of other chords (made with other scale degrees). ●

Cadences

Perhaps the most important thing to remember at this point is that chords do not move around randomly throughout a piece of music. Instead, they are arranged into phrases, following the outline of the melody, in much the same way that a paragraph of prose consists of several sentences, each made up of a complete thought. Furthermore, each phrase of the melody and harmony seems to come to its own point of rest, in the same way that sentences end with a period. Like a sentence, which can also end with a question mark or an exclamation point, these points of rest, or *cadences*, can vary in their strength and feeling of completeness. Understanding this concept of the cadence as a musical stopping point and identifying the types of cadences that most frequently occur are our next steps toward understanding tonality.

Regardless of the various types of cadences you may encounter in a piece of music (there are more than the four we will look at here), remember that cadences only appear at the ends of phrases. Every phrase of tonal music ends with a cadence. Therefore, to recognize cadences, first we must be able to recognize musical phrases. But even though every song is different, recognizing phrases isn't as difficult as it might seem at first. In fact, if you have sung or played through the examples in this book, you are probably already familiar with the concept of phrases in music. As you continue, just keep in mind that musical **phrases** are like sentences that make up a paragraph of prose. In the same way that the sentences of a paragraph relate to each other, the phrases of a melody combine to create a larger entity. Once you can see the phrases, the cadences at the end of each one will become clear.

A **cadence** is a momentary or permanent point of rest. Cadences occur both within a composition and at its conclusion; those in the middle of a piece are always at the ends of musical phrases. Often new musicians believe that V to I creates a cadence every time it occurs. This is not true. Cadences occur only at the ends of phrases.

Cadences can occur in both the harmony and the rhythm of a composition (though we will not go into rhythmic cadences here). The **harmonic cadence** consists of two chords. There are four types of harmonic cadences that occur most frequently in tonal music: the *authentic cadence*, the *plagal cadence*, the *half cadence*, and the *deceptive cadence*. Each cadence is a different formula of two chords, so each cadence can be heard as a *different* level of tension and resolution.

The Authentic Cadence

The **authentic cadence** in a major key is the chord pattern V–I; in a minor key it is the chord pattern V–i.

Authentic cadence, major key

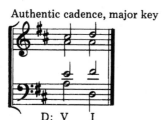

D: V   I

Authentic cadence, minor key

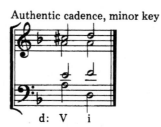

d: V   i

What makes a cadence work? A cadence gives the impression of stopping musically because of the interaction of the melody, the harmony, and the rhythm. Notice that while the chord pattern V–I can occur many times, as in the previous example, "Sur le Pont d'Avignon," not all occurrences create a cadence. Notice in the following example how the melody, harmony, and rhythm work together to produce a strong feeling of conclusion. The authentic cadence gives the strongest sense of conclusion of all the cadential patterns.

Hymn: Dundee

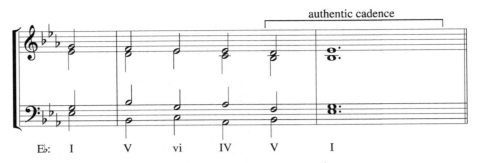

E♭: I   V   vi   IV   V   I

The authentic cadence is considered the strongest cadence because the sense of resolution—from the tension of the dominant triad to the restful nature of the tonic triad—feels most complete. This sense of resolution can seem even stronger if the tension of the dominant triad is increased. As we learned in the previous chapter, this can be accomplished by using the dominant seventh chord. The additional note, located a minor seventh above the root, adds extra tension to the dominant sound, which, in turn, is released with a stronger feeling of completeness when it moves to the tonic. Although dominant seventh chords can be used anywhere within a chord progression that seems appropriate, their most frequent use over the past three hundred years has been in the authentic cadence. Play and listen to the following two examples of authentic cadences that use the dominant seventh chords. Compare these examples to the previous one that used the dominant triad. Notice that the tension/release qualities of the cadence seem heightened when the dominant seventh chord appears.

Hymn: Winchester New

B♭: I   I⁶   IV   V   vi   ii⁶₅   V₇   I

Bach: Chorale, "Herr, ich denk' an jene Zeit"

E♭: I   V   I⁶   V⁶   I   ii⁶₅   V⁷   I

Pay particular attention to the sound of the authentic cadence and try to remember it. If you are successful, you will begin to notice how frequently it occurs in the music you hear around you every day. The authentic cadence is the most frequently used cadence in rock, jazz, country, and classical music. You can hear it everywhere if you remember what to listen for.

The Plagal Cadence

The **plagal cadence** is the chord progression IV–I in major or iv–i in minor.

Plagal cadence, major key

D: IV   I

Plagal cadence, minor key

d: iv   i

The plagal cadence is most familiar as the *Amen* ending of a hymn. This cadence, while also capable of producing a feeling of permanent rest, is not as strong as the authentic cadence. Consequently, it is used less frequently as the final cadence of a piece, except in hymns, where it has become commonplace.

Handel: "Lift up Your Heads" from *Messiah*

plagal cadence

He   is   the   King   of Glo - ry,   of   Glo - ry.

F: IV$_4^6$ I   IV   I$_6$ I   I   IV   I

The Half Cadence

The **half cadence**, or **semi-cadence** as it is sometimes called, conveys a feeling of stopping that is only temporary. The half cadence never functions as a true conclusion to a whole section or to an entire piece because the half cadence formula ends on a dominant chord (V). The V in a half cadence can be preceded by any chord, but in practice it is most often preceded by the I, IV, or ii in major and the i or the iv in minor.

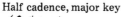

Half cadence, major key

D: IV   V

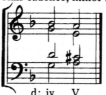

Half cadence, minor key

d: iv   V

The half cadence gives the impression of a pause, not a complete relaxation of tension. As such, it sounds best when it appears in the middle of a musical statement rather than at its conclusion. The following example has two short phrases. Notice that the first phrase ends on a half cadence, while the second phrase ends on an authentic cadence. This is the most common two-phrase sequence of cadences in tonal music. So remember, more often than not, the first phrase ends on a half cadence; the second phrase answers with an authentic cadence. This information will help you when you try to harmonize a melody in the next chapter.

Kuhlau: Sonatina in C Major, Op. 55, No. 1, II

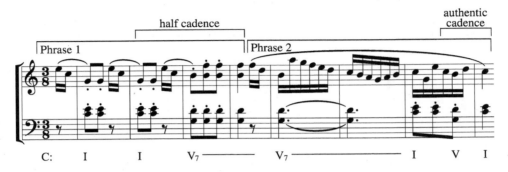

The Deceptive Cadence

The **deceptive cadence**, in its most common form, sounds at first as if it is going to be an authentic cadence. That is, the first chord of both the authentic and the deceptive cadence is a V or V$_7$, and our ear expects the final triad will be the tonic. Although this is true for the authentic cadence, it is not what happens in the deceptive cadence. Instead, the V or V$_7$ goes to an unexpected place, usually the vi, although other triads are possible. The result is that our ear has been deceived momentarily.

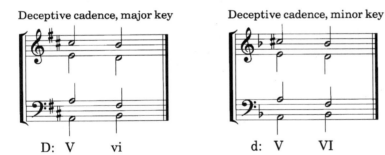

Ask someone to play the following example on the piano, first as written, then a second time substituting the tonic triad for the submediant triad in the cadence.

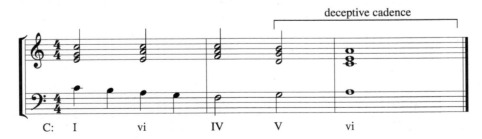

Notice that the authentic cadence created by the substitution of the I chord for the vi chord works well in this situation. In fact, our ear is led to expect it. This momentary deception of our ear allows the deceptive cadence to function as an *unexpected* point of repose. It cannot, however, function as the final cadence of a piece of music because the purpose of the final cadence is to bring everything to an obvious conclusion.

Now let's return to the hymn tune "Old Hundredth," first encountered in Chapter 12, to see how cadences function within a complete piece of music. Here is the hymn, this time with the chords and cadences indicated.

First, notice how regularly the cadences occur. Hymns generally have regular phrase lengths (in this case, three measures each) and a cadence concludes each phrase. Notice also the rhythm of the cadences. In each, the final chord occurs on the downbeat while the chord before it occurs on a weak beat. This is not happenstance, but planned, because cadences must *sound* right, both rhythmically and harmonically. Finally, notice the variety of cadences that conclude these four phrases. The first and fourth cadences are both authentic; they establish the key of G major most strongly. The middle two cadences, a half cadence and a deceptive cadence, conclude their phrases with a variety of sound and differing sense of completion that plays against the two authentic cadences.

The following excerpts contain examples of the cadences we have studied in this chapter. Listen to each excerpt several times and identify by ear where the cadences occur. Then analyze each cadence as to type, first by ear, then with the music.

Clementi: Sonatina, Op. 36, No. 3, III

Schumann: "Soldiers' March" from _Album for the Young_

2.

Bach: Chorale, "Ermuntre dich, mein schwacher Geist"

3.

(continued)

Kuhlau: Sonatina in C Major, Op. 55, No. 1, I

Anon., L'omnipotent from *"Genevan Psalter"*

Simple Chord Progressions

Exactly how do chord progressions function? As musical phrases move through various levels of tension and release, the alternation between activity and restfulness gives a feeling of movement to the music. This musical motion is supported by the melody, harmony, and rhythm; the interrelationship of these three elements allows the V–I progression, for instance, to function as a cadence at the end but not in the middle of a phrase. Harmony contributes to a feeling of motion through the variety of chords (and their level of tension) available. To some extent, every triad is active and tension-producing or passive and restful.

This alternation between harmonic tension and release can be heard in almost any example of tonal music. Pieces that use a large range of harmonic possibilities, however, are usually rather complicated and difficult; they are appropriate for more advanced theoretical study. Our discussion here will be limited to the concept of tension and release as it occurs in simple chord progressions.

Two-Chord Progression

The simplest chord progression consists of only two chords. In the majority of cases, these are the tonic triad and the dominant triad. The tonic triad, which is actually the center of gravity for *every* tonal chord progression, is the most restful sound. The dominant triad, on the other hand, is the most active sound. Therefore, a chord progression that simply alternates between the tonic and the dominant possesses a great deal of potential for musical tension and release.

Most folk songs, because they are intended to be sung and played by people with little or no musical training, use relatively few chords. Take the following example, "Tom Dooley." It has only two chord changes for the entire song: I–V–I. Notice that although the chords change slowly, the broken-chord style of accompaniment in the bass supplies a continual feeling of motion. Listen to someone from your class play this piece and concentrate on the accompaniment rather than the melody. Can you feel the change in tension when the V chord appears in measure 4? Notice how this level of tension is maintained for four measures before it resolves back to the I chord. This difference in tension levels, and the harmonic motion between them, allows such a simple chord progression to work musically.

F: I   V

(V)   I

Music in Action   Hearing Tonic and Dominant
The following melodies can be harmonized with only tonic and dominant chords. As a class, sing the melodies that you recognize several times and decide, by ear, which parts of the melody require tonic chords and which parts need dominant chords. If you play piano, you may wish to pick the melody out at the keyboard and add tonic and dominant chords to accompany it.

1. "Down in the Valley"
2. "London Bridge"
3. "He's Got the Whole World in His Hands"
4. "Wayfaring Stranger"
5. "Don't Let the the Stars Get in Your Eyes"
6. "How Much Is That Doggie in the Window?"
7. "Jambalaya"
8. "O Tannenbaum" ●

Three-Chord Progression

When a third chord is introduced into a harmonic progression, it is often the subdominant chord. Remember that the plagal cadence (IV–I) is considered not as strong as the authentic cadence (V–I), because the tension created between IV and I is not as great as that between V and I. Similarly, the subdominant chord is also less tension producing than the dominant chord. Thus, in the three-chord progression I–IV–V, the IV chord stands intermediate in tension between the active V chord and the restful I chord.

The subdominant chord usually appears in one of two patterns: I–IV–V–I or I–IV–I–V–I. The following folk song has the I–IV–V–I progression.

When used in this way, the subdominant chord contributes a first-level tension, which the dominant chord further increases to a second level. The harmonic tension is then resolved by the return to the tonic chord.

The next example of a three-chord progression uses the chord pattern I–IV–I–V–I.

"Michael, Row the Boat Ashore"

(continued)

Here the subdominant chord establishes a first level of tension, which is resolved by the return of the tonic chord. Then, a second level of tension is introduced by the dominant chord, which is also resolved by the return of the tonic. Sing this example in class, with half the class singing the melody and the other half singing the root of each chord. Do you notice the different kinds of tension produced between I–IV–I at the beginning of the progression and I–V–I in the second half of the progression?

Practice for labeling chord progressions and cadences is available in Practice materials 14-1 at the end of this chapter.

Music in Action — Accompaniments

The chord progressions for "The Wabash Cannon Ball" and "Michael, Row the Boat Ashore" are written in the previous examples as block chords in the bass clef to make them easier to see. In performance, however, they would never be played exactly this way. Ask someone in the class who plays piano and someone who plays guitar to perform one or both of these pieces, providing their own suitable accompaniment. As a class, discuss each accompaniment. What are the musical contributions of an accompaniment? Why don't the block chords written in the examples make a suitable accompaniment? ●

The 12-Bar Blues

Now, let's examine how chord progressions work in the 12-bar blues.

In the same way that the 12-bar blues is based on its own unique scale, it is also built around its own chord progression. In fact, this chord progression, which uses only the I, IV, and V chords, is so universally known that it may well be the most recognized chord progression in history. Although there can be variations on the blues progression, as there can be with the blues scale, the basic 12-bar blues harmonic progression has remained constant for almost a century.

Here is the 12-bar blues progression in the key of F major.

12-bar blues progression

Play it or listen to it played, first, with just the root of each triad, then with the entire chord. Even though an untold number of different melodies have been played over this progression during the past hundred years, the harmonic progression itself has remained more or less constant. The one significant alteration to the progression came from rhythm and blues, which substituted the IV chord for the V chord in measure 10 (as indicated above). Today you can hear the blues performed both with and without this alteration.

Take a look at the traditional "Good Morning Blues."

Traditional: "Good Morning Blues"

Notice that "Good Morning Blues" follows the blues progression precisely, using only the I, IV, and V chords in the proper order and place. This 12-bar progression gives the blues its characteristic harmony. Also notice that the pitches of the melody reflect the pitches of the chord. It is this interaction of the melody and the harmony that gives all music a sense of forward motion and of tension and release.

Music in Action

Hearing the Blues Progression

Listen to several recordings of the 12-bar blues by blues singers such as Bessie Smith, John Lee Hooker, Buddy Guy, and Robert Cray. (Not every song with the word *blues* in the title uses a real 12-bar blues progression, but many songs by these artists do.) Try to remember the progression so that you can recognize it in other songs. Keep in mind that even though the melody will change from song to song, the chord progression will remain the same. Once you have learned it, you know it.

Then, listen to several examples of early rock 'n' roll by artists such as Chuck Berry, Jerry Lee Lewis, Little Richard, and Bill Haley. Many of their songs are based on 12-bar blues progressions. Can you hear the blues progressions in these pieces? As a class, discuss how various styles of music can sound so different from each other if they all use the same chord progression.

As you listened to the blues progression, did you notice that it seems to group itself into three phrases, each one four measures long?

Phrase 1:	I	I	I	I
Phrase 2:	IV	IV	I	I
Phrase 3:	V	V	I	I

This division into three phrases is supported by the lyrics. We will explore this further in the next chapter.

Notice also that each four-measure unit ends with a tonic triad (a point of rest), while the start of each four-measure unit begins with a different chord (various degrees of tension). ●

Music in Action ● Song Building

Choose a partner from the class and try to create a 12-bar blues. If you both play instruments, one can play the bass line or the blues progression while the other tries to improvise above it using the blues scale studied in Chapter 11. If you sing, choose a partner who plays an instrument. If the majority of the class doesn't play an instrument, your teacher may want the class to sing the blues progression while individuals improvise a melody over it. It works best to not think in terms of "right" and "wrong" when improvising, but rather that some improvisations will be more successful than others. ●

A Final Note

Tonality is a system of musical organization that is relatively simple to comprehend, but mysterious and complex when attempting to describe it. Tonality, after all, is what turns a random collection of pitches into a melody or a group of individual chords into a musical thought. But how does it do this? What forces are at work?

In this chapter, we have begun the study of tonality: in our case, how all the individual elements of music work together to create the actual sound. We looked at the dominant/tonic relationship and explored the idea that all melodies and all chord progressions move through varying levels of tension and release. It is from this duality that a feeling of motion and a sense of tonal centering in music develops. Building further on the concept of dominant/tonic (tension/release), we explored the idea of harmonic cadences, that is, temporary and permanent points of rest. From there we looked at two-chord and three-chord progressions, ending with the 12-bar blues.

In taking this route, we have explored the essence of all harmonic progressions—the idea that music moves through varying degrees of tension (the progression) looking for resolution (the cadence). So far, we have looked only at simple progressions, but even there, we could see the underlying principles of tonality at work: a restful tonic chord, around which other diatonic chords (of varying levels of tension) move and interact, resolving each phrase with a cadence, and building musical structures from phrases. Keep in mind that this quality of harmonic motion takes place not only in the song as a whole, but also within the individual phrases that make up the song.

As you continue your work with chord progressions and tonal harmony, you will encounter many new chords and longer, more complex progressions that create subtle harmonic shadings far beyond the diatonic chords and progressions studied here. But no matter how complex the chord progressions may become, keep in mind that all tonal progressions have the same purpose and work the same way. The qualities of tension and release built into chord progressions and cadences translate into the feelings of expectation and fulfillment we experience in the music we love.

Practice 14-1

The following are short musical excerpts that use simple chord progressions. For the most part, they center around the tonic, subdominant, and dominant triads, although other diatonic triads may appear from time to time. When you have completed this chapter, analyze these excerpts in two ways.

- Begin by indicating the correct key in the space under the bass clef sign.
- Then, using chord symbol identification, indicate the correct chord symbol above each chord change.
- Then, using roman numeral analysis, indicate the correct chordal function below each chord.
- Finally, bracket and label all cadences above the treble-clef line.

Teschner: Chorale

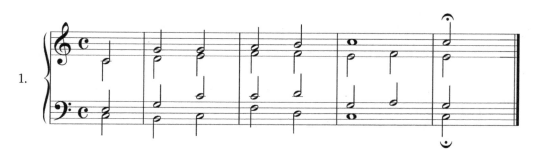

1.

Crüger: Chorale

2.

Beethoven: Sonatina

3.

(continued)

Practice 14-2

The following is a complete hymn from the Genevan Psalter, a collection of hymn tunes published in Geneva, in 1551.

- Begin your analysis by indicating the key under the bass clef sign.
- Then, above the example, write the chord symbol analysis.
- The cadences, which occur every two bars, are bracketed. Identify each of them.
- Finally, beneath the example, label the chord progression with roman numeral analysis.

Anon: Psalm 42

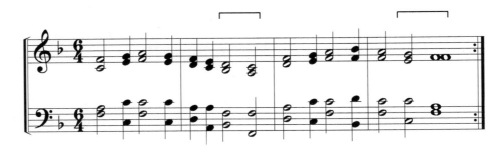

*This is not one of the four cadences we have studied, but it is related to one of them. Indicate the cadence it is related to.

Focus on Skills 7:
Triads and Progressions

 Visit Music Fundamentals in Action, at CourseMate, for interactive Focus on Fundamentals exercises.

1. Identify the root of each of the following triads, and label each as major (M), minor (m), augmented (A), or diminished (d) in quality.

   a.

   root   ____   ____   ____   ____

   quality   ____   ____   ____   ____

   b.

   ____   ____   ____   ____

   ____   ____   ____   ____

   c.

   ____   ____   ____   ____

   ____   ____   ____   ____

2. The following triads are in either first or second inversion. Identify the inversion, the root of the triad, and the quality.

   a.

   inversion   ____   ____   ____   ____

   root   ____   ____   ____   ____

   quality   ____   ____   ____   ____

   b.

   ____   ____   ____   ____

   ____   ____   ____   ____

   ____   ____   ____   ____

(continued)

3. Write the following triads in close position.

a.
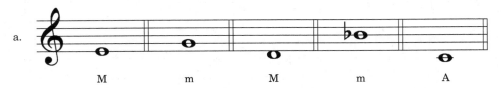
M   m   M   m   A

b.

M   A   d   M   d

4. Write the following triad in open position.

a.
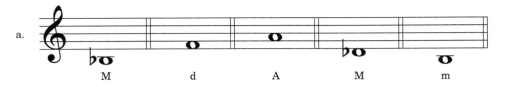
M   d   A   M   m

5. Complete the following triads and dominant seventh chords in close position.

a.
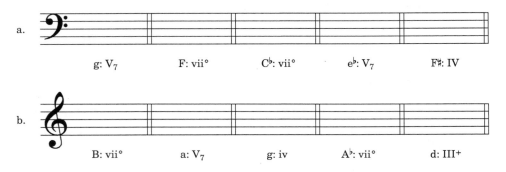
g: V_7 F: vii°   C♭: vii°   e♭: V_7 F♯: IV

b.

B: vii°   a: V_7 g: iv   A♭: vii°   d: III+

6. Analyze the chord progression of the following example by indicating the correct key, the roman numeral analysis, and the cadences.

Beethoven: Variations

Writing a Song

15

Writing a Song

Visit Music Fundamentals in Action, at CourseMate, to:
- Find many more practice exercises to help you succeed in this course
- See Tips&Tools for each chapter

Introduction

A song is a complex work of art. For a song to be successful its numerous parts must work together seamlessly, with the melody, harmony, and rhythm all complementing each other. Furthermore, the song must unfold over time in both a logical and a musically-pleasing way. Learning to write a song involves learning to combine these components in complementary ways that are pleasing to the ear. What makes it interesting is that some of what you need to know can be learned, but other aspects, the intangibles, are intuitive. Sometimes even the best songwriters don't know where a song came from.

In this chapter we will continue our study of tonality by considering the broader musical concepts that are most useful in writing songs: primary and secondary chords, harmonizing a melody, and musical form. In the process, we will look at four musical forms, or blueprints, for composing. Two of these, binary form and ternary form, are among the simplest forms used to create music; they have existed for hundreds of years. The other two, 12-bar blues and 32-bar song form, are musical forms used extensively today, particularly in popular music.

Primary and Secondary Chords

You may have noticed in the previous chapter how many different melodies were harmonized with only the I, IV, and V chords. This is possible because these three triads considered together contain *all* the pitches of the scale. Consider, for example, these three triads in C major:

I	C	E	G
IV	F	A	C
V	G	B	D

If the pitches in these triads are arranged in ascending order—C–D–E–F–G–A–B—they spell out all the notes of the major scale (C Major) on which the triads are based. Because these three triads (I, IV, V) contain all the notes of the scale, they can be used to harmonize most tonal melodies, and they are known as the *primary triads*.

The other triads (ii, iii, vi, and viiº) are known as the *secondary triads.* Their function is adding color, whereas almost any diatonic melody can be harmonized with only the primary triads (a good place to begin with any new melody), the secondary triads add much of the uniqueness and most of the color to the harmonization.

Harmonizing a Melody

The first step in harmonizing a melody is obvious—become familiar with it. Play it. Sing it. Listen to it. Try to locate the areas of tension and points of rest, to identify the musical phrases, and to decide where the cadences should go. Do as much of this by ear as possible; it's usually easier than looking at the written melody.

Let's begin with a melody that you may know, although you have probably never tried to harmonize it. It is by Stephen Foster, who lived between 1826 and 1864. Foster's contemporaries considered him the best songwriter America had ever produced. Today, some of his works have become America's folk songs. The melody we are going to harmonize, "Old Folks at Home," was written in 1851 and was Foster's most popular song during his lifetime.

Whether you know this melody or not, the first step in harmonization is always the same. Become familiar with the melody before going on.

Foster: "Old Folks at Home"

Once you feel you know the melody well, the next step (after you're sure you know what key it is in) is deciding where the cadences should occur. Remember, cadences happen only at the ends of phrases. Remember, too, that if you don't plan your cadences first, chances are good that your harmony will wander aimlessly and contribute little to the buildup of tension and the subsequent cadential release. Plan your cadences well, however, and the chord progression will not seem haphazard. Keep in mind that different kinds of cadences produce different levels of finality. And although the authentic cadence is the most final sounding of all the cadences, it should not be overused.

Our example, like many simple, diatonic melodies, is made up of four phrases, each of which is four measures long. Notice that the cadence points (measures four, eight, twelve, and sixteen) all contain whole notes, the longest note value of the melody. Another point to consider is that phrases one, two, and four are similar in sound, whereas the third phrase is different. This creates an AABA format for the four phrases that we will need to take into consideration when we harmonize it.

Foster: "Old Folks at Home"

Choosing cadences may seem difficult at first, but after you have harmonized several melodies, you will begin to see the same cadence patterns emerging in piece to piece. A good place to begin is to remember that when two phrases sound related, you can try ending the first phrase on a half cadence and the second phrase on an authentic or plagal cadence. This pattern is not always the best choice, but it appears frequently, and if it fits, it will make the first phrase sound somewhat incomplete and allow the second phrase to finish the musical idea.

In our example, the first phrase could end on a half cadence (the D can be a part of the G major triad) and the second phrase on an authentic cadence. The same is true of phrases three and four, although this type of symmetry is not always the best choice musically. Because we know we most likely want the piece to end with an authentic cadence, the only one we are unsure of is the cadence at the end of the third phrase. This could be a half cadence or an authentic cadence, since the G in measure twelve can be a part of both the G major and C major triads. In this particular case, however, the F major triad in measure eleven will allow us to use a plagal cadence, which will give us some variety and may be the best choice. Even though you should plan your cadences first, don't be concerned if you aren't certain which one to use at this stage. We know our possibilities for the third phrase of our example, and we can make a final decision after we fill in the other chords.

The next step in harmonizing a melody is to be certain that you correctly understand the **harmonic rhythm** of the melody—that is, how fast the chords change. Some pieces have a rapid, steady harmonic rhythm with chord changes occurring almost every beat. Others change every two beats, or every measure, and sometimes less frequently. In the case of a piece with a slow, irregular harmonic rhythm, it is easy to make the chords change too rapidly, which is frustrating because it feels as if *no* chord is appropriate. In such a situation don't try to force a chord change where none is needed.

Once you have planned the cadences and understand the harmonic rhythm, you are ready to fill in the rest of the chords. Although a great number of melodies can be harmonized with only the I, IV, and V chords (and an even larger number if the vi chord is also included), many melodies seem to require additional chords. If you find yourself working with this type of melody, keep in mind that any pitch can be a part of and harmonized in three different chords; for example, in the key of C, G can be the root of the V chord, the third of the iii chord, or the fifth of the I chord. If you have difficulty harmonizing a particular pitch in a new melody, begin by exploring these three diatonic possibilities.

Notice in the melody we are harmonizing that the harmonic rhythm changes about every measure. You can tell this by scanning the melody for chord outlines. Notice, for instance, that the melody spells a C major triad in measure 3, an F major triad in measure 11, and a G major triad in measure 9. Notice also in measures 7 and 15 that a C major triad is outlined in two beats, and the triad must change for beats three and four because D does not fit with the C major triad. Keep in mind also that chord changes will almost never occur in a perfectly symmetrical way. Although this can seem a bit arbitrary and confusing at first, practice and your ear will help you choose correctly.

Foster: "Old Folks at Home"

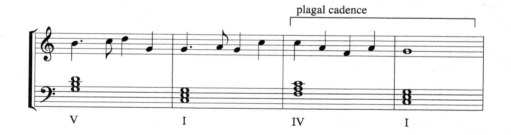

Tips for Harmonizing

As you find new melodies you want to harmonize, keep in mind that although they are different, the basic way of harmonizing them doesn't change. Although no formula ensures success, specific ways of working will point you in the right direction. Here, then, is a set of Tips for Harmonizing to help you go forward.

These tips reflect the work we have already done and suggest new possibilities to consider.

1. **Learn the melody.** Begin by becoming familiar with the melody you plan to harmonize. Is it a simple or complicated melody? Is it a diatonic or chromatic melody? This last point is significant because, in general, diatonic melodies are harmonized with diatonic chords, while chromatic melodies require chromatic harmonies. This distinction is important when you are first learning to harmonize—it means that some melodies are more difficult to get right than others.

2. **Find the phrases.** As you grow familiar with the melody, decide where the phrases occur. How many phrases are there? How many of them sound similar to each other? Can you create an outline of the phrase structure similar to the AAB pattern of 12-bar blues or the AABA pattern of the 32-bar song form? This level of understanding will prove of great help to you if you can master it.

3. **Plan the cadences.** When you understand the musical shape of the melody, you're ready to plan the cadences. In some ways, this is the most important step, because well-planned cadences give chord progressions a feeling of direction that keeps them from sounding as if they are wandering around. Remember not to use too many cadences of the same type.

4. **Determine the harmonic rhythm.** Once you have the cadences planned, determine the harmonic rhythm of the melody. Where do the chords change? How quickly or slowly does this happen? Is the pattern of change even or irregular? Scan the melody to see if it outlines triads or seventh chords at any point. If so, this is a good indication of what the harmonic rhythm might be.

5. **Begin with the primary triads.** Now, fill in the remaining chords, remembering that any melody note may become a member of three different diatonic chords (as the root, third, or fifth). As you harmonize new melodies, always begin with the primary triads first: I, IV, and V. Many songs, particularly folk songs, simple pop songs, and early rock 'n' roll, are based almost entirely on these three chords. You may find substitute triads later that better fit the music, but limiting yourself to the primary triads at first will give your preliminary harmonization a solid tonal grounding.

6. **Explore the secondary triads.** When additional triads seem to be needed for more subtle shading and tension—the minor sounds of ii, iii, and vi, for example, or the diminished quality of vii°—try substituting one of the secondary diatonic triads for a primary one. The ii chord will often substitute for the IV chord, for example, or the vii° for the V.

These suggestions are but a starting point, of course. You will develop your own unique ways of working as you practice and improve. The point is that harmonization skills, like most other aspects of music, have both an intellectual and a subjective side. So even as you learn new techniques, let your ear be your guide. If it sounds right, it probably is; the end result of any harmonization is how the music sounds.

Music in Action 🎵 **Song Building**

Choose one or more of the following melodies to harmonize. Use only block chords in root position (as in the previous example), and don't worry at this point about creating a suitable accompaniment. Begin by listening to the melody, planning the cadences, and establishing the harmonic rhythm. As you work, keep in mind that there is no one absolutely correct harmonization for most melodies. Some chord progressions do, however, sound more interesting than others.

"Mockingbird Hill"

"Red River Valley"

Additional practice for harmonizing melodies may be found in Practice materials 15-1, 15-2, and 15-3 at the end of this chapter.

Musical Form

Musical **form** is concerned with how music unfolds in time. It represents the blueprint of the composition, the road map that starts at the beginning of the piece and runs to its conclusion. Over the centuries, many different musical forms have been developed—some relatively simple, such as songs; others, more complex, such as symphonic movements, opera choruses, and string quartets. But regardless of the level of complexity, all musical form is an attempt to balance unity and variety as the music unfolds in time. For example, if all the phrases of a piece of music sound exactly the same, the piece will quickly lose our interest and grow dull to our ears, particularly with repeated hearings. If, on the other hand, each phrase is wildly different from the next, the piece will grow tiresome for the opposite reason, with too much variety and not enough repetition to allow the piece to hold together as a coherent musical statement in our minds.

Throughout the ages, certain musical shapes (or forms) have been developed and used so extensively that they have been given their own name. The *sonata allegro* form of Classical music, the *fugue* of the Baroque period, and the *theme and variations* (in use from the Renaissance until today) are three such examples. Here, we will look at four such forms. *Strophic*, *binary*, and *ternary* forms are simple musical shapes that have been used by composers for hundreds of years, while the *32-bar song form*, which can be traced back to the early 1800s (although it wasn't called that then), is perhaps the most-used musical shape for popular songs in all of the twentieth century and up to today. As you study the forms, make sure that you play them or listen to them played so you will have the sound of the form in your mind. It is not enough to simply look at the pieces on paper.

Strophic Form (12-Bar Blues)

The simplest form in music is probably **strophic form**. Many, if not most, folk songs exist in this form, that is, the song has a number of verses and each verse is sung to the exact same music. The surface of the song may, of course, change somewhat as the accompanying patterns or instruments change, but the melody, the harmony, and the rhythm stay the same, verse after verse. "Barbara Allen," "Erie Canal," and "Michael, Row the Boat Ashore" are examples of strophic songs that we have looked at. At this point, you may want to sing or play through several verses of a folk song that you know to get a sense of the form.

At first glance, the strophic form may appear to contain too much unity and not enough variety, because an outline of the form would be AAAA (assuming you sang four verses). In a way that's true; there is a lot of unity. This repetitive simplicity is a defining characteristic of strophic songs, particularly folk songs. But there is also another level of variety in strophic songs that occurs deeper inside the music within the phrases.

Consider for a moment the 12-bar blues, which is, after all, a strophic form in which both the melody and the harmonic progression repeat throughout the many verses. Inside this overall form, however, are three four-measure phrases that can be seen more clearly when we consider the lyrics. Here is the second verse from Bessie Smith's famous "Lost Your Head Blues" recorded in 1926:

Once ain't for always, and two ain't for twice.

Once ain't for always, and two ain't for twice.

When you get a good gal, you better treat her nice.

These lyrics, each line of which is sung to a four-measure section of the 12-bar blues progression, clearly show an AAB pattern that is also reflected in the harmonic pattern itself.

Lyrics: A _____   A _____   B _____

Progression: I   I   I   I   IV   IV   I   I   V   V   I   I

Additionally, this three-part division of the 12-bar strophic form is, as you will remember from the previous chapter, supported by the tension-and-release harmony of the chord progression.

Binary Form (AB)

Binary form is a two-part form that explores the principle of contrast. Consider the following, which is a short "Dance" by Beethoven.

A

Beethoven: "Dance"

B

Notice that this piece is divided into two separate parts, each of which is repeated. This pattern creates a binary, or two-part, form consisting of an A section of eight measures (sixteen when repeated) followed by a contrasting B section, also of eight (sixteen) measures. An interesting point worth noting is that the harmonic rhythm of the B section moves faster than that of A. In the A section, the harmonic rhythm generally moves at the rate of one chord every two measures. In the B section, there is a new chord every measure, sometimes two chords per measure.

Beethoven sustains the harmonic interest and achieves contrast by varying both the chord progression and the harmonic rhythm of the two sections. Section A is oriented around a tonic-dominant progression, while section B is tonic-subdominant oriented. Also, the faster harmonic rhythm in section B further differentiates the two sections, as does the introduction of chromatic pitches in the second part. Finally, notice that Beethoven supports the contrast between the A section and the B section with the accompaniment. In section A, for instance, where the harmonic rhythm moves slowly, Beethoven arpeggiates each chord to create momentum and provide constant forward motion. In the B section, where the harmonic rhythm moves faster, he ends the arpeggiation and uses quarter-note chords to punctuate the continually moving melody.

Although this "Dance" is written entirely in the key of D major, many binary pieces change keys at the beginning of the B section. When this happens, the original key will return by the end of the section so the piece can conclude in the same key in which it began.

Ternary Form (ABA)

Ternary form is a three-part form that explores the principle of contrast and repetition. It can be described as statement, departure, and return. The following, a "Waltz" by Schumann, is typical of many short instrumental and vocal works. Notice that this piece subdivides into three distinct sections:

A—measures 1–16

B—measures 17–28

Repeat of A—measures 29–44

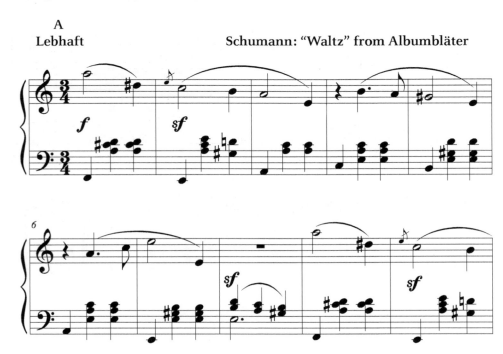

B

A

(continued)

The most important element of contrast in this example is the key change in the B section. Not all ternary pieces have so obvious a key change in the B section as this one, but almost all of them move to a temporary new pitch. In this example, both of the A sections are in the key of A minor, whereas the B section is in the key of F major.

Other elements create a contrast between the A and B sections. In the B section, the dynamics change from *forte* to *piano* and a new rhythmic pattern is introduced in the melody. In addition, the melody itself changes from phrases of irregular length to regular four-bar phrases.

Notice that when the A section returns in measure 29, it is an exact repetition of measures 1–16. Sometimes, however, composers will ornament and elaborate the A melody when it returns. Also notice that throughout the piece, the left-hand accompaniment remains the typical oom-pah-pah pattern associated with waltzes. This has a unifying effect on the entire composition.

32-Bar Song Form (AABA)

The 32-bar song form is a four-part form that also explores the concept of contrast and repetition. It can be described as statement, restatement, departure, and return, and is diagrammed as AABA. Because each of the four sections is of equal length, each section is eight measures long.

"Meet the Flintstones" is an example of 32-bar song form. Begin your study of this piece by singing through it several times and familiarizing yourself with the AABA structure.

Notice in this example that the first A section (measures 1–8) is immediately repeated (measures 9–16). It is then followed by a contrasting B section (measures 17–24), which, in popular music, is sometimes referred to as the bridge. This is then followed by a return to the A section (measures 25–32).

Barbera, Hanna, and Curtain: "Meet the Flintstones"*

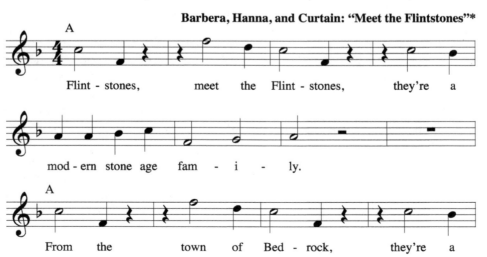

page right out of his - to - ry.

B

Let's ride with the fam - 'ly down the street,

through the cour - te - sy of Fred's two feet.

A

When you're with the Flint - stones, have a

ya ba da ba gay old time.

Many popular songs follow the 32-bar song form, or AABA format. "Body and Soul," "Ain't Misbehaving," "Satin Doll," and "Frosty the Snowman" are four such examples from the mid-twentieth century. Even though the melody, the rhythm, and the chord progression are different for each of these songs, they all exhibit a similar characteristic—the A sections provide the unity and the bridge (or B section) provides the contrast. In addition to a change in the melody, this contrast in the bridge can include changes in the rhythm, the accompaniment, and often the key. Although each piece sounds different, once you know what to listen for, you will begin to recognize the AABA pattern in many of the songs you hear every day.

Music in Action 🎵 Song Building

We know what we need to know now, so let's give it a try. Write a song in 32-bar song form. You may wish to write a song with lyrics that the class can sing or an instrumental piece that members of the class can play. Either way, keep in mind that each of the four sections (AABA) should be eight measures long and end with a cadence (with, perhaps, another cadence in the fourth measure of each eight-measure section if you are using shorter phrases). Also, remember that the bridge of your song should be a contrasting section in which the melody, the harmony, and perhaps the rhythm and the key are altered to provide a contrast to the A sections that surround it. When you have finished, arrange for a performance of your song, perhaps at a concert on the last day of class. ●

A Final Note

Here we are at the end of this book. I hope you have discovered that the study of tonal music and how it works is a fascinating topic full of many surprises and intriguing concepts. Although we have spent most of our time exploring the various components that make up music, it is important always to keep in mind that these individual components go together in some mysterious way to create an art form that is rewarding, imaginative, and never-ending. In music, there is always something more to learn and experience. So as you go forward, keep in mind that this book has given you a good beginning but it is only that, a foundation. If you are to continue to grow as a musician, you must build on what you have learned here. The fundamentals of music don't change, but the ways composers have used them through the centuries have changed, and an understanding of musical style will be essential to your continued development.

For some of you, the next step is a formal theory class; for others, it is independent work and study. To be successful, however, all musicians must understand the material contained in these final chapters. Chord progressions are the essence of tonal music. Their significance cannot be overstated. If you understand the concept of the simple chord progression, it will be easier to handle the more complicated progressions you will encounter later on. If you understand that all chord progressions (and their cadences) create varying levels of tension and release, then the chromatic patterns you encounter later will not seem so confusing or ambiguous.

All musicians should also be able to harmonize melodies. If you follow the steps we took earlier in this chapter, and practice, you should become successful at this. As you will recall, the steps are:

1. Learn the melody.
2. Find the phrases.
3. Plan the cadences.
4. Determine the harmonic rhythm.
5. Begin with the primary triads.
6. Explore the secondary triads.

Writing songs, on the other hand, does not have an easy formula for success. There are many different ways to go about it. But if you keep in mind that the phrases of your song must exhibit a balance of unity and variety, and that the melody, rhythm, and harmony must complement and support each other in ways illustrated in this chapter, you are well on your way.

Practice 15-1

Harmonize the following melody. Begin by singing or playing the melody until you know it. Then, plan the cadences and determine the harmonic rhythm before filling in the chords. Use only block chords in root position. This exercise deals only with melodies in *major* keys.

"Sweet Betsy From Pike"

Practice 15-2

Harmonize the following melody. Begin by singing or playing the melody until you know it. Then, plan the cadences and determine the harmonic rhythm before filling in the chords. Use only block chords in root position. This exercise deals only with melodies in *minor* keys.

"Johnny Has Gone for a Soldier"

Practice 15-3

Harmonize the following melody using lead sheet notation that we learned in Chapter 13. To do this successfully, you will need to go through the same process you did when preparing to write the actual chords. That is, learn the melody, find the phrases, plan the cadences, and determine the harmonic rhythm, all before filling in individual chords. Write your harmonization as chord names above the melody in lead sheet fashion.

"Scarborough Fair"

Graded Rhythms for Counting and Performing

Simple Meters

Compound Meters

37. 

38. 

39. 

40. 

41. 

42. 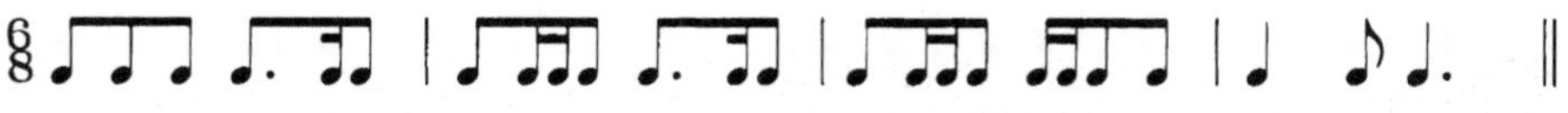

43. 

Less-Familiar Meters (Simple and Compound)

44. 

45. 

46. 

47. 

48. 

49. 

50. 

51. 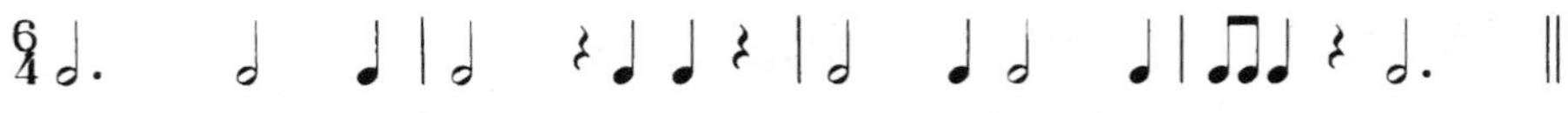

52. 

53. 

54. 

55. 

56. 

57. 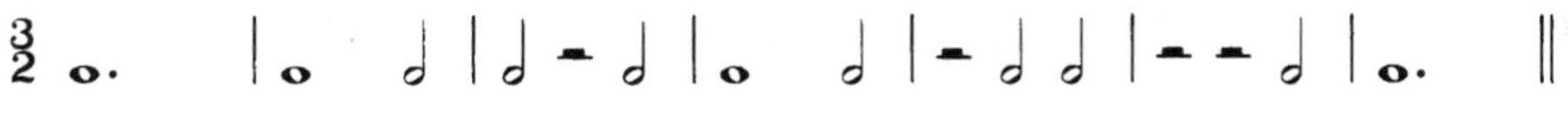

58. 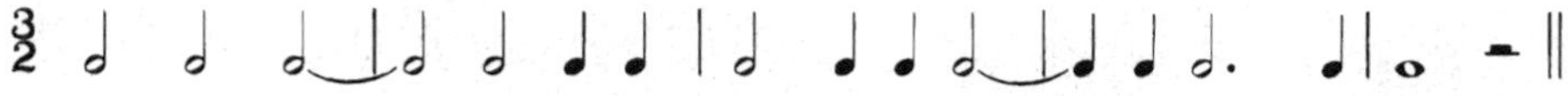

59. 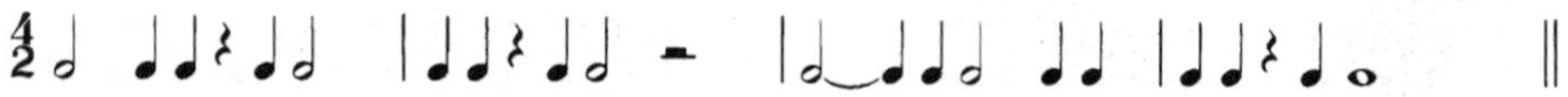

60. 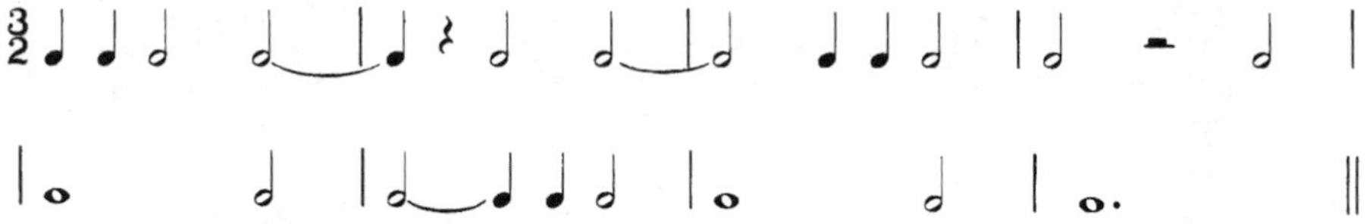

61. 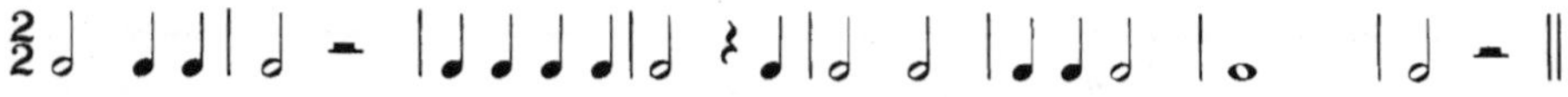

62. 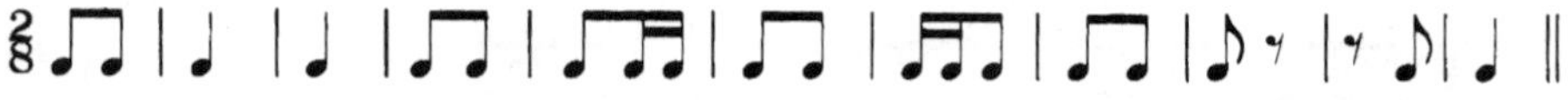

63. 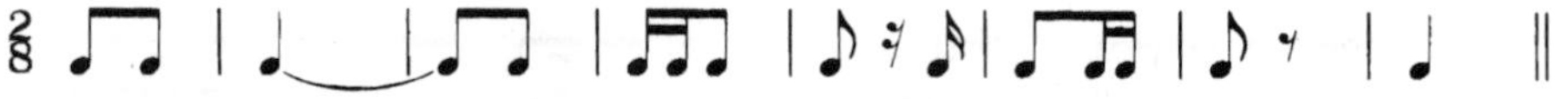

64. 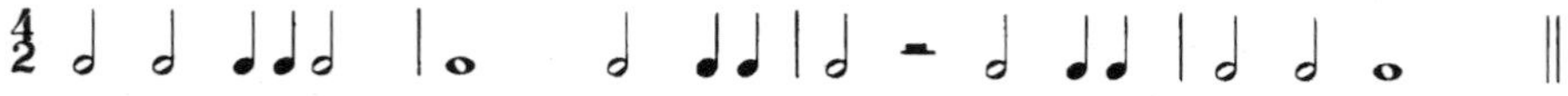

65. 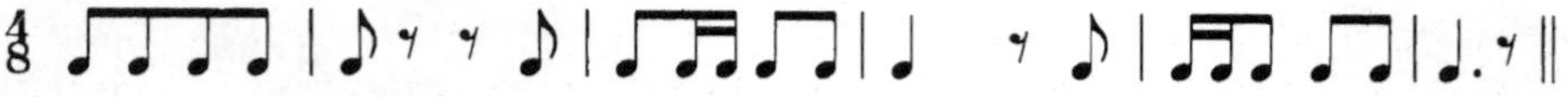

66. 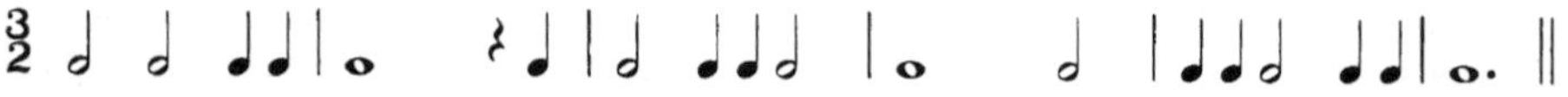

67. 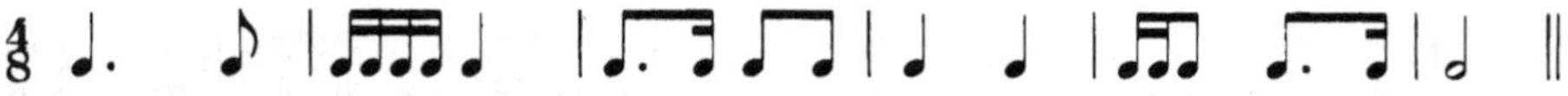

68. 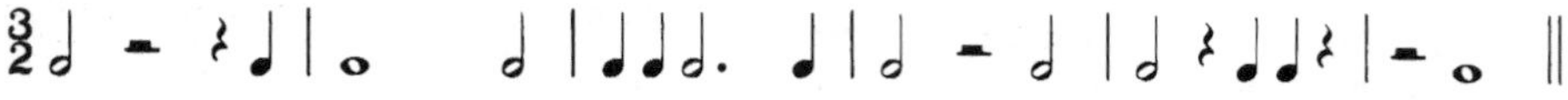

69. 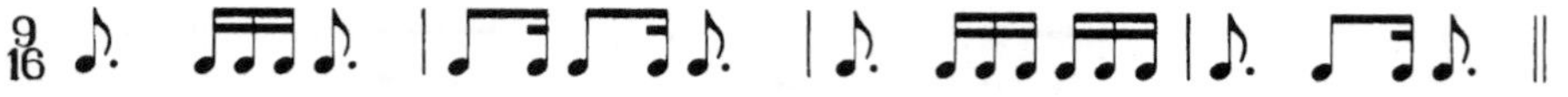

70. 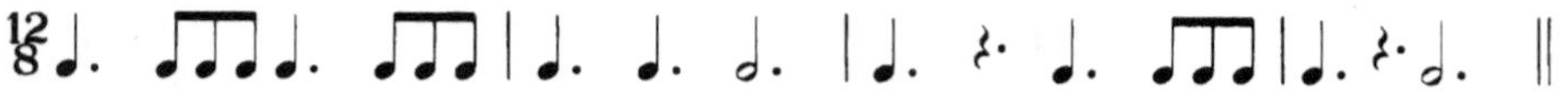

71. 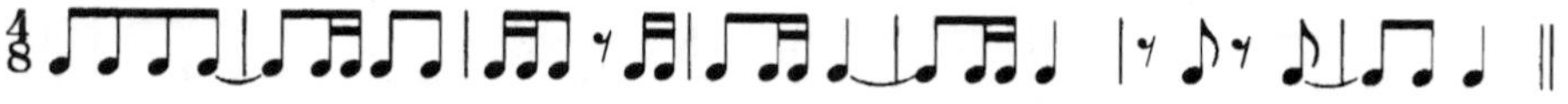

72. 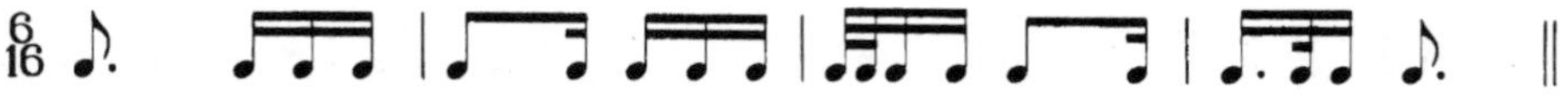

73. 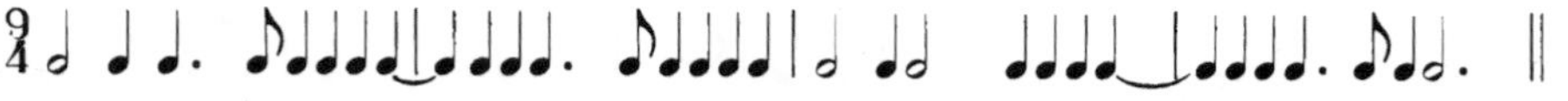

74. 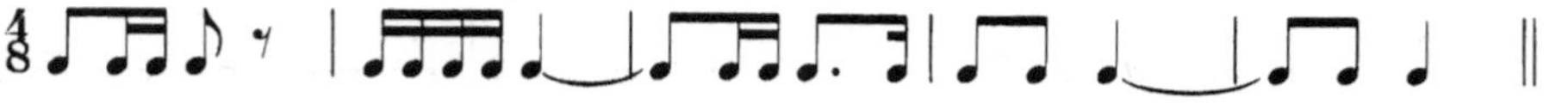

75. 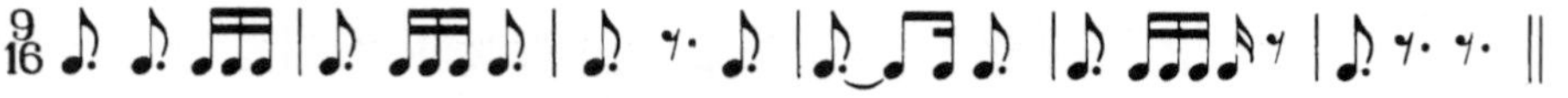

Graded World Rhythms in Two and Three Parts

The following two- and three-part rhythmic excerpts are adapted from a variety of musical styles and traditions throughout the world. They can be practiced with hand clapping or performed with "found" percussion instruments that students bring to class. Notice that many of the three-part patterns can be repeated a number of times. In these cases, adding or subtracting a voice on each repetition will increase the musical interest.

Two-Part Rhythms

Slowly (in 4)   Western Europe

13.

Stately   Eastern Europe

14.

Three-Part Rhythms

Fast   Africa

15.

Fast   South America

16.

Fast   Africa

17.

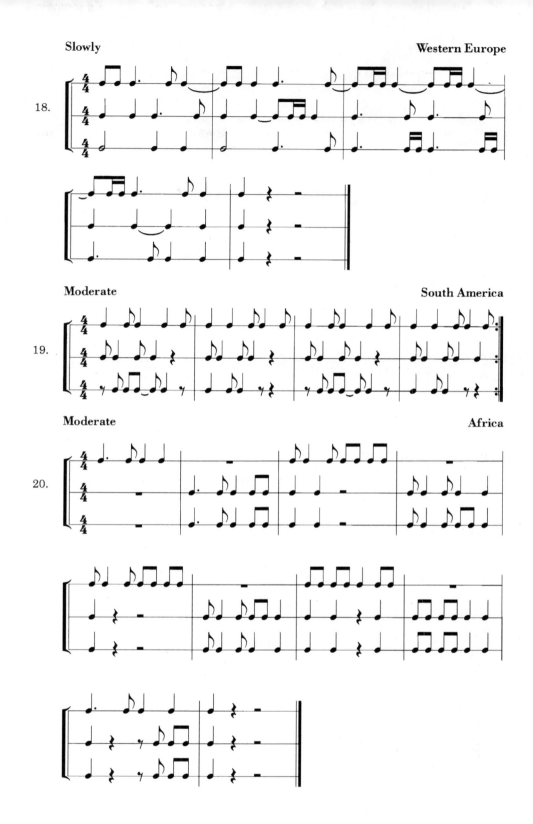

Syllables for Sight Singing Scales and Modes

Chromatic scale—ascending

1.
| do | di | re | ri | mi | fa | fi | sol | si | la | li | ti | do |

Chromatic scale—descending

2.
| do | ti | te | la | le | sol | se | fa | mi | me | re | ra | do |

Major scale

3.
| do | re | mi | fa | sol | la | ti | do |

Natural minor scale

4.
| do | re | me | fa | sol | le | te | do |

Harmonic minor scale

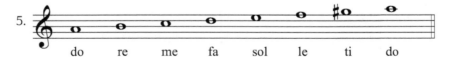

5.
| do | re | me | fa | sol | le | ti | do |

Melodic minor scale—ascending

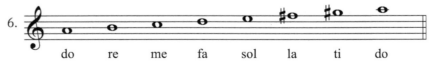

6.
| do | re | me | fa | sol | la | ti | do |

Melodic minor scale—descending

7.
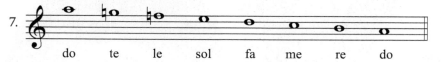
do   te   le   sol   fa   me   re   do

Dorian mode

8.
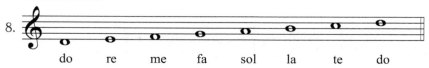
do   re   me   fa   sol   la   te   do

Phrygian mode

9.
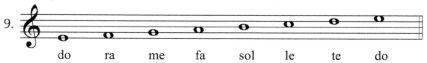
do   ra   me   fa   sol   le   te   do

Lydian mode

10.
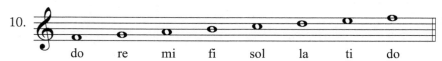
do   re   mi   fi   sol   la   ti   do

Mixolydian mode

11.

do   re   mi   fa   sol   la   te   do

Pentatonic scale (major)

12.

do   re   mi   sol   la   do

Pentatonic scale (minor)

13.

do   re   me   sol   la   do

Whole-tone scale

14.

do   re   me   fi   si   li   do

Graded Melodies for Sight Singing and Playing

Major Keys

Minor Keys

Chromatic Scale and Major Scale Fingerings for Keyboard Instruments

In the following staves, the top line of numbers gives the fingering for the right hand, the bottom line for the left hand. The numeral one, in either hand, always indicates the thumb.

Chromatic Scale

R.H. 2　3　1　3　1　2　3　1　3　1　3　1　2

L.H. 1　3　1　3　2　1　3　1　3　1　3　2　1

Major Scales

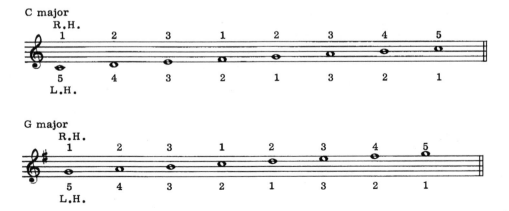

C major
R.H.
1　2　3　1　2　3　4　5
5　4　3　2　1　3　2　1
L.H.

G major
R.H.
1　2　3　1　2　3　4　5
5　4　3　2　1　3　2　1
L.H.

D major

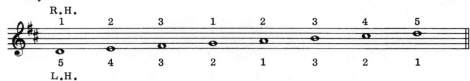

A major

E major

B major

C♭ major

F♯ major

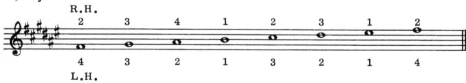

G♭ major

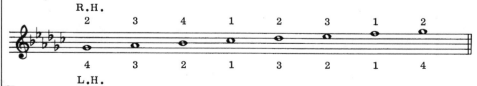

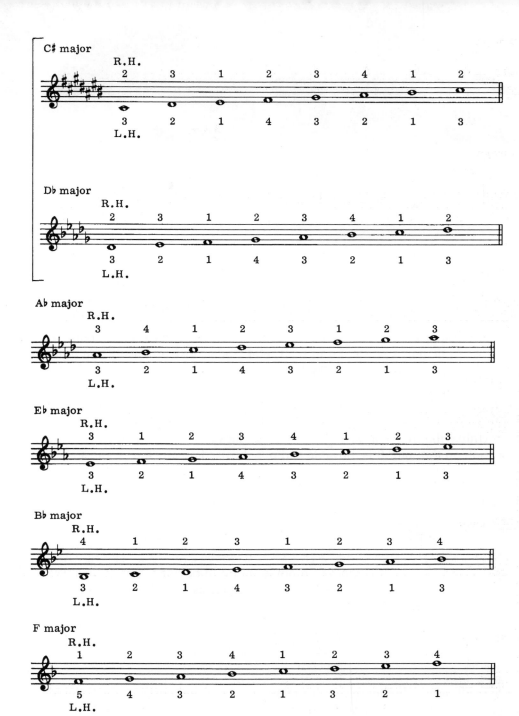

The C Clef

Although the treble clef and the bass clef are widely used, they are not the only clefs that appear in music. Several hundred years ago most music, both vocal and instrumental, was written in the **C clef**. Today, instruments of the modern orchestra such as the viola, cello, bassoon, and trombone use the C clef exclusively or frequently. It is also vital for the study of counterpoint. If you expect to study and perform early music, work with orchestral instruments, or continue your study of music theory, you will need to be able to read the C clef.

Unlike the treble or bass clef, the C clef does not always appear in the same location on the staff. It is movable and may be used on any line of the staff.

C clef positions

soprano   mezzo-   alto   tenor   baritone
             soprano

Today, however, it is most commonly found in one of two positions. When located on the third line of the staff, it is referred to as the **alto clef**; when located on the fourth line, it is known as the **tenor clef**.

alto clef   tenor clef

In all cases, whether in the alto, tenor, or some other position, the C clef identifies the location of the note C. Furthermore, this C is always middle C—the C in the middle of the great staff. In the following example, this same C is indicated in four different clefs:

Practice drawing the C clef in the alto and tenor clef positions. Make the C clef by (1) drawing two parallel vertical lines as long as the depth of the staff and (2) drawing two curved lines to the right of the vertical lines that meet the right-hand vertical lines above and below the third or fourth line of the staff, depending on which position is being drawn.

1. Draw two
   vertical lines.

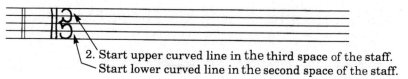

2. Start upper curved line in the third space of the staff.
   Start lower curved line in the second space of the staff.

Now identify by letter name the following pitches in the alto and tenor clefs. Remember that both alto and tenor clefs identify middle C.

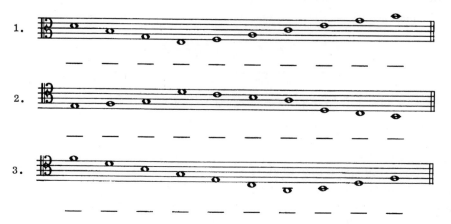

Now try the following: First identify the given pitch. Then rewrite the same pitch in the other clef.

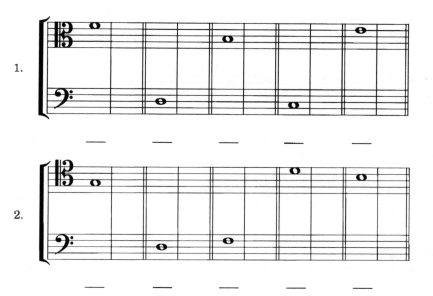

The following musical example is the opening of the chorale "Ein' Feste Burg" from Cantata No. 80 by Bach. Notice that in this excerpt the soprano, alto, and tenor voices all employ various positions of the C clef. The soprano voice uses a position of the C clef known as the *soprano clef,* while the alto and tenor voices use the two positions you have been working with. Here the variety of positions in which the C clef appears is the result of the composer keeping all the voice parts on or near the staff.

Bach: "Ein' Feste Burg" from Cantata No. 80

Following is a phrase from another Bach chorale, written in treble, alto, tenor, and bass clefs. In the space provided, rewrite the phrase in a single great staff, transferring the pitches from the alto and tenor clefs to the treble and bass clefs, as indicated. Be careful in your use of ledger lines. Your instructor or a member of the class can check your work by playing it on the piano.

Bach: "Heut' Triumphieret Gottes Sohn"

Other Scales and Modes

Modes

The modal system of the Middle Ages developed slowly over a period of several hundred years. Although each **mode** is a seven-note scale contained within one octave, just as major and minor scales are, they all sound different from each other because the combination of whole steps and half steps is different for each mode.

These modes, two of which are the present-day major and natural minor scales, were the basis of Western music from the Gregorian chant of the 900s until the tonal system began in the 1600s. They were revived in the twentieth century by composers around the world writing in a wide variety of styles. You are probably far more familiar with these scales than you think you are.

The modes are all seven-note scales based on patterns of five whole steps and two half steps. Each of the patterns has its own characteristic sound because the placement of the two half steps is different in each mode. Here is a chart showing where the half steps occur in each mode.

Ionian	3–4	7–8
Dorian	2–3	6–7
Phrygian	1–2	5–6
Lydian	4–5	7–8
Mixolydian	3–4	6–7
Aeolian	2–3	5–6
Locrian	1–2	4–5

Notice in the following that the half steps are always from E to F and B to C, but their position in the scale depends on which note is the beginning pitch:

Ionian mode (present-day major scale)

Dorian mode

(continued)

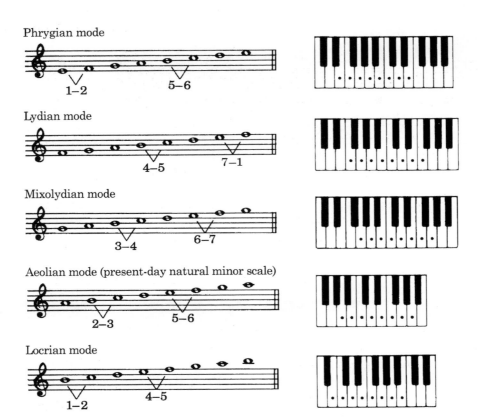

Phrygian mode
1–2   5–6

Lydian mode
4–5   7–1

Mixolydian mode
3–4   6–7

Aeolian mode (present-day natural minor scale)
2–3   5–6

Locrian mode
1–2   4–5

Medieval theorists divided the modes into authentic and plagal modes. Although a discussion of this concept is beyond the scope of this book, the distinction had to do with whether the *finalis*, or tonic as we would call it, was positioned at the beginning of the scale, that is, the first note, or in the middle. The modes we are studying are all authentic modes because the *finalis* is always the first note of the mode.

Transposing the Modes

For a while, the modes were not transposed when they were used musically. That is, composers always used D as the *finalis* when they wrote in Dorian mode, E as the *finalis* for Phrygian mode, and so on. Gregorian chant, for example, only allowed the use of one accidental, the flat sign, and it was only used to alter one pitch: B. But slowly, composers began moving the modes to other beginning pitches, mostly to adjust singing ranges to more practical levels. The result has been that, in the music of today, each of the modes can appear with almost any note as the *finalis*.

If your teacher wants you to learn how to transpose the modes, you will find some material for practice in Appendix H. It may be sufficient at this point, however, to know that the modes exist in transposed form, and that their characteristic sound stays intact as long as their interval pattern stays the same, no matter what the beginning pitch.

Whether you are planning to learn to transpose the modes or not, look at the following selection of modal melodies that span ten centuries (the tenth to the twentieth). Those that use a key signature are transposed, but you should still be able to identify the *finalis* of each.

Gregorian Chant

1. Pan - ge lin - gua glo - ri - o - si Cor - po - ris

my - ste - ri - um, San - gui - nis - Que pre - ti -

- o - si, Quem in mun - di pre - ti - um

Fru - ctus ven - tris ge - ne - ro - si Rex ef - fu -

- dit gen - ti - um.

"Henry Martin"

2.

Chopin: Mazurka in F Major, Op. 68, No. 3

Poco piu vivo

3.

p

(continued)

"The Drunken Sailor"

Chorus

Chant: "Dies irae" as quoted in Berlioz: *Symphonie fantastique*

"Old Joe Clark"

Chorus

Debussy: "L'Isle Joyeuse"

Un peu cédé

7.

p

The Whole-Tone Scale

The **whole-tone scale** is a scale of six pitches per octave, each of them a whole step apart. Because this scale contains only one kind of interval—the whole step—it is extremely ambiguous and, like the chromatic scale, lacks the feeling of a center of gravity. Centers of gravity can be established in whole-tone and chromatic melodies, however, by such devices as repeating certain pitches more frequently than others, or repeating accent patterns or harmonic backgrounds. Another peculiarity of the whole-tone scale is that it does not contain the intervals of a perfect fourth or a perfect fifth. Because these intervals are considered essential to tonal music, their absence makes whole-tone music feel unsettled.

Only two versions of the whole-tone scale exist:

Whole-tone scale

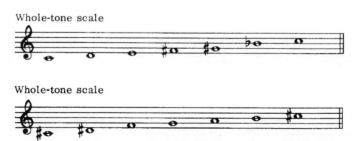

Whole-tone scale

Any other whole-tone scale is simply a reordering of the pitches in one of these two versions. The lack of the half-step interval allows any note within these two scale forms to function equally well as a tonic.

Although there are a few isolated examples of the whole-tone scale in the classical literature, it is found most extensively in music of the early twentieth century. Because of the whole-tone scale's ambiguity and harmonic vagueness, composers such as Debussy employed it to weaken the hold of nineteenth-century tonal practices, which they felt dominated music. Today, music based solely on the whole-tone scale is seldom written except as background music for movies and television.

The following examples show whole-tone music from the early twentieth century.

Debussy: *Prelude to "The Afternoon of a Faun"*

Debussy: "Voiles," Preludes, Book I

Debussy: *La Mer*

The Octatonic Scale

The **octatonic scale** is an eight-note scale (Greek *octa* means *eight*) that alternates between whole steps and half steps.

Octatonic scale

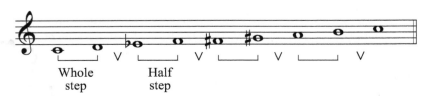

The octatonic scale is an invention of the early twentieth century and is known as a "synthetic" scale (as is the whole-tone scale), because it was intentionally created rather than allowed to develop naturally over time (as did the major and minor scales, the pentatonic scales, and the modes).

Jazz musicians sometimes refer to the octatonic scale as a diminished scale because it is constructed from two diminished seventh chords and a diminished seventh chord can be built on every pitch of the scale.

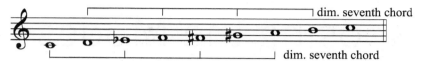

In addition to the continued use of the octatonic scale by jazz musicians, they were used by a number of twentieth century composers such as Oliver Messiaen and Béla Bartók.

Transposing the Modes

In transposing the modes, we will concentrate only on the authentic ones: Dorian, Phrygian, Lydian, and Mixolydian. In these the *finalis,* or tonic, coincides with the first note of the scale. These four modes are easy to recognize when they occur on the white keys. But if transposed to another beginning pitch, as they often are today, recognition becomes more difficult. Let's begin our study with the following example.

"Scarborough Fair"

A hasty glance at this piece might lead you to believe that it is in A natural minor (the key signature and last note are clues). Notice, however, that the eighth measure contains an F♯. If we begin on A (the beginning and ending pitch of the song) and construct a scale based on the pitches of the melody, we find that "Scarborough Fair" is, in fact, in Dorian mode:

One way of learning and recognizing the modes in their transpositions is to remember where the half steps are:

Mode	Half steps
Dorian	2–3, 6–7
Phrygian	1–2, 5–6
Lydian	4–5, 7–1
Mixolydian	3–4, 6–7

If it is still difficult to distinguish the modes, it may help to relate the modes to the major and minor scales, with which you are already familiar. Thus, *Dorian mode* is similar to the natural minor scale but with a *raised sixth degree*:

To write Dorian mode on A, we write the A natural minor scale but with a raised sixth degree:

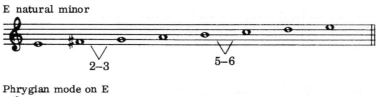

Phrygian mode is similar to the natural minor scale but with a *lowered second degree*:

To write Phrygian mode on A, we think of the A natural minor scale, but we lower the second degree:

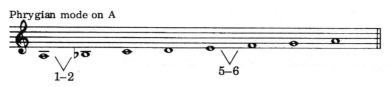

Lydian mode is similar to the major scale but with a *raised fourth degree*:

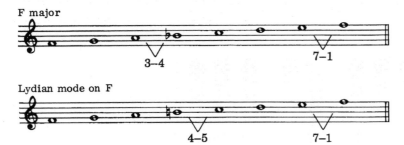

To write Lydian mode on C, we think of the C major scale but with a raised fourth degree:

Mixolydian mode is similar to the major scale but with a *lowered seventh degree:*

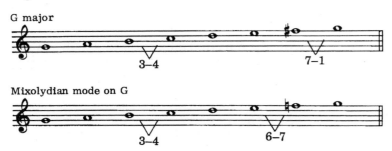

To write Mixolydian mode on C, we think of the C major scale, but we lower the seventh degree:

An alternative way to remember the modes is to relate each of them to the major scale. In this system, Dorian mode uses the pitch content of the major scale, but uses the second scale degree as the beginning pitch. Phrygian mode, likewise, can be thought of as a major scale beginning on the third scale degree; Lydian mode as a major scale beginning on the fourth degree; and Mixolydian mode as a major scale beginning on the fifth scale degree.

Using this system, it is relatively easy to transpose a mode to a different beginning pitch. If for example, we wish to write Dorian mode beginning on B♭, we need only to think of B♭ as the second scale degree of a major scale, in this case the A♭ major scale, and then use the accidentals of that scale. Since the accidentals for A♭ major are A♭, B♭, D♭, and E♭, Dorian mode beginning on B♭ would be B♭–C–D♭–E♭– F–G–A♭–B♭. A similar process works for the other modes.

Write the indicated modes starting from the given pitch. Before beginning, mentally note the relationship of each mode to the major or natural minor scale. Mark the half steps in each mode you write. A keyboard is provided to help you visualize each scale.

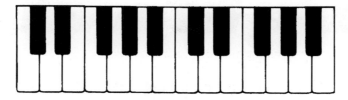

Dorian mode

1.

Dorian mode

2.

Phrygian mode

3.

Phrygian mode

4.

Lydian mode

5.

Lydian mode

6.

Mixolydian mode

7.

Mixolydian mode

8.

A Brief Introduction to Timbre

Timbre refers to the unique sound quality of an instrument or voice that allows us to distinguish it from other instruments playing the same pitch. Timbre is determined, in part, by the way in which the sound is produced, the size of the instrument, and the design of the instrument.

When an instrument or a voice produces a tone, we hear it as a single pitch. In actuality, the tone is a composite of a fundamental frequency and a series of **overtones**. We hear a single pitch because the overtones are not as loud as the fundamental. This phenomenon is known as the **harmonic series**, and it consists of a fundamental pitch plus its first fifteen overtones.

The term **partials** refers to all the pitches within a harmonic series, including the fundamental. When the reference is to *overtones*, however, the fundamental is considered a separate element. Thus, the following example, showing the harmonic series for the pitch C, is said to have either a fundamental and fifteen overtones or sixteen partials.

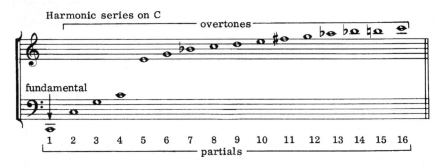

For instance, when a violin string is played, it begins to vibrate. Not only does the entire string vibrate, but shorter vibrations occur simultaneously over various lengths of the string. The vibration of the entire string produces the fundamental pitch we hear, while the shorter vibrations (the overtones) color the sound.

One instrument differs from another in timbre because each instrument is designed to amplify certain overtones and suppress others. Therefore, the design of an instrument accounts, in large part, for its characteristic timbre.

Two other factors influence instrumental timbre: the size of the instrument and the way in which the sound is produced. In general, the larger the instrument, the lower the pitch range. Mentally compare the pitch ranges of a violin and a string bass or a trumpet and a tuba. Both sets of instruments produce pitches in the same way. In each case, it is the size of the instrument that gives one a soprano range and the other a bass range.

Orchestral instruments are grouped into families according to how the sound is produced (strings, woodwinds, brass, and percussion). Members of each family of instruments sound related because their similar way of producing sound helps create a similarity in timbre.

Strings: Violin, Viola, Cello, String Bass

A string instrument produces sound when a string is set in motion by a bow or is plucked by a finger. The vibration of the string is amplified by the body of the instrument. Pitch is determined, in part, by the length of the string—the longer the string, the lower the pitch. The diameter and the tension of the string also affect pitch.

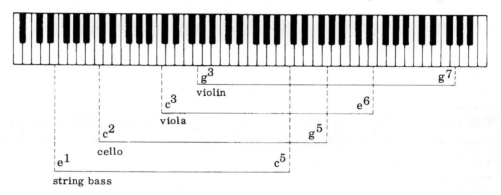

This illustration and those that follow show the approximate pitch range for each family of instruments.

Woodwinds: Piccolo, Flute, Oboe, English Horn, Clarinet, Bass Clarinet, Bassoon, Contra Bassoon

A woodwind instrument produces sound when the column of air inside the instrument is set in motion. Because this is done in a variety of ways, the sound of the woodwind family is less homogeneous than that of other families of instruments. The air column in a flute or a piccolo is set in motion by blowing across an air hole; in a clarinet or a bass clarinet by blowing against a single cane reed; and in an oboe, an English horn, a bassoon, or a contra bassoon by blowing against a double cane reed. The pitch on all woodwind instruments is controlled by finger holes on the instrument, which allow the performer to control the length of the air column—the longer the air column, the lower the pitch.

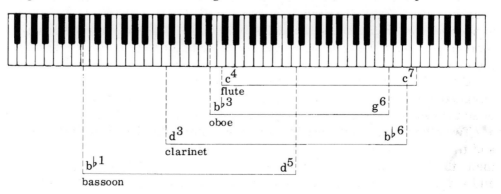

Brass: Trumpet, French Horn, Trombone, Tuba

The air column inside a brass instrument is set in motion when the performer buzzes his or her lips into a cup-shaped mouthpiece. Pitch on the trumpet, French horn, and tuba is controlled by three valves that open and close various lengths of tubing, thereby making the air column longer or shorter. Pitch on the trombone is controlled by the slide, which varies the length of the air column.

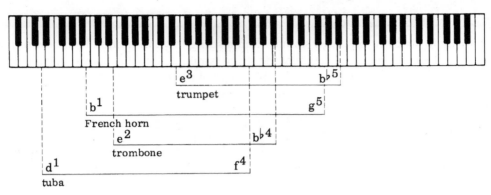

Percussion

Sound is produced on percussion instruments by striking them, usually with a wooden stick or a felt- or yarn-covered mallet. Some percussion instruments produce definite pitches, among them timpani (kettledrums), marimba, vibraphone, xylophone, chimes, and orchestra bells. The percussion instruments that produce an indefinite pitch include snare drum, bass drum, cymbals, and gong.

Voices

Human voices are classified into four main categories, by range: soprano, alto, tenor, and bass. The average range for each classification is as follows:

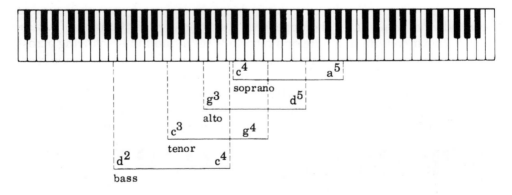

A further subdivision of voice types, shown here, is often made, particularly in opera, to indicate which vocal technique and which portion of the range are stressed.

I. Soprano
   A. Coloratura—emphasizes agility and range
   B. Lyric—emphasizes a more gentle voice quality
   C. Dramatic—emphasizes dynamic range
II. Mezzo-Soprano—a high alto/low soprano
III. Alto—the term *contralto* refers to a very low female voice
IV. Tenor
   A. Lyric
   B. Dramatic (*Heldentenor* in German)
V. Baritone
VI. Bass-Baritone—has some of the baritone's high tonal qualities and some of the bass's low tonal qualities
VII. Bass

A Brief Discussion of Acoustics

Acoustics may at first appear an unlikely topic for a book concerned with music fundamentals. But acoustics is becoming more relevant every year. The dramatic increase in the number of synthesizers and in the use of home computers to make music has brought the study of acoustics to the forefront.

Every musical sound has four characteristics: pitch, volume, duration, and timbre. On a mechanical level, these components are manipulated when we play an instrument or sing. The same is true on an electronic level for synthesizers and the music programs of computers. Sounds are created on these instruments by altering and adjusting the four basic characteristics of sound. If you plan to become involved with programming synthesizers or in composing with computers, you will need a solid understanding of acoustics.

Frequency

Musical sounds, in fact all sounds, are made up of physical vibrations of air molecules. The air molecules themselves do not move forward. Instead, they vibrate back and forth in repeated patterns called *oscillations*. These patterns in the air are similar to the ripples in a pond created by throwing in a stone.

Air molecules are set into motion in a number of ways. Saxophone players do it by causing their reed to vibrate; string bass players pluck a string; trombone players buzz their lips inside the mouthpiece. Once the sound is begun, air molecules near the vibrating source are set into motion, and they in turn transfer this pattern of motion to adjacent molecules. This is how sound travels through the air.

It may be difficult at first to think of a musical pitch as a vibrational pattern of air molecules, but that is what it is. Furthermore, the faster the vibrating pattern, the higher the pitch; the slower the pattern, the lower the pitch. When thought of this way, the more accurate term for pitch is *frequency*.

Frequency is the number of times a vibrational pattern repeats itself. This repetition is generally measured in vibrations per second, and the term for this is Hertz (normally abbreviated Hz). When musicians talk about the pitch the orchestra tunes to as A-440 (the A above middle C), they are actually referring to a frequency of 440 Hz, that is, an air displacement of 440 vibrations per second.

Another interesting characteristic of pitch is that when the frequency is reduced by one-half, the pitch we hear descends by one octave. While the A above middle C vibrates at 440 Hz, the A directly below middle C vibrates at only 220 Hz, and the A below that at 110 Hz. The vibrating frequencies for all the As on the piano follow.

3,520 Hz

1,760 Hz

880 Hz

440 Hz

(middle C)

220 Hz

110 Hz

55 Hz

27.5 Hz

Amplitude

The pitch or frequency of a sound is determined by the speed of the vibrational patterns. But the speed of the vibration does not determine how loud a sound is. In other words, the dynamics can change without affecting the pitch. Loudness, known as amplitude, is controlled by how far each air molecule is displaced. That is, the more air movement in the initial displacement, the farther the displacement will carry through the air, and the louder the sound will appear. Scientists measure amplitude in decibels; musicians use less precise terms like *mezzo piano* and *forte*.

An important point to remember is that excessive volume, particularly when listening on headphones, can cause permanent hearing loss. This has been thoroughly documented. Although many people enjoy loud music, it is important to use caution when listening at high volume, because a loss of hearing can never be corrected.

Duration

Musical sounds have three distinct parts—attack, sustain, and decay. The initial attack describes how the sound begins. It can be quite sudden and forceful, as when a trumpet player moves his or her tongue and releases air into the instrument. Or it can be more gentle, as when a pianist lightly touches the keys. Most instruments are capable of a variety of attacks.

Once a sound is begun, the second stage is the sustain stage. Some instruments, such as the organ, can sustain a sound indefinitely. Others, such as a clarinet, can sustain only as long as the breath of the performer holds out. Other instruments, such as the xylophone, have a sharp attack but almost no sustain time at all.

Once a sound begins to fade, it is considered to be in the decay stage. Musical sounds normally come to an end in one of two ways: There is a gradual loss of amplitude until the sound is no longer audible, or the sound is cut off abruptly by stopping the air or muting the string.

Synthesizers and the music programs of computers work by controlling the attack–sustain–decay characteristics of a sound. By manipulating one or all of these elements, well-known sounds, such as the sound of a flute, can be created electronically, or new sounds can even be invented.

Timbre

You will remember from Appendix I that every instrumental sound is really a composite consisting of the fundamental pitch plus the overtones of the harmonic series. Each instrument, including the human voice, emphasizes certain overtones and suppresses others. This creates a unique vibrational pattern for each instrument, but it does not alter the frequency. Therefore, two instruments, such as the flute and the oboe, can play the same pitch (frequency) but still maintain their own characteristic and distinct tone color (timbre).

Basic Guitar Chords

Because of the way it is tuned, the guitar is easier to play in sharp keys than in flat keys. Consequently, a complete chart of all possible guitar chords is of little use to someone just learning to play the guitar. Rather, it is better to learn the easy chords first and, after developing fluency with those, add the more difficult chords as needed.

Below are the tonic, subdominant, and dominant chords for the easier keys. You will be able to play many of the songs in this book using these three chords.

Major Keys

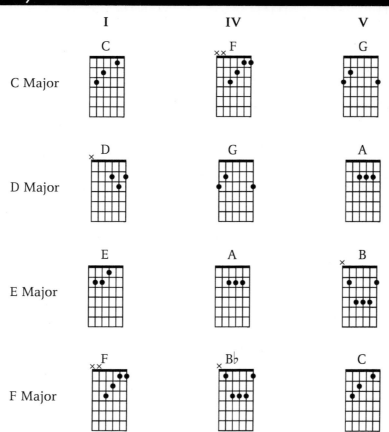

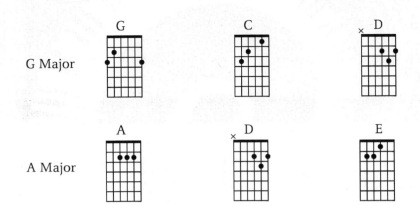

G Major

A Major

Minor Keys

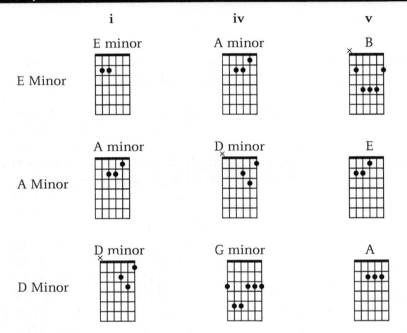

	i	iv	v
E Minor	E minor	A minor	B
A Minor	A minor	D minor	E
D Minor	D minor	G minor	A

x = do not play this string.

Glossary

Terms are **boldfaced** in text.

Accelerando (*accel.*)   A tempo marking indicating a gradual change to a faster tempo.

Accent mark (>)   A sign that indicates that the note above or below it receives more stress than the surrounding notes.

Accidentals   A set of signs that, when placed in front of a notehead, alter the pitch of that note chromatically. See also **Sharp sign; Flat sign; Double sharp sign; Double flat sign; Natural sign**.

Adagio   A tempo marking indicating a slow tempo.

***Alla breve* (₵)**   A simple-duple meter with a half-note pulse, that is, **²⁄₂** meter.

Allegro   A tempo marking indicating a fast tempo.

Alto clef   See **C clef**.

Anacrusis   One or more pickup beats that begin the first incomplete measure of a piece of music.

Andante   A tempo marking indicating a moderate tempo, about walking speed.

Articulation   An indication of how musical phrases are to be played. Articulation is controlled by a set of words and symbols that indicates various types of attack and whether the line is to be played short and separated (*staccato*) or smooth and connected (*legato*).

Augmented interval   The increasing of a perfect interval or a major interval by one half step.

Authentic cadence   A momentary or permanent point of rest in a harmonic progression created by the two-chord progression V–I in major or v–i in minor.

Bar lines   Vertical lines, placed immediately before the accented pulse, that divide written music into measures. The meter is more easily read when music is divided into measures. Compare with **Double bar lines**.

Bass clef (F clef) (𝄢)   A sign that locates the note F on the fourth line of the staff. This F is then used as a reference point for locating other pitches.

Beat   The primary pulse of a piece of music.

Binary form (AB)   A two-part form that explores the principle of contrast.

Blue notes   The lowered third, fifth, and seventh scale degrees. These notes are used extensively in the 12-bar blues and jazz.

Blues scale   A six-note scale in which the second and sixth scale degrees are missing, the third and seventh degrees are lowered, and a lowered fifth degree is added to the existing fifth scale degree.

Broken chord patterns   Block chords played one note at a time in some repeating pattern, usually occurring as an accompanying figure.

Cadence   A temporary or permanent point of rest at the end of a musical phrase.

C clef (𝄡)   A sign that locates the note middle C on the staff. This sign is movable and may appear on any of the staff's five lines. Today it is commonly found on the third line (alto clef) or the fourth line (tenor clef). In either position the C becomes a reference point for locating other pitches.

Chord   The major component of tonal harmony; three or more pitches sounding simultaneously. See **Triad**.

Chromatic half step   A half step that involves two pitches of the same letter name and staff location, such as G to G♯, A to A♭, or E to E♯. See also **Diatonic half step**.

Chromatic scale   A scale formed by the division of the octave into 12 equal half steps.

Clef   A sign that locates a particular pitch on the staff. This pitch is then used as a reference point for other pitches on the staff. The commonly used clefs are treble clef, bass clef, and C clef.

Common time (C)   A simple-quadruple meter with a quarter-note pulse.

Compound interval   Any interval greater than an octave in arithmetic distance.

Compound meter   Any meter in which the basic pulse is normally divided into three equal parts.

Crescendo (*cresc.* or ◁▭▷)   A dynamics marking indicating that the musical passage is to grow louder.

Cut time   See *Alla breve*.

Deceptive cadence   A temporary point of rest in a chord progression, in which an unexpected chord, usually vi, follows a V or V_7 instead of the tonic triad that is expected.

Decrescendo (*decresc.* or ▷▭◁)   A dynamics marking indicating that the musical passage is to grow softer.

Diatonic half step   A half step that involves two pitches with adjacent letter names and staff locations, such as A to B♭, G♯ to F, or B to C. See also **Chromatic half step**.

Diminished interval   The decreasing of a perfect interval or a minor interval by one half step.

Diminuendo (*dim.* or ▷▭◁)   A dynamics marking indicating that the musical passage is to grow softer.

Dominant   The fifth tone or triad of a major or minor scale.

Dominant seventh chord (V_7)   The chord formed by adding a fourth note, a minor seventh above the root, to the dominant triad.

Dotted note   A dot placed beside a note increases the value of the original note by one half. Thus, a dotted half note is equal to three quarter notes. Any note can be increased by half its value by adding a dot.

Double bar lines   Two vertical lines used in written music, most commonly to indicate the beginning of a new section in a large work or to mark the end of a work.

Double flat sign (♭♭)   An accidental that, when placed in front of a note, lowers the pitch of that note by two half steps (one whole step).

Double sharp sign (✕)   An accidental that, when placed in front of a note, raises the pitch of that note by two half steps (one whole step).

Downbeat   The strongest beat of any meter, always written as the *first* beat of the measure.

Duple meter   A division of the musical pulse into a recurring pattern of one strong and one weak pulse.

Duplet   A borrowed division in compound meter, in which a note normally subdivided into three equal parts is subdivided into two equal parts.

Duration   The length of a sound in time.

Dynamics   A characteristic of musical sound involving degrees of loudness and softness. In written music, volume is indicated by specific words and abbreviations.

Enharmonic pitches   The use of two different letter names for the same pitch. C♯ and D♭, F♯ and G♭, E♯ and F are examples of enharmonic pitches.

F clef   See **Bass clef**.

Fixed *do*   A system of sight singing in which the note C is always *do*, regardless of the key.

Flat sign (♭)   An accidental that, when placed in front of a note, lowers the pitch of that note by a half step.

Form   The organizing principle, or structure, of a piece of music. Form in music can be compared to the blueprint of a building. It controls how music unfolds in time. Most musical forms that are used to any extent have been given their own names. These include binary, ternary, strophic, and sonata forms, as well as fugue, theme-and-variation, and rondo forms.

Forte (*f*)   A dynamics marking indicating *loud*.

Fortissimo (*ff*)   A dynamics marking indicating *very loud*.

G clef   See **Treble clef**.

Great staff   A treble clef staff and a bass clef staff joined together by a vertical line and a brace. It is employed in music that requires a range of pitches too wide for a single staff, such as piano music.

Guitar tablature   See **Tablature**.

Half cadence   A temporary point of rest in the harmony of a piece of music created by a momentary pause on the dominant chord. The half cadence itself is a two-chord progression, the most common being IV–V or I–V in major and iv–V or i–V in minor.

Half step   The smallest interval in tonal music. On the piano, it is the distance between any key and the key immediately above or below it.

Harmonic cadence   A momentary or permanent point of rest in the harmony of a piece. There are several types, each a different formula of two chords.

See also **Authentic cadence; Plagal cadence; Half cadence.**

Harmonic interval   The musical distance between two pitches sounded simultaneously. See also **Interval.**

Harmonic minor scale   An altered version of the natural minor scale. The seventh degree is raised a half step to create a leading tone. This, in turn, creates the interval of an augmented second between the sixth and seventh degrees of the scale.

Harmonic rhythm   The rate of change—fast or slow, steady or irregular—of the chords in a piece of music.

Harmonic series   A fundamental frequency plus a series of overtones, heard as a single pitch. All musical pitches contain the harmonic series or parts of the series.

Harmony   Harmony generally refers to the horizontal progression of chords that takes place throughout a piece of music. The harmony is generated directly from the scale, or scales, on which a piece is based.

Interval   The musical distance between two pitches. Intervals may be harmonic (sounding simultaneously) or melodic (sounding successively). Interval quality may be perfect, major, minor, augmented, or diminished.

Interval size   The letter-name distance between two pitches. The interval size identifies the basic interval (third, fourth, and so on), but not the interval quality (major, minor, and so on).

Key signature   A grouping, at the beginning of a composition, of all the accidentals found in the major or natural minor scale on which the piece is based.

Largo   A tempo marking indicating a broad, very slow tempo.

Leading tone   The seventh tone or triad of a major, melodic minor, or harmonic minor scale; a half step below the tonic.

Ledger lines   Short lines above or below the staff that function to extend the pitch range of the staff.

Lento   A tempo marking indicating a slow tempo.

Major scale   A seven-note scale based on an interval pattern of five whole steps and two half steps, the half steps occurring between the third and fourth and the seventh and first tones.

Measure   A division in written music that allows the meter to be seen more clearly. Measures are created by bar lines placed immediately before the accented pulse.

Mediant   The third tone or triad of a major or minor scale.

Melodic interval   The musical distance between two pitches sounded in succession. See also **Interval.**

Melodic minor scale   A scale developed to avoid the augmented second of the harmonic minor scale. In the ascending form, the sixth and seventh degrees of the natural minor scale are raised; in the descending form, they are lowered to their position in natural minor.

Melody   A consecutive horizontal line of pitches that contains a contour (or shape), rhythmic motion, and cadences (or arrival points of rest). The interaction of these elements can produce an infinite number of melodic possibilities.

Meter   The division of the musical pulse into a recurring pattern of strong and weak pulses. The most common patterns or meters are duple meter, triple meter, and quadruple meter.

Meter signature   Two numbers, one above the other, that appear at the beginning of a piece of music. The top number indicates the meter of the music; the bottom number tells which note value represents one beat.

Metronome   An instrument invented in the early 1800s that produces a certain number of clicks per minute. Because each click can represent one beat, it is a more precise way of indicating tempo than the Italian terms also commonly used to mark tempo. The metronome marking in written music is given by the symbol M.M., which stands for *Maelzel's metronome.*

Mezzo forte (*mf*)   A dynamics marking indicating *moderately loud.*

Mezzo piano (*mp*)   A dynamics marking indicating *moderately soft.*

Minor scale   A seven-note scale, of which there are three versions. See also **Harmonic minor scale; Melodic minor scale; Natural minor scale.**

Moderato   A tempo marking indicating a moderate tempo.

Modes   A group of seven-note scales consisting of five whole steps and two half steps. By changing the placement of the two half steps, seven modes were created (Ionian, Dorian, Phrygian, Lydian, Mixolydian, Aeolian, and Locrian). These scales, from which the present-day major and natural minor scales were drawn, were the basis of Western music until the early 1600s.

Modulation   The act of moving from one key center to another within a composition. Sometimes this is done by using a double bar and a change of key signature. Other times, the key signature remains the same, but accidentals are introduced into the music that actually change the key.

Motive   A motive is a part of a melody, and is a short arrangement of pitches that is identifiable as a melodic unit. The motive usually lends itself well to further transformation or development. Some melodies consist of several short motives.

Movable *do*   A system of sight singing in which the tonic of any scale is always *do*, and the subsequent syllables are assigned to each succeeding pitch of the scale.

Natural minor scale   A seven-note scale consisting of five whole steps and two half steps. The half steps occur between the second and third tones and the fifth and sixth tones.

Natural sign (♮)   An accidental that, when placed in front of a note, cancels (for that note) any existing sharp, flat, double sharp, or double flat.

Noteheads   The small oval shapes drawn on the staff to represent particular pitches.

Octatonic scale   An eight-note scale consisting of alternating whole steps and half steps.

Octave sign (8va)   A sign indicating that the notes below it are to be performed one octave higher than written (8va———┐) or that the notes above it are to be performed one octave lower than written (8^va____┘).

Overtones   The pitches above the fundamental pitch in the harmonic series.

Parallel keys   A major key and a minor key with the same tonic but different key signatures.

Partials   All the pitches of the harmonic series, including the fundamental.

Pentatonic scale   A scale with five pitches per octave. A variety of pentatonic scales exists; the most well-known version contains no half steps.

Perfect pitch   The ability to always recognize by ear any pitch when it is sounded. See also **Relative pitch**.

Period   A combination of two or more melodic phrases. If a period consists of two phrases, the first generally ends with a feeling of incompleteness that the second phrase acts to complete.

Phrase   The phrase is the basic building block of a melody. It gives a feeling of completeness. Historically, phrases have tended to be symmetrical in length, that is, two, four, or eight measures in length. Melodies are often built of two or more phrases.

Pianissimo (*pp*)   A dynamics marking indicating *very soft*.

Piano (*p*)   A dynamics marking indicating *soft*.

Pitch   The frequency at which a given sound vibrates.

Plagal cadence   A momentary or permanent point of rest in the harmony of a piece of music created by the two-chord progression IV–I in major or iv–i in minor.

Poco a poco   A dynamics marking meaning *little by little*, as in *dim. poco a poco* (gradually softer).

Presto   A tempo marking indicating a very fast tempo.

Pulse   The constant, regular beat in music. It can be represented visually by a line of quarter notes, half notes, eighth notes, and so on; it is felt as the beat to which you tap your foot.

Quadruple meter   A division of the musical pulse into a recurring pattern of one strong and three weak pulses.

Related keys   A major key and a minor key with the same key signature but different tonics.

Relative pitch   The ability to identify a second pitch or pitches once a reference-point pitch is known. See also **Perfect pitch**.

Repeat sign (‖: :‖)   A sign consisting of double bar lines plus two large dots either before or after the bar. This sign occurs in written music at the beginning and the end of measures that are to be repeated immediately.

Rest   A musical sign used to indicate duration of silence. Every note value has a corresponding rest sign.

Rhythm   Rhythm organizes musical sounds into patterns of time duration. Strictly speaking, *meter* refers to a recurring pattern of strong and weak beats, while *rhythm* means the various arrangements of irregular durations within the metrical pattern.

Ritardando (*Rit.*)   A tempo marking indicating a gradual change to a slower tempo.

Scale   A group of pitches, generally in patterns of whole steps and half steps, that form the basic pitch material for a composition. See **Major scale, Minor scale, Modes, Pentatonic scale**, and **Whole-tone scale**.

Semi-cadence   See **Half cadence**.

Sharp sign (♯)   An accidental that, when placed in front of a note, raises the pitch of that note by a half step.

Simple interval   Any interval that is one octave or smaller.

Simple meter   Any meter in which the basic pulse can be normally divided into two equal parts.

Slur   A curved line, extended over two or more notes of different pitch, used to indicate a smooth, connected style of playing or singing.

Staff (pl. staves) A set of five parallel lines on which music is notated. The five lines, the four spaces between the lines, and the spaces above and below the staff are used to indicate pitch. Normally, the higher on the staff a symbol is located, the higher the pitch.

Strophic form A musical form with repeating verses, each verse of which is sung to the exact same music.

Subdominant The fourth tone or triad of a major or minor scale.

Subito A dynamics marking meaning *suddenly*, as in *subito p* (suddenly soft).

Subject The melodic material of contrapuntal compositions such as inventions and fugues.

Submediant The sixth tone or triad of a major or minor scale.

Subtonic The seventh tone or triad of a natural minor or descending melodic minor scale; a whole step below the tonic.

Supertonic The second tone or triad of a major or minor scale.

Syncopation Occurs when an accent is placed on what would otherwise be a weak beat.

Tablature A form of musical notation that indicates what action to make rather than what sound to expect.

Tempo The speed at which a piece of music moves; the speed of the pulse. In written music, Italian terms or a metronome marking are used to indicate the tempo.

Tendency tones The apparent attraction of various scale degrees to one another. In general, the need for active tones, that is, the fifth, seventh, and second, to resolve to less active tones, that is, the tonic.

Tenor clef See **C clef**.

Ternary form (ABA) A three-part form that explores the principle of contrast and repetition.

Tetrachord Sequential four-note patterns in scales. In the C major scale, the notes C-D-E-F form the lower tetrachord, while G-A-B-C form the upper tetrachord. The term comes from ancient Greece and the tuning system for the lyre.

Texture Indicates the density (thickness or thinness) of a musical line. There are three primary musical textures: *Monophonic texture* is one melodic line without accompaniment. *Homophonic texture* is one predominant melody with accompaniment. *Polyphonic texture* is two or more equally important melodic lines occurring simultaneously (also called *contrapuntal texture*).

Theme The melodic material used for classical works such as sonatas, symphonies, theme-and-variations, and other generally homophonic compositions.

Tie A curved line connecting two notes of the same pitch; used for creating notes of long duration.

Timbre The unique sound or tone color of an instrument or voice. The timbre is determined, in part, by the size and design of an instrument, and by the way in which its sound is produced.

Time signature See **Meter signature**.

Tonal music Music in which both the melody and the harmony are derived from major or minor scales.

Tonic The first note or triad of a major or minor scale; the pitch to which the other tones of the scale seem to be related.

Transposition The act of moving a piece, or a section of a piece, from one key level to another. Often, singers will transpose a piece to another key in order for it to be in a range better suited to their voice.

Treble clef (G clef) (𝄞) A sign that locates the note g¹ on the second line of the staff. This g¹ is then used as a reference point for locating other pitches on the staff.

Triad The basic chord of tonal music. A three-note chord constructed of two superimposed thirds. Four qualities of triads are possible—major, minor, augmented, and diminished.

Triple meter A division of the musical pulse into a recurring pattern of one strong and two weak pulses.

Triplet A borrowed division in simple meter, in which a note normally divided into two equal parts is divided into three equal parts.

Upbeat The beat before the downbeat, that is, the final beat of a measure.

Vivace A tempo marking indicating a quick and lively tempo.

Volume A term used to indicate the degree of loudness of a sound.

Whole step An interval consisting of two half steps.

Whole-tone scale A scale consisting of six pitches per octave, each a whole step apart.

Subject Index

This index includes topics discussed in text. See *Index to Musical Examples* for names of composers and titles.

D melodic minor scale, 182
D minor guitar chords, 320
D minor triad, 206, 211
D natural minor scale, 145, 176
D natural minor triads, 210
D sharp harmonic minor scale, 179
D sharp melodic minor scale, 182
D sharp natural minor scale, 175
Da capo al fine, 85–86
Dal segno al fine, 85–86
Deceptive cadences, 242–243
Decrescendo (*decresc.*), 83
Diatonic half step, 94
Diminished fifth intervals, 124
Diminished intervals, 122, 124
Diminished triads, 207–209
Diminuendo (*dim.*), 83
Dominant scale degree, 99–100
Dominant seventh chords, 225–226
Dominant/tonic relationship, 237–238
Dorian mode, 289, 301, 309, 311
Dotted notes, 39–40
Double flat, 29
Double flat sign, 35
Double sharp, 29
Double sharp sign, 35
Downbeat, 45
Drawing
    C clefs, 298–300
    F (bass) clefs, 16
    G (treble) clefs, 15
    note values, 10
Duple meter, 7, 8, 11
    compound, 57–58
    simple, 44–45
Duplet, 66–68
    counting methods for, 67–68
Duration, 317–318
Dynamics, 82–83

E

E flat major scale, 104, 297
E flat natural minor scale, 176
E harmonic minor scale, 178
E major guitar chords, 319
E major scale, 103, 296
E melodic minor scale, 181
E minor guitar chords, 320
E natural minor scale, 146, 176, 309
Ear training, 101–102
    compound meter, 70
    defined, 101
    intervals, 131
    major scales, 100–102
    minor and major key signatures, 150
    minor scales, 168, 171–172
    pitch, 14
    rhythm, 6
    simple meter, 47
    triads, 231–232
Eighth notes, 9, 10–11
    beams, 9–10
    equivalency to quarter note, 11
    flags for, 9
    illustrated, 9
    rhythm tree, 11
Eighth rests, 12–13
Enharmonic keys, 151
Enharmonic pitches, 78–79

F

F clef, 16–18
    See also Bass clef
F major guitar chords, 319
F major scale, 104, 145, 297, 310
F major triads, 210

F sharp, 27
F sharp major scale, 296
Fifths
    as interval, 121, 123–124
    major circle of, 113–114
    minor circle of, 151–152
Figured bass, 227
Fixed *do*, 98
Flags
    beamed together, 9
    illustrated, 9
Flat major keys, 112
Flat minor keys, 147–149
Flat sign, 35
Flats, 29
    enharmonic pitches and, 78–79
Flute, 313
Forte (*f*), 83
Fortissimo (*ff*), 83
Fourths, as interval, 121
French horn, 314
Frequency, 316–317
    See also Pitch
Frets, 224

G

G clef, 15–16
    See also Treble clef
G flat, 78
G flat major scale, 296
G major guitar chords, 320
G major scale, 96, 103, 114, 146,
    295, 310
G sharp harmonic minor, 165, 179
Grand staff. *See* Great staff
Great staff, 18–19
Guitar chords
    guitar tablature, 223–225
    major keys, 319–320
    minor keys, 320
Guitar tablature, 223–225

H

H (higher in pitch), 14
    See also L (lower in pitch)
Half cadence, 241–242
Half notes, 9–11
    equivalency to quarter note, 11
    illustrated, 10
    rhythm tree, 11
Half rests, 12–13
Half steps, 28, 123–126
    chromatic, 96, 164
    diatonic, 94, 96
    major scales and, 93–94
    minor scales and, 161
    modes and, 301
Harmonic cadence, 239
Harmonic intervals, 119
Harmonic inversion of intervals, 129–130
Harmonic minor scales, 164–166, 288
Harmonic rhythm, 266, 268, 272
Harmonic series, 312
Harmonizing a melody, 264–267
    tips for, 267–268
Harmony, 210, 211

I

Interval pattern, 93–94, 119
Intervals, 28, 119–141
    augmented, 122
    compound, 128
    defined, 119
    diminished, 122
    harmonic, 119
    harmonic inversion of, 129–130

    major and minor, 122, 125–127
    melodic, 120
    perfect, 123–124
    quality of, 122–123
    scales as, 93–94
    simple, 128
    size of, 120–122
Inversions
    labeling, 212–213
    of seventh chords, 226–227
    of triads, 211
Italian dynamics, 83

K

Key signatures
    defined, 109
    flat major keys, 112
    minor, 145–157
    relative major and minor scales,
        145–147
    sharp major keys, 110
    See also Accidentals; Major key signa-
        tures; Minor key signatures
Keyboard, 25–33
    black keys, 27
    musical distances, 28
    octave identification, 81–82
    pitch and, 87–88
    scales and, 97
    sight singing and, 173
    white keys, 25–27

L

L (lower in pitch), 14
Largo, 49
Lead sheet, 2, 278
Leading tone scale degree, 99
Ledger lines, 18, 79–80
Lento, 49
Lydian mode, 289, 301–302, 310, 311

M

Major intervals, 122, 125–127
Major key signatures, 109–116
    circle of fifths, 113–114
    flat keys, 112
    parallel keys, 150
    sharp keys, 110
Major keys,
    guitar chords, 319–320
Major pentatonic scale, 185–189
Major scales, 288, 309
    ear training, 101
    elements of, 94–95
    fingerings for keyboard instruments, 295–297
    intervals of, 125
    naming scale degrees, 99–100
    sight singing, 97–99
Major triads, 205–206
Major-minor relationship, 145–151
Major-scale method, 123
Measures, 8
Mediant scale degree, 99
Melodic intervals, 120
Melodic minor scales, 166–168, 288–289
Melodies, 19–20
    graded melodies for sight-singing and
        playing, 290–294
    harmonizing, 264–268
Meter signature. *See* Time signature
Meters, 7–8, 11–12
    compound, 280–281
    defined, 7
    feeling the, 8
    less-familiar, 281–282
    simple, 279–280

two-chord progression, 247–248
See also Cadences; Chord progressions;
    Tonal music
Tonic chord, hearing, 248
Tonic scale degree, 99
Transposing modes, 302–305
Treble clef, 15
Triads
    augmented and diminished, 207–209
    close and open positions, 206–207
    in actual music, 227–231
    inversions of, 211
    labeling, 219–225
    labeling inversions, 212–213
    major and minor, 205–206
    scales and, 210–211

seventh chords, 225–227
structure of, 204–205
See also Chord progressions;
    Chords
Triple meter, 7, 8, 11–12
    compound, 57–58
    simple, 45
Triplet, 66–68
    counting method for, 67–68
Trombone, 314
Trumpet, 314
Two-chord progression, 247–248

U
Unison, intervals of, 123
Upbeat, 45

V
Viola, 313
Violin, 313
Vivace, 49
Voices, timbre and,
    314–315

W
White keys of keyboard,
    25–26
Whole notes, 9–11
Whole rests, 12–13
Whole steps, 28
    major scale and, 94–99
Whole-tone scale, 289, 305–306
World rhythms, 283–287

Index to Musical Examples

Prelude to "The Afternoon of a Faun" (Debussy), 306
"Preludio III" from *Well Tempered Clavier*, Book I (Bach), 109, 110
"Psalm 42" from *Genevan Psalter* (Anon.), 256–257

R
"Red River Valley," 269
"Rondo" from *Sonatina in G Major*, Op. 36, No. 4 (Clementi), 230–231
"Rondo" from *Sonatina in G Major*, Op. 36, No. 5 (Clementi), 229
Ronda from Sonatina Op. 20, No. 1 (Kuhlau), 80–81
Rossini, G. *William Tell*, Overture, 186
Russian Folk Song, 51

S
"Sakura, Sakura," 190
"Scarborough Fair," 46, 278, 308
Scarlatti, A. G. Sonata in C Minor, 169
Schumann, R.
   "Poor Orphan Child, The" from *Album for the Young*, 172, 246
   "Siciliana" from *Album for the Young*, 85–86
   "Soldiers' March" from *Album for the Young*, 245
   "Wild Rider, The" from *Album for the Young*, 171, 247

"She'll Be Coming Round the Mountain," 43
"Siciliana" from *Album for the Young* (Schumann), 85–86
"Skip to My Lou," 22
"Soldiers' March" from *Album for the Young* (Schumann), 245
Sonata in B♭ Major, K. 570, III (Mozart), 80
Sonata in C Minor (Scarlatti), 169
Sonatina, Op. 36, No. 1 (Clementi), 84–85
Sonatina in C Major, Op. 55, No. 1, I (Kuhlau), 246
Sonatina in C Major, Op. 55, No. 1, II (Kuhlau), 242
Sonatina Op. 36, No. 3, III (Clementi), 244
"Sourwood Mountain," 46
South American rhythms, 71
"St. James Infirmary," 223
"Star Spangled Banner, The," 168
"Sur le Pont d'Avignon," 98–99, 238
"Sweet Betsy from Pike," 17–18, 277
"Sweet Genevieve" (Tucker), 68
Symphonie fantastique (Berlioz), 304

T
Techner, Chorale, 255
"This Old Man," 17
"This Train," 188
"Three Blind Mice," 59, 168

"Tom Dooley," 248
Traditional
   "Behind Closed Doors," 191
   "Blues and Booze," 192
   "Careless Love," 2
   "Worried Man Blues," 224
Tucker, Henry, "Sweet Genevieve," 68

V
Valses nobles (Schubert), 227
"Voiles," Preludes, Book I (Debussy), 306

W
"Wabash Cannon Ball, The," 166, 249
"Waltz" from *Albumblätter* (Schumann), 272–274
"Wayfaring Stranger," 21, 64, 189, 221–222
Western European rhythms, 283–287
"When Johnny Comes Marching Home," 59
"Wild Rider, The" from *Album for the Young* (Schumann), 171, 247
William Tell, Overture (Rossini), 186
Winchester New (Hymn), 240
"Worried Man Blues," 224

Y
"Yellow Rose of Texas, The," 44